The Waiting Heart

Also by Yvonne Rodney:

Getting Through
Let It Go

To order, **call 1-800-765-6955.**
Visit us at **www.reviewandherald.com** for information
on other Review and Herald® products.

The Waiting Heart

Yvonne Rodney

REVIEW AND HERALD® PUBLISHING ASSOCIATION

Since 1861 | www.reviewandherald.com

This book was
Edited by Penny Estes Wheeler
Copyedited by Judy Blodgett
Designed by Emily Ford / Review and Herald® Design Center
Cover art by © Thinkstock.com
Typeset: 11/13 Minion Pro

PRINTED IN U.S.A.

17 16 15 14 13   5 4 3 2 1

Library of Congress Cataloging-in-Publication Data
Rodney, Yvonne, 1959-   .
  The waiting heart: conversations with single women / Yvonne Rodney.
     p. cm.
  1. Single women—Fiction. I. Title.
   PS3618.O3574W35 2013
   248.8'432—dc23
                                    2012024155
  ISBN 978-0-8280-2694-9

For Colleen, who asked a really good question!

Preface

What prompted the writing of this book? Here's what happened. One day my friend Colleen came by my house for a visit. In her typical way, she rattled on about this and that, filling me in on what she'd been up to since last we connected. She recounted how she'd watched a television program on which the host said, "If you are not married by now, and you wanted to be, have you ever asked yourself why?"

Well, that provocative question would not leave my mind. I don't know why it kept bothering me. After all, I've been married for more than 20 years. But stay with me the question did! Finally I posed it to my unmarried girlfriends (I have many), and each one wanted me to write *her* story!

In the end, as with all unleashed ideas, it became *nobody's* story except that of the characters—Quilla and her interviewees, whose issues and situations dictated what you now hold in your hands. For them, I became the messenger, and only after they had told their stories did I allow myself to edit and refine.

Then I did the next necessary thing: I asked a couple never-married, wanna-be-married women whose opinions I value to read the story. I waited for their verdict with bated breath, wondering if I'd missed the boat entirely. "Don't change a thing!" they said. I argued that I couldn't have gotten all of it right, but they stood firm.

So here it is: Quilla's story. Or the story of a friend, sister, niece, the woman next door, or the colleague at work.

And the biggest surprise of all? This story spoke to this long-married author in a real way. I think God uses my writing to tell me things I won't hear any other way, such as "I love you, Yvonne," or "I've got you, Yvonne," or He tells me how He is single-mindedly devoted to a love relationship with me. His is the real "Waiting Heart." And because I don't always believe myself worthy of such undying devotion, I need to be reminded again and again.

May you, too, experience the constancy of this *awesome* Lover within these pages and be reminded that *you* are indeed treasured by the God of the universe.

Chapter 1

Quilla

I'm 44 years old, five feet six inches (sorry, my metric conversion abilities are not great) and decent looking. At 135 pounds I'm not exactly weight-challenged. I have good teeth, practice excellent hygiene, dress well, work out two or three times per week, don't publicly pick my nose, and have been told that I'm a nice person. Dogs lick my hands, and most children don't run screaming in the other direction when I talk to them. I am a down-to-earth kind of Christian (as opposed to a "holier than thou") and consider myself reasonably intelligent. So why am I not married by now?

I had it all planned. I'd finish school, get a good job, and sort of establish my career before I settled down. It wouldn't hurt throwing in a little bit of travel, too, while I was at it. I wanted no regrets once I settled down to domestic bliss. My wedding dress would not be too . . . oops! I'm so sorry. My mother raised me better than this. Here am I rambling on like an idiot and haven't even introduced myself. It's just that this question is bothering me. When things bother me, I blabber a lot. I worry the thing to death.

It all started when I got dragged by my friend Susan to this women's symposium at the convention center. I don't do these women thingies. Too much emotion! Somebody always breaks down in front of the audience and blabs out personal stuff better left unsaid. But like I said, I got dragged against my better judgment. Susan can be a pest sometimes when she doesn't get her way, so she begged me and begged me to go with her.

Susan isn't married either. She's getting desperate because she says her biological clock isn't just ticking; it's on permanent alarm mode, and no amount of hitting the snooze button is getting it to shut up. Susan wants to have a kid. Badly.

Me? I'm not so sure about the kid thing. I'm reconciled to the fact that I've missed that boat. But I'd like to be married while my skin still has some elasticity left in it. Already I'm seeing danger signs. Lately when I wake up in the morning I find that the side of my face I slept on is starting to remain longer with that slept-on look. Kinda like how your hair flattens against the side of your head when you sweat on it at night. Last Friday morning it took two face washings and some brisk cheek slapping to get things to slip back into position.

Anyway, as I was saying, Susan and I went to this convention center thing. You name the topic, they had a session: "Finding the Hero Within You," "Saving the Best of Your Self." In one day you could learn which part of your body not to lift; choose from any number of massage treatments; experience spa happiness; and discover the latest in diet, exercise, or yoga techniques. For every topic there was a guru waiting to tell you the path to total personal fulfillment.

Yeah, yeah! Like I'm going to exercise any more than I do now. I wish I loved to run on stationary machines or bicycles without leaving the building, but I hate that stuff. Play me a good game of tennis or some kind of sport. Machines and I don't get along. Last time I tried to get off a moving treadmill I went flying onto the elliptical machine where some old guy was sweating up the equipment. Just my luck! Why couldn't it have been a young, muscled, good-looking male specimen who'd snatch me from the jaws of embarrassment by looking into my eyes and shouting, "Kismet!"

Anyway, as I was saying, Susan made me go to this session for single women. Actually the speaker wasn't bad. Her name is . . . Did I ever get around to telling you my name? No? Pray for me, please. I need therapy. Early-onset dementia must be the reason. My name is Tranquility. No, I'm not kidding. That really is my name. Actually my full name is Tranquility Victoria Adeline Hazelwood. Everyone calls me Quilla (well, not quite everyone—my mother sees nothing wrong with the "beautiful" name she gave me). And yes, I sometimes get called tequila, and I don't like it.

What's in a name? My mom says my name reminds her of peaceful days in nature. I personally think she gave me that name while the childbirth drugs were still in her system. When I rail at my dad for agreeing to that stupid name he shrugs his shoulder in that way that reminds me that what Dru Hazelwood wants, Dru Hazelwood gets. So I've learned to tolerate the name but not the meaning. I am not a tranquil person, at least not on the inside. It's important that you understand that right up front.

I'm a nurse. I really wanted to be a physiotherapist but got turned off by the machines. Don't even go there. Telling me that there's more to physio than machines is preaching to the pew. I know that. Lately I'm feeling testy. I need to rant. That's why when the woman in the session, the one who looked like she had done a lot of "coming to terms" in her life, told the audience of 37 single women (I know there were 37 because I counted them) to ask themselves "Why am I not married?" I got up and left. Susan, not wanting to stay by herself, left too. But she was not happy with me. We nearly had a fight over that stupid question.

"Why am I not married?" Is that some kind of twisted way of blaming the victim? It's like saying I have control over things and should be able to weave my web and catch a guy out of thin air just like that! Upset is what she made me. I don't normally get irritated like this. But . . .

I can hear what you're thinking. *Woman has issues! That speaker sure hit a nerve!* What do you know about my life? Nothing, that's what! Maybe you need to be asking yourself why you picked up this book to read. You think you could ask yourself that? Just say, "Self, why did you pick up this book?" and see what answer you get.

Well! *That* was totally uncalled-for. I take it all back. Don't listen to me. I really don't mean to offend you. God knows I truly don't. I'm a nice Christian woman who is single and not happy about it. Not happy at all. Never in my wildest imaginings did I believe that I, Tranquility Hazelwood (Quilla for short), would still be unmarried at 44. How did this happen to me? So please forgive me. I'm just having a hard time reconciling myself to this unplanned-for singlehood, and the "Why am I not married?" question is driving me nuts. And before you ask, let me tell you the questions that have plagued me since that convention center session two weeks ago Sunday:

1. Was there something or a set of somethings I *did* to end up still single?
2. Was there something or a set of somethings I *didn't* do to end up single?
3. Is there something I *can* do about my single state, and if so, how badly do I want to get married?
4. Can I live with being a never-married woman?
5. Where does God fit into my current unwed state, and if my being married would have been good for me, wouldn't He have sent someone my way by now?
6. How do I deal with the pain of loneliness and lack of sexual fulfillment?
7. Is there a defect in me that turns men off?
8. Are my expectations about the qualities I want in a husband too high, not grounded in reality? And if so, how do I know that for sure?

9. What am I prepared to do about my single status?
10. Am I marriage material?

There! I have 10 questions. I'm sure you can think of some I haven't thought of, so bear with me as I take a good hard look at these questions. I don't know where the answers will lead, but if you're willing to take the journey with me, maybe together we can discover answers we can live with.

One more thing. I must tell you what happened to me last Tuesday evening at the park. I was sitting on a picnic table near the big maple tree by the river reading a book. I'm thinking of applying for a nursing position with the city's Department of Public Health, and the job requires you to do school visits—update vaccines for kids and stuff like that. Anyway, I was refreshing my brain on the major contagious diseases kids get, and call me weird, but I was really getting into the treatment and diagnosis of the many versions of hepatitis when it gradually dawned on me that someone had entered my space. Sure enough, a woman had sat down at my table.

Strange, I thought. There were at least two other free tables close by, and shaded, too. Why is this person at my table? Now, before you start on me, I know this is a free country, but you just don't come to a park and sit beside a perfect stranger when there are other seating options. So I put on my best frown and turned my head in the direction of the interloper, 'cause that's what she was, only to see this sweet face smiling up at me.

"Hi," she said. "I saw you sitting here and decided to come join you. You don't have to talk to me, but I just needed to be in the company of someone. I hope you don't mind. Some people like to have their private space, you know, and get upset when others come inside."

Well, talk about hitting the nail on the head. What do you say to something like that? What would you have done? If you say "I'd get up and find myself another seat," I thought about doing that. But you know how it is when you've found the perfect sitting position and have yourself arranged in just the right way so no body part is being unduly stressed? The last thing you want to have to do is to shift that position. So no way was I going to move. Plus, as I said before, I am a Christian. I try to do the right thing, even when I don't feel like it. I couldn't just walk away, even if I wanted to, from the plea of a perfect stranger for the pleasure of just being in my company. I couldn't! So I nodded to her and said, "It's OK," and got back to my reading.

But my concentration was shot. Neither hepatitis A, B, nor the HPV could engross me, so I shut the book and examined my company. Even though her face was turned toward the river, I could tell that the water had transported her mind away someplace very far. She looked to be in her mid-70s. She had a light shawl draped around her shoulders and shoulder-length hair, all salt—not even a hint of pepper. Her elbows, resting on the table, meandered to surprisingly beautiful slim fingers, nails clean and cut short—tapered-like. Something about the shape of her nose made me guess her to be of Eastern European descent. Her face, set in profile, had many wrinkles demarking life passages. *Fascinating*, I thought. A face in repose can so beg for speculation, so many questions to be asked. I watched her as she watched the river, and I wondered.

She turned suddenly, and before I could shift my eye to a point above her head and pretend that I, too, had been gazing at my own unseen memories, I was caught. I smiled weakly.

She smiled back. That same sweet smile she'd used to greet me earlier. Why have I never really thought about smiles? The fact that they are gifts we share with others? And that in the sharing there is a kind of acknowledgment of a person that says, "Yes, I see you, and we are on this planet together." That's what her smile did for me.

Well, to make a long story short, we started talking. She asked about the book I was reading, and I ended up telling her that I was planning to apply for a new job. Of course, one thing led to another, and before I could help myself, the question that's been plaguing me came out. I told her about the session at the convention center; I even mentioned the questions I listed earlier—not all of them, and certainly not in the order I have them written here.

Well, Natasha, that's her name, Natasha Nowakowski, listened with her lovely face that looks so beautiful even in profile, and when I had wound down to the end of my litany of woe, revealed all my pent-up anger against the poor convention center presenter who has no idea of the catalyst of introspection she'd provoked, Natasha nodded and sighed. Then she leaned in to me as if about to reveal a top-secret message for my ears only, and this is what she said in her soft accented voice.

"Quilla [no, I did not tell her my full name], one day you reach a certain age and discover that parts of your life are different from what you expected. You're single when you thought you'd be married with children. You expected to have grandchildren to keep you company in your old age, but you have none. Your dream to be a great artist is covered in spiderwebs somewhere in a dark corner of your mind. I think these things we expect to happen, they shape our picture of the future. And when they don't happen, we feel like . . . like we lost something, something important that should have happened but didn't. And this loss is like severing, like death—but there's nobody to mourn with you."

What do you make of that! When she said the part about "the loss is like severing, like death"—I got goose bumps all over my brain. Right there in the July heat I felt cold all over.

Do you believe that God sends people your way to teach you things? I do. By the time Nat and I finished (she told me to call her Nat), I knew what I had to do. I was going to have more of these conversations. I would use my God-given smile of acknowledgment and ask women just like me the question. Maybe in their stories I will find a way of reconciling myself to my single state of affairs and make contentment my new partner. Maybe. At least it will keep me busy for a while. Again, please accept my apologies for the earlier rant. Now that I've put some thoughts down to see in black and white, I somehow feel better.

Oh, before I forget to mention it, Natasha and I are going to stay in touch. I don't know where she lives and she didn't offer any contact information, but we made plans to meet at the park whenever our paths took us there. We will sit in the same seat or close to the same area so that we can visit with each other and share company. Go figure!

Chapter 2

Mara

Meet Mara. She's been coming to our church for about five years, ever since she emigrated from her native island of Jamaica. With skin the color of dark-brown honey kissed by sunshine, shoulder-length kinky locks, and a verbal speedometer that could challenge a Formula I racer, you always know where you stand with Mara. She's 34 years old, and is an executive assistant at a management consulting firm downtown.

Once I decided on this investigative assignment (my mission, or project, if you want to call it that), Mara was one of the first persons I thought of—she and my friend Susan. I could count on Mara for the straight goods, so to speak. She's pretty open about being single and hating it.

I called her soon after I ran into Natasha, and we agreed to meet the following Thursday evening after work. Seeing that this was her interview and I wanted her to feel comfortable, I asked her to pick the meeting place. She suggested her apartment, about a 25-minute drive from my place, located on the side of the city where Susan lives. If Mara and I finished early, I could go look Susan up, even though she's still a bit peeved at me from the convention center incident.

Mara lived on the eleventh floor of one of those lifestyle high-rises with all the so-called amenities. All it needed was a valet service and a people-oriented concierge. I rang the lobby telephone, and the door opened silently to let me in. I was taken on an equally cushioned elevator ride to the eleventh floor, where the automated elevator voice announced my arrival.

No sooner had I entered Mara's apartment, which was tastefully decorated with warm island home paintings of white-sand beaches and African carvings, than she offered me something to eat.

"Do you eat ackee? I haven't had dinner yet, so if you want to join me, that's what's on the menu."

I felt my taste buds react, and trust me, the reaction was not positive. I vigorously abhor that dish. Why Jamaicans get so passionate about that yellow tofu-scrambled egg yolk-looking mushy concoction to which they've added salted cod, of all things, and made it a national dish is beyond me.

Give me a mango any day, or even some fried dumplings, but ackee? Yuck!

"Thanks, Mara, but it's not one of my favorite foods."

"Chile [child], you don't like ackee? Half you life gone den! Obviously you haven't had it made for you by a professional."

Oh, no. I'd offended the Jamaican pride. Next thing she'd be insisting that I must try *her* version of the dish, and I was going to have to say no. Not a good start to my interview.

"Trust me, Mara, I've tried almost every recipe from every single Jamaican at church. I guess I just don't have the taste for it."

She shrugged. "Suit yourself. I have some mango nectar. You like mangoes?"

"Yes. I love mangoes!" I enthusiastically replied, grateful for a shared likeness for something.

"Well then, maybe only a quarter of you life gone." Indicating one of the chairs at her round, four-seater dining table, she invited, "Come. Sit down and chat with me while I eat. I'll get you that drink. I typically add a bit of ginger beer and some ice. That OK with you?"

Never having tried that combination, I nodded anyway. Well, let me tell you, when that drink hit my taste buds it woke up my mouth! I heard the rush of waves against a beach, reggae beats thudding in the distance, and I simply closed my eyes. I had just tasted paradise punch.

Mara's killer smile flashed. "I see you like it. Maybe next time you might try some of my ackee. Just because you've had several bad experiences with something doesn't mean you should rule out everything in that category. Just remember that, Quilla girl."

I took another sip of the drink, and this time I felt the heat of the sun and saw a handsome stranger of the male species walking toward me with a look that suggested I was his destiny. "Are you sure it's just mango nectar and ginger beer you have in this drink?"

She ignored my question. "It does make you want to lie on a beach and chill out, doesn't it?"

"Oh, yes."

Finishing her meal, Mara cleared the table. "Let's go sit on the sofa and get comfortable." Once we were settled she said, "Tell me again exactly what you want to talk to me about, just so we're clear."

I repeated the story about the incident at the convention center, including my wrath at the audacity of the woman's question—"Why am I not married by now?"—and my subsequent thoughts on the subject, along with my decision to interview a few single women. Mara, who had taken a seat in a high-back wicker chair that sported a bright-yellow padded seat and cushioned backrest, tucked her legs under her and listened attentively. When I finished my intro, she looked at me keenly.

"Did God send you here?"

"Huh? What do you mean?"

"I mean, did you ask God which person you should talk to about this topic, and He suggested you talk with me?"

"No, of course not! I just thought of you. I didn't ask God anything about this."

"Well, you should have."

This is what I mean when I said you get the straight goods from Mara. "You're right. I should have," I agreed.

"He must have sent you anyway. I'm having issues with Him on this very topic, so I've not been talking to Him much recently. He knows I'm mad, so He sent you!" Mara nodded as if having a conversation with a voice in her head. "Cool. I can deal with that. Let's see how this intervention of His plays out. Where do you want to start and how do you want to do this?"

She had the most fascinating accent. One minute she sounded totally Jamaican, and the next it sounded something like a cross between Canadian and British. Taking a deep breath, I got straight to the point. "So why do you think you're not married, assuming you want to get married?"

Mara pursed her lips and tilted her head my direction. A brown lock of hair fell over her left eye. Instead of replying, she turned the question on me.

"You want to get married, Quilla?" Her question, asked in that caring voice of hers, touched something vulnerable in me.

"Yeah," I nodded, feeling a strong urge to cry. Mara did not press.

"Me too, chile. Since I was 23 years old I knew for sure—sure I wanted to get married. Sometimes I'd see a couple walking down the beach hand in hand with one or two kids running behind them, and I knew I wanted that for myself one day."

Four questions rushed to my mind. Was it marriage that she desired, or the image of happiness that the couple with their kids presented? Had a man ever proposed to her? Had she been in serious relationships? Were there no eligible men in her home church back in Jamaica? It then dawned on me that asking these women why they had not yet married, which on the surface seemed such a no-brainer, might be entering a path of pain for some. I must tread carefully.

Mara, however, did not need for me to tread carefully. She continued her talk as if she'd rehearsed for the moment. "It's not like I've never been asked, you know. If you discount Buddy, who proposed to me when we were 8 years old, then I've had two—no, make that three—proposals in the past 10 years."

I was shocked. Three! Wow! I had managed almost one, and some days I wonder if it was really ever one at all.

But I could see how she'd get that many. A face that was blemish-free, she had immaculately outlined eyebrows, rounded cheeks, full lips, and a killer smile.

"So what happened, Mara? Why, when you want to get married and you had three proposals, are you still single?"

"That's easy to answer. One of the guys was already married, though I didn't know it during most of the short time we dated. When I confronted him, he tried to convince me to wait for him—he'd already begun divorce proceedings. He also claimed to be a fellow Christian. The second guy cited incompatibility just six weeks before our wedding. And the third— well, I broke that one off when I realized I didn't love him enough. He was not my soul mate, plus he wasn't a Christian. I just couldn't go there. He also wanted to get into bed. But then again, all of them wanted that—well, except guy number two. He wanted us to wait until marriage."

Again my mind dumped several questions into my consciousness. Three proposals! Three incompletes! It's enough to make you question your own desirability or wonder about the kind of men you attract. I ignored my mental questions and continued with the interview.

"And after all that, you still want to get married?"

Mara smiled sheepishly. "Shoot me for being a fool, but I still do. And that's what got me so mad at God recently. Quilla, I'm 34 years old. I want to have kids. I want to be that picture of the family on the beach. Why isn't God making that happen for me? What do I do with my sexual feelings? A 34-year-old virgin! Nowadays that could make front-page news. Then there are certain times of the month when I think that if I don't have sex I'm going to go nuts. God and I are usually pretty tight, but lately"—she made a sucking sound with her teeth—"I'm just mad at Him.

"The other night after work the guys invited me to join them at a club where they hang out. I usually say no, but that night I just couldn't face coming home to this empty apartment. I'm trying to do the right thing, but every day it gets harder and harder. And to add insult to injury, last Sunday morning I was starting to feel guilty for neglecting God for so long—you know? I miss our times together. So I picked up my devotional book to at least read a little something. Guess what the text for the day was? Guess what it was?"

I took a shot in the dark. "'Wait on the Lord'?"[1]

Mara jumped out of her chair. "How did you know? The text I read was a different one but with the same message. 'But they that wait upon the Lord shall renew their strength.'[2] I could have flung the book through the window. WAIT! What have I been doing all these years if not waiting? Sometimes God's responses make me want to scream! So I told Him, 'I can't deal with this today. I've been waiting way too long as it is, so I really don't want to hear nothing about waiting and renewing my strength. I want to hear that while I am yet speaking, You've already dispatched the angel Gabriel to bring me a man. How's that!' But as usual, when I ask for things that really matter to me, God seem to zip up His lips!"

Mumbling under her breath, Mara made that teeth-sucking sound again as if she was reliving the incident with God. "Good thing Stelle called and invited me out for brunch at Papa John's. I wanted to break things, I was so mad. Do you get where I'm coming from, Quilla girl?"

Did I get it? Oh, I got it, all right. I could so relate, but I don't know about shutting down ties with God just because we don't get what we want. What if the thing we want is not the best thing for us? And come to think of it, did you notice how Mara just skipped over guy number two? I bet there's a lot of pain there. But should I ask about it? Is it my business?

"I completely get you, Mara," I said.

Honestly, though, I really wanted to know about guy number two. Mentally I asked God if I should go there. Before I had a clear answer, however, my mouth was asking the question. "What exactly happened with the second guy? What did he mean by incompatibility reasons?"

Mara did not answer. Back in her chair again, she leaned her locks against the bright-yellow padding and stared into space. Now I'd gone and done it. I'd offended her. Why can't I ever wait to let my mind dictate my actions rather than running my mouth off? Looking for a way back to the friendly give-and-take of a few minutes earlier, I decided it was not fair to expect the people I interviewed to do all the disclosing. I needed to own up to a few things as well.

"Mara, I'm 10 years older than you are, and I still struggle with the issue of not being married. I question God as well on this. It's not like there are very many . . . Let me rephrase that. There are very few single men in the church, let alone eligible ones. That said, I've done a bit of dating, and here I am still single. Forty-four years old! Did I do something to cause this? Sometimes I wonder if I have some inherent flaw that no one's told me about that keeps men from approaching me. And as for those guys who took the time to take me out on a few dates, I wonder what they discovered about me that sent them running the other direction? What is it about me? Am I not marriage material? Am I not worth the journey of discovery? Am I not beautiful enough? not smart enough? What is wrong with *me*, Mara?" I heard the catch in my voice, and shut up.

Mara, bless her heart, did not offer me a tissue. Instead she looked at me, sincerity written all over her face, and said, "Sometimes men are just plain stupid, Quilla girl. They don't have the ability to recognize gold when they see it. And you are pure gold, Quilla. Pure gold. I've been watching you from the time I came to church. If anyone is perfect wife material, you're it."

I couldn't help the next question. "If that's true, Mara, then why am I still single?"

As soon as I'd asked the question, I realized my mistake. I was becoming the interviewee. Not good. I'm compromising my objectivity. Back up, Quilla. So I begged off to go to the washroom—partly because I needed to go and partly for some stock taking. There in the bathroom I made mental notes.

What do you make of Mara so far?
Here's my list:

1. She's lonely and sexually frustrated. (*I can relate to that!*)
2. She's mad at God, and her devotional life is on pause.
3. Guy number two might be a clue to some of her anger.
4. It's getting harder to hang on to her virtue, and she expects God to do something about her situation: a miraculous intervention.

By writing down what I'm observing about Mara and all the other women I plan to interview, I am hoping to get some kind of clarity on this question: "Why am I not married by now?" Here is Mara at 34, thinking she's too old to be a virgin. What do you think about that? What would she say if I told her that at 44 years old I've never actually had sex? That one time—let's call it a near miss—doesn't really count.

---

[1] Ps. 27:14.

[2] Isa. 40:31.

Chapter 3

When I returned to the living room, Mara had opened the doors to the covered balcony abutting the room, and now she beckoned me to join her. Enclosed in glass, the balcony allowed for opened windows and fresh air, unusual in a high-rise. A slightly awkward silence developed as we both stared out the window at the somewhat smog-covered skyline.

"It's not that I didn't hear your question, you know," began Mara. "I just hadn't anticipated going there in our little chat."

Quick to repair lost ground, I added, "No, I shouldn't have asked. This interview, however, is taking me down some paths I hadn't anticipated. I don't know that I can be as objective as I need to be while doing it."

"So don't be objective," Mara said firmly. "How can you be objective about something that's so close to your heart? I think as long as you're sensitive to people's feelings and give them time to come to terms with some of the memories your questions trigger, you'll be fine. As long as you realize that by going down this road and asking what seems like a simple question *on the surface*, it's going to force people to dig back to some sticky stuff in their past. Are you prepared for that, Quilla girl?"

The summer breeze was back in Mara's voice, so I knew we were going to be OK. Quilla girl—is that my new name now? I didn't mind it, though. Coming from Mara, it felt right. "No, I'm not prepared, but I'm hoping that in the process of talking to people like you I might get some clarity for myself and come to terms with what is left of my life."

"Then in that case the quest is worth it for all of us, Quilla."

A buzzing sound sent Mara scurrying for her telephone.

"Yellow," she answered. "You're downstairs? Well, come on up. You're just the person we need to provide some guidance on this subject Quilla and I are discussing." Turning to me she said, "Quilla girl, you're going to meet my good friend Stelle. She can be cou___ on to be the voice of reason on any topic, this one included. Plus I ha___ ___ested interest in seeing if it's possible to ruffle those always-smooth f___ ___rs of hers."

Stelle

I greeted Stelle with some interest. My first impression of her put me in mind of the PR woman on the old TV show *The West Wing*. Tall, shoulders slightly rounded from probably growing too tall ahead of her peers, she exuded an air of confidence and calm assurance. After Mara's introduction she regarded me with a quizzical look.

"Quilla," she mouthed my name. "Is that short for something? And is it spelled q-u-i-l-l-a, like the feather pen with an a at the end? I suppose if you were Spanish it would sound more like 'Keeya.'"

Mara rolled her eyes good-naturedly as she led us back to the living room. "There she goes. Everything, my dear Quilla, is open for the investigative probing of one Stelle Kingswood! Feel free to disregard her question." Then to Stelle: "Not even a minute in my house, and you're harassing my guest."

"It's OK. I don't mind," I said. "My full name is Tranquility Hazelwood. So Quilla—(like the feather pen)—would be the most likely short form for my name and the one I answer to. However, I've been called Keela, Keelover, Tequila, Sea breeze, and everything else associated or not associated with tranquillity. And for the record, I am not a tranquil person."

Stretching out a long hand with nails graced by a French manicure, Stelle greeted me warmly. "It's my pleasure to meet you, Quilla, as in the feather pen with an a at the end." Then seating herself on the same couch I'd previously occupied, she asked Mara, "Did you make any ackee today?"

Mara's eyes narrowed at her. "Yes, I have yours set aside and was planning to give it to you tomorrow at lunch. What? You couldn't wait till then?"

Stelle licked her lips as she shook her head. "Can I have some now? Please, man, ah beg you!"

Mara glared at her, arms akimbo. "Stelle, that accent is awful. How many times must I remind you that under no circumstances should you attempt to speak like a Jamaican? We are an accommodating group of people, but that hurts both the ear and the other sensibilities. I don't know how come you eat so much and it shows nowhere. Your belly must have a deep gully in it occupied by a fat tapeworm."

Stelle ignored her. "Is it in the same container in the fridge?"

Defeated, Mara sat down. "Help yourself. Then come back out here and earn your supper, you breathing excuse for a beanstalk!"

Stelle sashayed off to the kitchen to find her food. "You work with Stelle?" I asked Mara.

"No. We met at the fitness center over by York Street a couple years back. Stelle is big on fitness, life balance, and eating right. Her only concession to meat of any kind is fish, and since she tried my ackee she's been hooked. Despite the fact that I rag her a lot, she's a good egg. We get along pretty well, and she's very respectful of other people's beliefs. I must warn you, though! She's as curious as nine cats and wants to know every turn of phrase or idiom that comes out of your mouth."

Stelle returned with a small plate of the ackee and rice. She did not look happy. "I couldn't find any whole-wheat fried dumplings," she stated grumpily.

"I didn't make any."

"But . . ."

"Do you recall the saying about beggars and choosers?" Mara interrupted.

Stelle sighed, sat down, and dutifully began to eat, a small cloud settling over her countenance.

Mara relented. "You're such a spoiled brat! Fine. Come Sunday I'll make you some fried dumplings. Happy now?"

Sunshine broke out on Stelle's face as she nodded happily. "Now what project did you want me to help with?"

"Why are you not married by now?" Mara announced.

Stelle choked on her rice. "Why am I not what?"

I jumped into the conversation before it got out of hand. "Not you personally." I then retold my experience at the convention center and without going into too much detail, quickly brought her up to speed on my questions and the discussion so far.

"What do you say, Stelle?" Mara asked. "That being single at this point in your life is *your* choice?"

Stelle raised her fork to signal she needed to complete her chewing. "Of course," she finally replied.

"I guess you don't want to be married, huh?" I asked.

Stelle finished the last morsel and rested the plate on the side table next to the sofa. "I did not say I don't want to be married. I agreed with Mara's question that being single so far has been my choice."

I wanted clarification. "By that you mean that you could have been married by now if you'd wanted to?"

"That's right," said Stelle. "But the question is do I want to be married for the sake of being married? Do I want to be married to have easy access to sex? Do I want to be married in order to have children, for companionship, or to satisfy some societal expectation? Personally, I want to be married to someone who's going to accentuate me, not someone who thinks he's going to complete me. I feel pretty complete by myself. But I would, when I get married, want to be with someone who respects my personhood and with whom I could do the same."

I thought back to Ken, my one near-miss marriage proposition. I met Ken on a visit to Boston nine years ago. I had attended a nursing conference in Boston and decided to tag some vacation time to the end of the conference. That weekend when I attended the local church, Ken was one of the greeters at the door. He asked my name and where I was visiting from. He made sure I was welcomed from the pulpit and arranged for me to join a few church members for lunch. Dear sincere, kindhearted Ken. After the church service and lunch, he drove me back to my hotel and volunteered to show me around his city. His black Honda Accord came to fetch me at least four times during my 10 days in Boston, and at the end of my vacation he asked if he could come visit me sometime.

"St. Catharines, Ontario, is a far way from Boston," I told him.

"I want to see more of you, Quilla," he'd replied. "I'm sure you can tell I find you an alluring woman."

Yes. He actually used those words to describe me. Alluring woman. No man had ever described me this way before. Not even Sam, the guy from church whom I'd dated on and off while I was in college.

And how was I feeling about all this attention, you ask? Amused mostly, and maybe indulgent. Ken reminded me of a puppy our family once had. I don't mean that in a bad way. He just had that eager-to-please look about him. Just by smiling in his direction I could make his day. During the following months Ken visited me several times, and I went back to Boston a few times, eventually to meet Ken's family. His parents were older and pretty simple folk. And Ken had an older sister living at home with her two kids, following a divorce from her husband of six years. The family welcomed me with open arms. I brought their son much happiness, his dad told me.

So one Sunday morning, as Ken was getting ready to take the long drive back to Boston after visiting me for the weekend, I walked him to his car. Back then I was still living at home— renting the basement of my parents' place. Ken stayed upstairs with them during his visits. They took a liking to him. Anyway, as I was saying, Ken and I walked to his car holding hands in comfortable familiarity. Looking over his shoulder to see if he was being observed by my folks, he drew me to him and kissed me. Ken was a good kisser, and my heart always did a little flutter when he kissed me. I just wished he wasn't always so proper, you know.

After he kissed me he opened the door to his black Honda and sat at the wheel. He started the engine and then turned it off. Looking up at me from where he sat, he asked, almost conversationally, "You ever think about us getting married, Quilla?"

I must confess the question caught me off guard. Was this a marriage proposal? If I answered yes, would that make me seem too eager? If I said no, would I seem uncaring? Where was the declaration of undying love and devotion?

I hedged. "It's crossed my mind. You?"

"Every time I do this long drive I want you home with me instead of my coming all this way to see you. We're good for each other, don't you think? We get along, and we share the same beliefs and values."

And that, for the most part, is the beginning and the end of my simple tale. I received no "you are the woman of my dreams," no ribbons in the sky, just an image of us living together in placid contentment, rubbing noses from time to time like two friendly puppies.

But I wanted more. I wanted romance and heart palpitations and serenades along the Seine. I wanted candlelight dinners, walks in the park, "champagne breakfast" with a red rose for passion. I wanted a man who commanded my attention—not a kind puppy of a husband who would wear tube socks to bed.

So as time went by, the visits became fewer. The question was never asked again, and one day we both decided to end it. Actually he called and, being the decent person that he was, told me he wanted to explore a new relationship closer to home. And at the ripe old age of 37, my one last train to the Zion of matrimony left the station without me.

Why am I not married by now? Like Stelle said, I think I also wanted a soul mate. But to tell the truth, I'd give anything at this point in my life for the occasional kiss to flutter my heart and a mate who would wear socks with me to bed. For that matter, since that day of the almost proposal, no man has ever approached me for other than the occasional date with the implied hop into bed afterward. But a hop into bed is not my choice for date nights. Instead I go to bed alone with no one to warm my feet. At times the loneliness feels so cold that turning up the heat and donning thermal underwear couldn't ward off that kind of chill. Surely God must have another plan for my life than this.

"Stelle, do you ever listen to yourself?" Mara flared. "You must have an extremely low libido. What is wrong with marrying someone for sexual companionship?"

Stelle's reply was as calm as her face. "And after the sexual appetite is satisfied, Mara, what then?"

Mara sputtered. "You talk, you take walks, you plan your future together. Stuff like that! Duh!"

"You've just made my point, Mara," replied Stelle. "You are looking for more than just a sexual partner. You just described a life partner. The question, however, that you're probably getting at is the weightier issue of what to do with your sexual feelings while you wait for your life partner or soul mate. And your situation is even more complicated since your religious beliefs dictate that you abstain from sex prior to marriage."

"So what do you do?" Mara shot back.

"About my religious beliefs?"

"Don't play with me, Stelle," Mara growled. "I mean what do you do with your sexual feelings when you get them—Miss cool-as-cucumber under all circumstances?"

"I acknowledge them, then ignore them."

"Come again?" I asked.

"Even though I don't live under the religious constraints of no sex before marriage, I still think one should not just jump into a sexual relationship. Sex is too personal and intimate for me to share it casually. Maybe that's why your church recommends waiting till marriage. As to what I do with my sexual feelings, I suppose that not all women are the same when it comes to their sex drive. I suspect that some have higher, as you mention, libidos than others. However, unlike hunger, no one is going to die from not having sex. Technically, the human species will eventually die off if nobody procreates to perpetuate our kind, but the individual doing the abstaining will not die from lack of sex." She gave a dismissive snort. "Despite what some guys would have us believe. The sex urge is just what it is. An urge. Ignore it, and it goes away in time. Indulge it, and you need to keep feeding it. Don't feed it, and eventually you hardly feel the need for it at all."

I disagreed wholeheartedly. "Don't you have certain times of the month when you feel strong urges for sex?"

Mara did not give Stelle time to respond. "You might be content with leading a celibate life or waiting in the wings for Mr. Soul-mate to come," she retorted, "but that's crazy making. Seriously, Stelle, like Quilla asked, how do you deal with the loneliness? Man, I am trying hard to be a good Christian girl and hold off on the sex thing till I get married, but some days the longing and need is enough to make you grind your teeth down to the gums."

Stelle waved her beautifully manicured hand dismissively in our direction. "Those are just your high-fertility days. The hormones are hinting that they're ready and waiting just in case you need them. By the way, Mara, is that why you went to the club with the guys the other day? That's not your typical scene."

"So you were actually paying attention to what I was saying! I tell you, Stelle, your mind is a steel trap. I thought that all you got out of that litany of woe was my accidental reference to a shame tree. But you actually heard something! Well, next time, try to hear things when I'm saying them and not four whole days after the fact. If that was a life-and-death situation and I was Jewish, I'd be dead and long buried by now!"

"What's this about a shame tree?" I asked. "What's a shame tree?"

"Not you too!" cried Mara

"See," gloated Stelle. "Quilla is just as fascinated with the expression. Maybe you can explain it again. I want to make sure I have the context right if I need to use it in conversation."

Mara rolled her eyes. "God bless the poor hearer. Whoever it is will probably have to check herself into a madhouse after they hear your awful accent. For your information, Quilla, I was recounting to my good friend here an incident I was subjected to at the club the other night. There I was, already regretting my foolish decision to accompany the guys, when I became aware that the main attraction for the night was one of our former church sisters. Her stage name is Velvet. Following her performance—that had me looking anywhere but at the stage—she actually came to our table to say hello to me with that 'aren't we bad girls' kind of smile. To add insult to injury, Peter, one of the guys from work, asked to be introduced to her. I could have sunk through the floor.

"Have you ever seen a really dark-skinned person blush, Quilla? Well, my skin turned red. I'm sure even my teeth showed a tinge of pink, so embarrassed I was. But not so for our fallen star. Oh, no. She was in her element. *How does one fall so far from God?* I thought. *How did she get from church to this place?* Anyway, I was recalling the incident along with my embarrassment to Ms. Curiosity here, and I just mentioned that the woman's shame tree must be dead. Did I get any sympathy from her? No. All I got was a 20-item questionnaire about what a shame tree was!"

"So what exactly is it?" I demanded.

Mara groaned while Stelle gave me a righteous smile.

"All right. Here we go again. But, Quilla, my girl, for your peace and happiness, I caution you not to question my every turn of phrase. It will make me very unpleasant to be around. I talk the way I talk, and that's that!" She paused for emphasis. "Now, a shame tree is technically not a tree."

"So why—?" Mara's glare at my interruption made me swallow the rest of my question.

"It's more like a bush that grows wild in the country. However, all Jamaicans call it a shame tree, so don't go there asking people to show you a shame bush. What's special about this plant is that as soon as you touch it, the leaves curl inward, making the bush look completely withered, bashful-like. It doesn't respond that way to a strong wind. Only to a touch. So when someone behaves brazenly or shows no embarrassment at something that ought to be shameful, we say that their shame tree is dead." She folded her arms. "Happy now?"

"Isn't that fascinating?" murmured Stelle. And just at that moment a muffled voice announced into the conversational pause, "You are one with the universe."

"That's me," responded Stelle, reaching for her handbag.

Mara looked at me. "No. You're not going nuts. That's the ringtone on her phone."

Stelle checked the caller ID and returned the phone to her bag.

"Would that be Brad?" Mara pried.

Stelle sighed. "Yes. That would be Brad."

"And you just ignored him?" Mara pried some more.

"I'll see him tomorrow, or I can call him later. I hate it when I'm in conversation with people and they insist on answering their phones and having what should obviously be a private conversation while I sit there and try hard not to listen. It's just bad manners."

Being a sucker for a romantic story of any kind, I couldn't help asking, "Is Brad someone special?"

Mara leaned toward Stelle, eyes twinkling. "Quilla girl, remind me to fix you up with a special batch of mango nectar before you leave. That, my friend, is a wonderful question and asked with such pure innocence that it could not be contrived. Stelle! Please tell us, Is Brad someone special?"

Stelle calmly picked up her plate and purse, looked at her watch, and remarked. "Look at the time. Let it not be said that I've overstayed my welcome. Good night, Quilla. It was a pleasure meeting you. Good luck with your project. I'll be interested in hearing how the interviews are going, so next time you meet with Mara, have her tell me so I can continue to add my two cents. Mara, dear, I'll retrieve the rest of my lunch from your refrigerator and be on my way. I'll see you Monday. I'm not available for lunch tomorrow."

Mara nodded. "So that's the way you're going to play this game, eh? Cool. I'm cool with that. Catch you later. Just remember that my memory is even longer than that of an elephant's."

Stelle let herself out. I stood up as well. "Mara, I really appreciate you taking the time to talk. If you think of anything else to add to the discussion, just call, and I'll schedule another visit. Especially if you promise to serve that mango punch again."

"No problem. But before you go, do you mind saying a word of prayer? I'm not talking to God right now, but that doesn't mean I've thrown Him over, you know. But I don't feel right talking to Him when I'm so mad."

"But that's when you need to talk to Him most, Mara. Don't you think God is big enough to see beyond your anger to the pain and loneliness you're feeling? I think God would rather we speak to Him in anger than not at all."

"Maybe you're right. But right now the anger is a much better partner than trying to discern the ways of the Lord. At least it's something I recognize."

So I took Mara's hand, and we bowed our heads. "Dear God of the universe," I prayed, "You who sits high and looks low, You whose eyes are on little sparrows and tender lilies and who can number the hairs on our heads, You Holy One who knows us all by name, and at the creation of the universe set in motion a series of events that could take us to this moment in time. Please draw near to us now. We stand before You as women who desire to do Your will but find the yielding part, the waiting part, the understanding part, difficult.

"How long, Lord, we want to know, must we live in loneliness and want? Is it something that we're not doing that we need to do before You can bless us with the desires of our hearts for life mates and family? Is it

Your desire for us to walk alone so that we can best fulfill Your destiny for our lives? Is there something in our past that we need to understand and deal with? Speak, Lord. Even though we might not want to hear what You have to say, speak to our hearts and reveal Your will for our lives. Until You make your message clear to us, however, help us to remember that Your grace is truly sufficient for us. And let us claim the words You said to the apostle, 'My strength is made perfect in weakness.'*

"Console my friend and Your daughter Mara. You know her heart. You know her pain. Continue to surround her as only an understanding Father can, and in the fullness of time lead her gently back to true communion with You, I pray in Jesus' name. Amen."

Mara's grip on my hand tightened almost to the point of pain. I opened my eyes and saw that hers were shut tight but not tight enough to hold back the tears. I took her other hand in mine and allowed her to squeeze that one too just as tightly. When she'd gotten herself under control, she gave me a wet smile and a hug, and we parted—me with a question on my lips. Dear God, what have I started?

---

* 2 Cor. 12:9, NKJV.

Chapter 4

It was close to 9:30 when I got home from meeting with Mara and Stelle, but after a shower and a short devotional I found sleep elusive. I make it a point to be in bed no later than 10:30 on weeknights, and a good book after my time with God is typically my ticket to dreamland. Tonight, however, my mind kept doing somersaults. I felt an ache in my heart. Something was bugging Mara. But how to help her? Did it have anything to do with guy number two?

Earlier in the week I'd learned that my favorite TV talk show was doing a special on the single woman syndrome, so I recorded it. And since sleep would not come, I went downstairs to watch the program. Forty minutes into the show I concluded it had nothing new to say on the issue. There were just as many single women outside the church bemoaning the lack of good man material as there were in. But one thing got me thinking. The expert, a psychologist they'd brought in for the show, said that some people are relationship phobic. He said that negative experiences in our early life, the critical time when we should be forming our sense of connectedness, can sometimes leave permanent scars. These scars, he said, can prevent us from developing and maintaining healthy relationships with others.

When I heard that statement, I thought about a particular foster child (he had to be less than 2 years old) that someone had brought to church for a while. What a beautiful boy he was! Obviously of mixed heritage, I guess Italian/Afro Canadian, he had the most soulful eyes I've ever seen. What I found most unusual about that little boy, however, was that I never heard him cry or whine or insist, as children do so well, on having his needs met. If he was put into the playpen in the mother's room while the person he was with went into the service, he'd just stand there holding on to the playpen rail, staring at you with those soulful eyes. If you reached out your arms to pick him up, he gladly came to you. And when you put him back, it almost seemed that he just accepted it. It's as though he had learned at that very early age not to expect loving care.

But shouldn't that be the right of every child? Growing up with the assurance that he or she is loved and that their little lives matter? What happened in such a short life to make this child believe what he did about the world? As suddenly as he appeared at our church, he was no longer around. I often wonder about him and how he's doing. And every time I think of him I feel a pain around the vicinity of my heart. We failed him. I know we did. As a church and as a society, we failed him. A child should not have such a low expectation of people at such a young age.

So how does this relate to the talk show I was watching? It's like this. When these children, these unloved or unconnected children, grow into adulthood, can they truly be intimate with another person? Could it be that some of my single sisters, and even a few of those who are married, have intimacy issues? Could it be that without meaning to, they give off signals that say, "Touch me not. I don't expect you to be around, so if you leave me, that's what's supposed to happen"? Or these unconnected boys who grow up to be men and run from one woman to the next, these guys who are attracted to the sense of belonging but without the internal resources to give and take—is there a deep-down reason for their behavior?

Oy! My head is hurting. By the way, did I tell you I got the public health nurse job? No? Well, I did. I start in three weeks—August 22. Hopefully I'll be able to get most of my interviews done by then. Who am I kidding? There are so many loose ends to tie up at work before I leave that I'll be hopping until the very last day. Thank God that tomorrow is Friday and I'm off this weekend. I don't know about you, but I'm going to bed. I'll trust God to help me calm my frantic thoughts. I suggest you do the same. Tomorrow night I'll call Susan and see what she's been up to. She, for sure, will be my next interviewee.

Susan

What can I tell you about my good friend Susan? She's the complete opposite of me. I set goals and methodically go after each one. Susan, on the other hand, is a dabbler. Not content to wait for life to happen or for things to come to her, she makes the change she desires. I've known Susan for years. We grew up in the Niagara area together, attended the same church, and once we finished our nursing program at Niagara College, we conspired on a strategy to present to our parents as to why they should give us their blessing to leave home at age 21 and move to the big city of Toronto. We even shared an apartment there for a few years. When my dad developed MS, I moved back to St. Catharines for about three years to help

Mom manage his care. It was during that time that I met Ken, but then I've already told you about him.

It was Mom who finally came to me one day and told—not asked—me to go back to Toronto. That while she appreciated all the help I'd given, I needed to get working on my life—not theirs. I remember looking at her in astonishment.

"Go, Quilla," she'd ordered. "Go back to Toronto or wherever you want, and start creating a life for yourself. Find a nice man, get married, and have us some grandkids. Daddy will be around for a while, and I've already made arrangements for a nurse to come in three days per week to help me."

"But Mom," I'd protested, "having a nurse three days a week will cost a fortune."

"Yes, it will. But your rich brother is footing the bill. Since he cannot be here to physically assist, he is sending money. Already he's deposited enough money in our account to pay the nurse for the next six months. That plus our insurance will take good care of our finances. So listen to your mother. Go, sweetheart. We'll be OK."

Daddy had looked at me wistfully as I'd hugged him goodbye. We'd always been close, and it had been hard for me to leave him. He now relied on a wheelchair for mobility; his weak-muscled arms had sluggishly hugged me, and his eyes had teared up. But Dru Hazelwood had spoken. And what Dru Hazelwood wanted, she got.

One of the good things about being a nurse is that your job is very portable and is always in demand somewhere. Within a week of returning to Toronto, I had a job lined up working 12-hour days at the women's hospital. Four days on, three days off. The long workdays were demanding, but I ended up with at least two weekends off each month, sometimes three. I bunked with Susan for the first three months (she'd kept the apartment), but after that I felt the need to have my own space. So I went house hunting and bought a small townhouse (you know the kind, they're more like row houses) for a small fortune in the west end of downtown Toronto. It came with a one-car garage, so my fuel-friendly small domestic car fitted in perfectly with my urban lifestyle, allowing me the freedom to leave the city on days off or on weekends. For city traveling, however, it's usually much easier to take the public transit. Susan still lives in North York, about a 30-minute drive from my place.

Yes, you don't have to remind me. I already started to talk about Susan, but as you can tell by now, my mind travels a lot and not always in a predictable pattern. And maybe I'm not as methodical as I like to believe.

At least now you have a better context for things, wouldn't you say?

So Susan and I go way back. Even during the time I had gone back home to help with Dad, we kept in touch. Most weekends I'd visit Susan, and we'd go to church together and then do whatever else came to mind. Ken came along with us a few times, but Susan never quite took to him. They were chalk and cheese.

I think I mentioned before that Susan is desperate to have a kid. To tell the truth, she's starting to worry me. Even though she's only 11 months younger than me, some days I feel like her mother. How do I tell this most-of-the-time reasonable woman that because of her advancing age, she may want to let go of this obsession of giving birth? She's 43 years old, for crying out loud! Even if she met a guy today and he proposed tomorrow, and allowing for a minimum six- to eight-week courtship, then planning the wedding, and let's say she got pregnant right away, the fact is that she'd be close to 45 by the time she was ready to birth this child. But no!

Lately she's taken to calling me The Voice of Doom. A few weeks ago I thought her natural reason was reasserting itself when she actually agreed that Mr. Right might not be anywhere in sight. Boy, the sigh of relief I breathed almost cleared the kitchen floor of the week's accumulation of dust. But it was a wasted sigh. In the next breath she mentioned that she had done some Internet research on sperm banks and was seriously considering that option. Her rationale was that for her, having children took a higher priority than getting married. Then she added, "And also, with a sperm donation I won't be breaking any biblical laws about premarital sex, *and* I won't have to deal with the complication of an interfering daddy figure."

Pray for me, please! I love this woman like a sister from my mother's womb, but there are some days . . . words fail me, especially when I talk about my friend. Bear with me while I connect with my inner hero.

Jesus is my friend. I can do all things. I will not get upset. I will be patient and kind and long-suffering and tenderhearted and slow to anger and abounding in all good things. Yes, yes, yes, Jesus is my friend.

I'm OK now.

Susan's coming over tomorrow. Actually I'm having a few people over for lunch after church. She has been pouting about the convention center incident, but after I spouted off about the sperm bank thing, I'm sure she's using our little tiff as a way of making sure she hears no more of my "option-killing, fear-mongering, non-out-of-the-box-thinking, joy-stealing kind of talk." That's what she said when I raised such practical issues as what she would tell the child about the father. What about genetic diseases and stuff like that? I even asked her if she thought this was a morally right thing to do. Would God approve of her decision? Seriously, I was not trying to preach to her, but this was my girl, my sister in Christ, my pal—I had to try to reach her! And appealing to her spiritual nature . . . well . . . I just had to go there. That's when she used all those "ing" words I just told you about.

What else can I tell you about my friend Susan? (I almost wrote the word "fiend" instead of "friend." Dr. Freud would certainly pounce on that one.) My friend Susan (oh, no—I first wrote "fiend" again—what's that about?) is what I call a man magnet. Mara would say that "she pretty like money." That woman can attract men like metal attracts magnet. You'd think that would give her an edge in the matrimony department!

Now, I'm no psychologist, but between you and me I think Susan has intimacy issues just like that little kid I was telling you about. She can attract the men, but she can't hold on to them. There must be something preventing this beautiful woman from being married. And while for people like me it might have to do with lack of interested men to choose from or whatever else I don't know about, that is not Susan's situation. Doctors, lawyers, janitors, carpenters, shy nerds as well as brazen salesmen, deacons, elders, and unmarried pastors have all dated my friend. So you tell me, what is your diagnosis?

I have to document what happened today at lunch before it completely slips my mind. Not that there's any hope of that happening!

I'd prepared a few vegetarian dishes. Nowadays I find it easier to cook vegetarian when I have company, because I don't know when friends are going to turn on me. One week they're staunch carnivores, and the next they've swung completely to the other side and are extreme vegans. I err on the side of cooking for the lacto-ovo veggies. I love my cheese and milk.

Anyway, I'd prepared a broccoli bake, some seasoned wild rice, and one of those mock-meat roasts that have way too much salt to be healthy but taste really good with mushroom gravy. Wendell brought a cornbread (Wendell, married to Gloria, makes a mean cornbread), and Susan a salad. Susan always brings salad. Not always the good-for-you kind of salads, mind you. She specializes in calorie-filled greens. She'll toss in nuts (one day I think she will kill someone at my table who's allergic), cranberries, nacho chips, beans, peas, you name it. I don't know what she does, but even when I'm skeptical about eating one of her creations, I'm always pleasantly surprised that the combinations actually work.

So for lunch there was Susan, Wendell, Gloria, Edward (Wendell's nephew visiting from Atlanta), and me. When Susan arrived bearing her glass dish and salad fixings, I saw poor Edward's eyes nearly pop out of his head, and I can't say I heard much from him during the first part of the visit. Yes, Susan has that effect on men. Women hate her, and most men become mutely mesmerized.

The food was a hit. Wendell and Gloria, married forever and both great conversationalists, kept us entertained during the meal. Then Wendell asked a question that got the table quiet. He asked, "When you pray, do any of you listen for God to talk back to you?"

Talk about a conversation stopper. We all thought about it. Finally I shook my head. Susan was shaking hers, too, and Edward, well, he mumbled something incoherent.

"This is Wendell's latest quest," supplied Gloria. "He's been reading about stuff like that recently. What's the name of the guy you're reading now, honey?"

"Eldredge. John Eldredge," Wendell replied. "In his book called *Walking With God* [I wrote down the name and title] the author makes a pretty good case for how we can hear the voice of God and seek His direction, and not just for the big things in life but for the little day-to-day things, too. Like 'Should I vacation in the Maritimes or go up to the cottage?'"

"How about 'Will I get married in the next year or never?' Will He specifically answer me that?" Susan asked all serious as she tends to get about this subject.

"I'm not sure," Wendell answered. "I think God speaks to all of us differently. But let me tell you something that happened to me last week. Eldredge," he nodded toward Susan, "in this book, said that instead of picking up the Bible and reading a text each day or methodically following a yearly Bible reading plan, he challenged the reader just to ask God what text or passage He wants you to read that day. So being the experimentalist that I am, I decided to try it. Right there on my bed with Gloria sleeping beside me, I closed my eyes and tried my best to quiet my mind. Then I asked God what He would have me read from His Word."

"And?" Susan questioned impatiently.

But Wendell would not be rushed. He actually looked sheepish and excited at the same time. "And before the prayer had spoken itself in my thoughts, I heard as clearly as the August sun is shining outside, 'Matthew 8.'"

Wendell's excitement was getting contagious. I was so caught up in his story that I blurted out, "All of Matthew 8?"

"No, that's not the end of the story," he said. "I picked up my Bible—it was lying on the bed—then asked God, 'Did I hear You say Matthew 8?' Again I heard just as clearly, 'Matthew 8.' 'Which verse?' I asked. Again, just as clearly, 'verse 24.' By now my heart was racing and my brain spitting out all kinds of explanations, but I was committed to seeing this through. But even as I turned the pages I was doubting. How do I even know that Matthew 8 has a twenty-fourth verse? For the life of me I couldn't remember. If there was no verse 24, my experiment had failed and maybe proved that God does not really speak to people, at least not to me in that way. I wanted it to be true, even as I doubted it could happen."

As I tried to recall if there was a verse 24 in Matthew 8, Edward took a small NIV Bible out of an inner pocket and quickly flipped to the verse. He handed the book to me, and I read: "'Suddenly a furious storm came up on the lake, so that the waves swept over the boat. But Jesus was sleeping.'"

"'But Jesus was sleeping.'" Wendell's eyes shone with emotion. "That, my friends, hit the nail on the head. 'But Jesus was sleeping.' You see, all week long I'd been having difficulty sleeping. We're going through a big restructuring at work, and tensions are high. Would I have a job? What would change? What about my staff? How could I help them? Etc. All kinds of anxious thoughts had taken over my mind and were robbing me of sleep. So when I read that Jesus was sleeping, with waves sweeping over the boat, it was like a lifeline. In that instant I knew that I didn't need to worry. I serve the Master of ocean and earth and sky. I could sleep with the full assurance that God's in control of my life, and though storms rage I need not be anxious. I could sleep."

"So what did you do?" Susan asked.

"Right there I talked to Him in my mind. I told Him everything that had been keeping me awake, plus some other things, and for the first time in my Christian experience, I felt that I really mattered to God. Oh, yes, I believed I mattered to Him in the big scheme of the plan of salvation, but for the first time I knew that my little life, my personal situations, my happiness, mattered to God and that He actually looked forward to hearing from and talking with me."

"Wow," I said. "That's awesome, Wendell. Have you asked God anything else since then?"

A little of the light went out of his eyes. "To tell the truth, I'm afraid. What if the first time was just a fluke?"

Gloria slapped him on the arm. "Oh, you of little faith. God comes through for you, and still you doubt!" Using her fork to move around the dozen or so grains of rice left on her plate, she said, "I think talking to God is less about asking for stuff and more about the daily conversations. Since Wendell told me his story, I've been thinking about myself. I usually schedule time to 'have worship' or to pray, but maybe if I could get into the habit of talking to and listening to God even in the middle of work and day-to-day stuff, I'd spend each moment of my day with Him, and not just some scheduled time. So that's what I've been trying, and it works! Once we open the door to God and keep it open, He can speak with us, and we with Him anytime, anywhere."

Wendell's eyes twinkled in merriment. "See why I married her? She's not only beautiful but smart too." They shared a look, and we all looked away.

Oh, I thought, *to one day experience that kind of loving intimacy with a man of my very own!*

"Did Quilla tell you about her latest project?" Susan asked. She didn't wait for an answer. "She's asking single women past a certain age to speak to the question 'Why am I not married by now?' I'm her next interviewee. You think God might have something to say on this subject?"

Edward's eyes became alert. "Really? But why just single women? Why not single men?"

Susan beat me to a response, and her answer had an edge. "Because men can get married anytime they please, and most of them, when they do, marry younger women."

"Come again?" Edward asked.

"In any given year, and ruling out countries that practice gender selection, China and India to name a couple, the birth rate of men to women is something like 105 male babies to 100 females. My understanding is that males have a higher mortality rate than females and are a little bit more susceptible to disabilities that afflict children."

I was impressed. "When did you learn all this stuff?"

"Quilla. *You* know I research everything."

"Stupid of me. Of course I know that."

"By the time those males and females reach puberty, the ratio of males to females is about one to one, so it should follow that there should be a man available for every woman. Agreed?"

"Well, not quite," replied Gloria. "Not all men are heterosexual."

"Point taken," said Susan. "But neither are all women. So, all things considered, there should be a heterosexual man available for every heterosexual woman."

"A lot more men than women are in prisons," Wendell thoughtfully added. "And there are fewer men than women in the church. Plus with the wars going on, fewer single men are circulating in the population."

"Wendell, could you let me finish? The point I'm trying to make is that even though there should be one female for every male within one's age group, older men tend to marry younger women. So as the women get older, men their age do not see them as desirable. That's the biggest reason there are fewer men our age available for unmarried women—not because there are fewer men, but because they are off chasing after some young thing."

"Well, older women should marry younger men then," countered Wendell. "It's only fair. Tit for tat and all that."

"Yeah, right!" I said.

"What do you mean, 'Yeah, right'?" asked Wendell. I know he was playing with me but I couldn't help rising to the bait.

"Because a man of 80 can get away with marrying a 25-year-old. Yes, we might call her a gold digger and him a dirty old man, but society tends to be more accepting of it. Let an older woman marry a man that much younger than her!"

"That's an extreme example," Edward said. "Whether it's the man or the woman, such an age difference is just plain weird."

"So how many years older than you would you accept in the woman you marry?" Susan asked. The edge was back in her voice. Had she taken an instant dislike to him?

He didn't seem to notice, but he did stop to think for a moment, then said, "It would depend on the woman, what she's like, and how we relate to each other. Stuff like that. But I think I could handle a 10-year difference."

Susan's voice dripped sarcasm. "Yeah! Till your friends start making references to your woman being your 'auntie' or some similar put-down. Then you'd drop her like a hot potato. Face it, most men like the young thing that looks pretty clinging to their arm, and whose body parts still point east, not droop south. They don't care much for what's in a woman's head, her heart, and her soul. They don't want a woman who's going to challenge them, who's comfortable in her own skin, and whose life does not revolve around them and their needs! What do guys know about what's in a woman's heart?"

"Susan," I interjected, "we're just having a discussion here."

"Maybe your friend has been hanging around the wrong kind of guys," Edward said as he picked up his plate and headed toward the kitchen.

Susan followed hot on his heels. She had that look in her eyes. Oh, boy! Poor Edward was in for it.

"Wendell," I hissed. "Do something! She's going to have him for dinner."

Wendell did not move. Actually he looked amused, enigmatic even. "Oh, Edward can hold his own."

In panic I appealed to Gloria. "Gloria, please go deliver your nephew. You know how Susan gets when she's challenged. Men always assume that because she has a pretty face that she's a pushover, but . . ." I stopped midsentence. I might as well have been speaking to the wall. Gloria, too, looked like she had no intention of rescuing the poor, young man.

So I got up to follow them. But no sooner had I left the chair than Edward reentered the room and took his seat.

"Excuse me!" Susan stormed back in. "You just don't walk out on a person when they're talking!"

"Is that what you were doing?" he asked calmly. "It sounded more like you were shouting. "Plus," he continued just as calmly, "I went to put away my plate, and you followed *me*. I came back to sit with our other guests. Why don't you rejoin us?"

If I had not seen it with my own eyes, I would not have believed it. Susan opened and closed her mouth several times and then, to my astonishment, she actually sat back down. This man, this apparition from Atlanta, actually got my friend to shut up! I glanced at Gloria and Wendell to see if they looked as stupefied as I felt, but they didn't. Wendell actually passed his hand across his face as if he was trying to hide a grin. Who was this Southern stranger?

For the next little while, this Edward Grainge (I found out later from Gloria that he was 35 years old and single), with the tact of a Henry Kissinger, waxed eloquent on all the things women could do to reverse the preformed ideologies preventing them from finding fulfillment in life. For example: Why do we never question the validity of our assumptions regarding what our mate must be like? When did we make the decision that our marriage partner should be of a particular age or race or height or coloring? that they should have a particular job, be in a particular income bracket, drive a certain car, or dress a certain way? What if the man or woman who could be our soul mate comes in a different guise from the image we have in our heads? Would we be able to recognize him or her?

These were really good questions. Before I even had time to process them fully, and I'm sure there were other things he talked about that I missed, he made a statement that hit home for me. He said—and it is so etched in my consciousness that I quote it word for word—"God might have another ministry for some people's lives that precludes marriage." Then he went on to say something to the effect that maybe we just assume that because everyone else is married or getting married (whether or not they're happily so), and it's the thing to do when one comes of age, we impose this pressure on ourselves, and society does as well, to conform to that pattern. "Is it the destiny of every woman to be a mother and wife? Could it be that God's plan for your life precludes that option?"

Again my head filled with the typical million and one thoughts and questions. But I needed time to process all this. Reflection time to go through each piece of it, one by one. I took a large sip of water to quench my rising thirst at the same time Susan rediscovered her voice.

"Tell me, Edward," she said, matching his unruffled calm, "do you have normal sexual urges?"

I gagged, spewing water all over Wendell and Gloria, who were sitting directly in front of me. Now I know these dear friends love me very much, but no one relishes being spat on—even accidentally. Consistent with their blessed ability to take life in stride, they dried themselves off and assured me that worse things had happened to them. My embarrassment was acute, and my gratitude to them for their thoughtfulness immense. Such great examples of sermons in shoes!

And what of our sparring partners during my moment of crisis? Even as I was rushing to get towels for Wendell and Gloria, Edward, who was stacking the dishes at the table, calmly said, "Every day the Lord sends, my sister."

"Dessert, anyone?" I squeaked.

Wendell raised his hand. Gloria shook her head. Edward nodded, and Susan stared at him. Obviously she was not finished.

"So one could conclude, then, Mr. Reasonable [yes, she called him that very name], that you're destined to be married. Why else would God torture you with sexual longings when you haven't a prayer of satisfying them?"

Right then I felt a strong need to let my knees unlock and plop down on the floor. Maintaining an erect posture during this conversation was too taxing, and I certainly did not trust myself to ingest anything else that could be spewed out of my mouth.

"Sexual urges, or the means to gratify them, should not, in my opinion, be a primary reason for entering into marriage," Edward said calmly.

He and Stelle would make a great pair, I thought.

"Then pray tell me what should be?"

Now I know she was arguing for argument's sake. But why wouldn't she let this go? It was as if the rest of us were not even in the room. I wanted to jump up and wave my arms, but obviously that would be a waste of time. This had gone beyond us.

"Come on, Susan," Edward said, motioning to me to pass my plate, "how many people do you know who, with lust raging in their loins [yes, he used that very word], have hurtled down the aisle of matrimony and lied before God and witnesses that they would love, honor, and cherish the man or woman? But then, at the first sign of adversity or when a more appealing prospect came along, they leave the lust of their lives for greener pastures? Let me go a step further. How many are still in the burned-out remains of these marriages with nothing to nurture them but the ashes of regret—making lives hell for themselves and the children they just as uncaringly brought into the fray to suffer for their mistakes? How many?"

Susan said nothing.

Edward rested the pile of plates on the table. "You're quiet, Susan."

Still she refused to answer, and for the first time since the start of the after-lunch debate, Edward seemed to lose his calm. Not by much, but obviously this topic had become personal.

He sat back down at the table. He tapped his forehead gently with his forefinger and released a hard sigh. "Too many of us," he began, looking at no one in particular, "and I speak for my gender now: Too many of us Christian men allow our decisions to be made by our loins and not our minds. Minds that are brought under submission to the will of God. Those of us not actively engaged in nonmarital sex choose the next-best thing, using marriage as a means of getting access to morally legal sex. But hey, God invented sex. That already tells me He's a fun guy. But a marriage based just on sexual desire is destined to fail.

"When I marry, it will be because I love that woman with my mind first of all. I want to make a commitment to her in the heat of the noonday sun, with no lurking darkness or candlelight to mute the edges of my reason. Because when I make that decision, I will be making a commitment to seek what's best for her. I'll be making a decision to allow her to be who God designed her to be, not a remodeled version of my fantasy. And yes, there will be sexual attraction, but it is just one of the essential requirements for a marriage to work. How do I know that, you ask? I've seen it in my own parents, and you need look no further than the couple sitting across from you at this table."

Wendell brought Gloria's hand to his lips and kissed her ring finger, causing her to squirm with embarrassment.

Turning to Susan, Edward continued. "Do you know what's so tragic about all this?" He did not wait for her to answer. "Of the many marriages I've seen and observed up close, these two examples are the only ones I can cite as marriages to aspire to."

Susan stood up and briefly applauded. "Well said, Mr. Reasonable. You've made your case."

Then she excused herself and headed to the bathroom. I wanted to applaud too, but something about the way she held herself reminded me of the time she found out she was adopted. What monster had this well-spoken man awakened?

By the time she returned to the dining table, Edward had already helped me lay out the tray of summer fruit I'd arranged for our dessert—mangoes, strawberries, cherries, melons, grapes, and pineapples. Everyone dug in, even Gloria, who'd probably expected one of my more decadent creations. We chatted about this and that for a while longer, and by 5:30 the group broke up. I received hugs and hearty thanks for another lovely dinner.

As she was leaving, Gloria said to me, "I think your project is a good one, Quilla. My friend Lynn might be a candidate for you to interview. Let me ask her and get back to you."

Edward gave me a hug along with his thanks. To Susan he offered a slight incline of the head. Eyes twinkling, he thanked her for being an excellent conversationalist and said that he looked forward to meeting her again.

Chapter 5

Susan and I watched them walk to their car and waited till they drove off. Then we went back inside to clear the table and wash up. When all the dishes were loaded into the dishwasher and the table and countertops cleaned, I poured a glass of water and went to the back porch to sit down. Susan put the leftover salad in a plastic container and placed her bowl by the front door so she'd remember to take it with her. Then she joined me.

We sat in silence, each of us preoccupied with our own thoughts. These last two days of August were proving to be just as hot as the beginning of the month. Thankfully, I'd installed an umbrella on the porch that could be adjusted to block most of the sun. The sky was a perfect blue. No smog warning today. A walk along the waterfront would be ideal for later, but I'd wait to see how the rest of the evening played out. Susan was still too quiet for comfort.

"You OK, Sue?" I finally asked.

She didn't answer. These days a lot of people don't directly answer questions when you ask them. Why is that? There you are waiting for the answer to a perfectly straightforward question and they ignore you. Or they start talking to you about something completely different. Do you have any logical explanation for why that is?

Susan eventually began to speak. However, something about the way her voice sounded—a flat tone, a lack of effect—made me abandon my mental conversation. Her tone had a feel to it . . . almost like the way she'd held her body earlier, as if her insides needed to be carried carefully lest they slosh over the rim of their containment and make a mess.

"So many men have told me that I'm beautiful," she began. "I was 9 when the first older man, someone as old as Daddy, told me so. For some reason the way he said it made me *not* want to be beautiful at all. What do you think, Quilla? You're my oldest and dearest friend. You think I'm beautiful?"

What is happening to me on this holy Sabbath day of rest? Apocalypse now? To tell the truth, I hate when Susan starts looking inward. It means that I have to look right along with her, and I don't feel up to it today. I still needed to process the conversation from lunch. There was Mara's guy number two, Natasha's "like severing, like death," and my own future, but despite the tiredness in my bones, my body acquiesced with a soft sigh. No. I would not be one of those people I just ranted about. I would answer my friend's question.

"Most women would die to have a face as stunning as yours, Susan. I've told you that before. But you're my friend, and I don't see your face. I see your heart. I watch people when you walk into a room, especially men. When you come into a room ordinary-looking women like me don't seem to exist."

"And you still love me?" Her flat voice held just a hint of inflection, changing the words to a question.

"What kind of a question is that? Of course I love you. You're my best friend."

"And you don't resent the fact that guys ignore you? For me?"

My thoughts shot heavenward. Did she want the honest answer, or should I give her the kind one? I opted for honesty. "Yes, sometimes I wish I had some of the attention you get. Actually, many times I wish that. But you didn't choose your looks. I've also seen that sometimes it's a burden to be so pretty. So I take it in stride, but no, while I sometimes wish for your beauty I can honestly say I don't resent you."

"So if I'm so beautiful, why am I not married by now? Can you tell me that?"

"No, Susan. I wish I could." I need to tread gently here, so I intentionally temper my tone to softness. "I get the feeling that you know the answer, though. Do you?"

Susan shucked the summer sandals off her feet and placed her nicely tanned legs on the chair across from her. She picked at a piece of fluff on her white peasant skirt. Her dark relaxed hair hid her face, hiding the expression in her eyes when she answered.

"Twenty-nine marriage proposals. That's how many I've received. I started keeping track when we moved to our first apartment in Toronto. Remember then?"

"*Susan!* You've had 29 marriage proposals? I'm positive you didn't tell me about that many!"

"I didn't."

"But why?" I screeched. "I'm your best friend!" My voice held enough intonation and cadence for both of us.

"What purpose would it serve, Quilla? Wouldn't you think I'm showing off or being really insensitive?"

I looked into my heart. Yes. I would think so. Hey! I was barely batting one lousy proposal, and she had 29! Twenty-nine!

"OK. Point taken. But why are you telling me now?"

"Because of your project. It got me thinking. I've had 29 marriage proposals, and for argument's sake, let's say that even three of those were worth considering. The question still remains—why haven't I married? I think the answer is me."

"Tell me why you think so."

"I'll tell you if you stop using that therapist voice. I can recognize that tone from across great distances. You don't need to kid-glove me on this. You're my best friend, but there are a few things that even you don't know about me. One of them is that I'm marriage-averse."

"Say what?" Gone was the borrowed voice of the inconsistent therapist. "Are you not the same person who's been husband-obsessed since . . . whenever?"

Again my question got ignored.

"Ever since I found out that I was adopted, I've felt as though I lost myself. It's as if everything I believed about me is a lie. My eyes do not come from Mommy. My height does not come from Daddy. I love them, Quilla, but I don't know who I am. Did I get my 'beautiful' face from a rapist? Was he a child molester? Was she a prostitute, or was she a teenage girl from the church who couldn't face raising a child alone? Who am I, Quilla? This best friend of yours, do you know who she is?"

"But Susan, who *you* are is not defined by your parentage. It's based on who God created you to be. And God, knowing the circumstances under which you would enter the world, sent you the right kind of adoptive parents to nurture that potential in you."

But I might as well have kept my mouth shut.

"It's not like I haven't tried to find them, you know. I've searched for years and years. I even paid a private detective three months of my wages trying to find them. The guy guaranteed 85 percent success rate. But mine was part of the untraceable 15 percent. Unsuccessful. We couldn't find any records of a disclosure veto, no 'no contact veto.' Nothing. Quilla, I live in Ontario. This was the fourth province in Canada to open up adoption records. So why can't I find my parents? Or at least my birth mother! Are they dead? Did they just drop off the face of the earth? How is it possible for a child to be born, given up for adoption, and have no one curious, even now, about the woman she's become? I even put my name out there indicating I wish to be contacted, but no one has come forward."

Droplets of tears fell in measured intervals onto Susan's royal-blue blouse, but all that changed in her voice was an added wetness to the flatness.

"I want to be married. I want children. So many good and kind men have asked me, and God knows that at least twice I longed to say yes. But always I thought, *I have nothing to give; no history to offer my child or a husband.* I can't bring 'nothing' into a marriage. I know things are different now than when I was born 43 years ago, but I still don't understand why Mommy and Daddy didn't keep something that would help me be able to find my birth parents. Didn't they think I'd want to know? And then to tell a 13-year-old that she was not their child by birth."

I wanted to go to her, but I wanted her to talk even more. This was the first time she'd talked about this—at least to me. Something must have triggered it, and if I went to comfort her now, the moment might never come again for her to vent this, much less get past it. Trying hard to sound less like a therapist and mostly like her friend, I decided to challenge her.

"But Susan, your parents dote on you. When *is* a good time to tell your child that she's adopted?"

"But they must have known that I would ask, once they told me."

"They didn't tell you, Susan. Remember? You told me that you and your mom had a big argument. I can't recall what about. You screamed at her something to the effect that 'you're not my mother' and 'I wish you were dead,' so she thought that somehow you'd found out the truth. Later she came to your room and told you about your adoption and how much she loves you. Remember?"

"What does it matter how I found out? It doesn't change anything. I still have nothing to offer anyone, definitely not a husband."

"Come on, Susan. Thousands of people who were adopted are happily married and leading rich, fulfilling lives. Take Gloria. She's adopted. Look how she and Wendell love each other and their son, Chris. And Ben Simmonds. You remember him? He was in our biology class in high school. He's adopted. He married Francine Brooks right after they finished high school and moved to Port Credit. They're still married too. Recently he found me on LinkedIn, and we've e-mailed each other a few times since then."

Susan raised her beautiful head and gave me a watery smile of defeat.

"Logic won't work here, Quilla. I know all that. As I said before, it's me. Only me. I can't seem to get beyond the barriers and break free. This loving companionship that I want so much it makes me ache, I can't take when it's offered to me. But thanks for being my staunchest friend over the years."

I watched helplessly as she slowly pulled her lovely feet off the chair and returned them to the sandals—royal blue, just like her shirt. Then just as slowly, she hoisted most of her body to a standing position, the head still bowed, the shoulders refusing to lend support to the neck. She was going to leave. And I could not find the right words to get her to stay. Worse yet, I could not find the will to try.

My precious friend opened the sliding-glass doors and entered the house, darkened by twilight. She turned on no lights.

Go, I begged my feet. *Get up! God, what do You want me to do? I can't move.* As the heaviness in me increased, Susan, salad bowl in hand, returned. Her beautiful brown eyes posted a vacant sign while the rest of her body advertised "for sale."

"That's why the sperm bank makes sense in a way," she continued. "I wouldn't have to deal with a husband. You see, I might be able to scrape up enough substance to make a decent love gift for a small child. But I don't think I can do that for both a husband and a child. Anyway, I just wanted to let you know that. You deserve an explanation."

The heaviness fell from me like a cracked body-mask split apart by internal pressure.

"Which part of this sorry tale is an explanation, Susan? From the day we left St. Catharines to come live in Toronto, all I've seen you do is this mad hunt, day in and day, out for a man to marry. And like metal to magnet, they come— the hunters and the hunted. Jason was too pushy, Ethan was a milquetoast, Kevin not the right temperament, Max the mechanic—too earthy. Then the pastor guy, what's his name—Dudley, he . . . what was the problem with him, anyway? I never understood why that one had to go. Then you get upset with at me for dragging your sorry behind out of that convention center session, and now, *now*, you tell me that after 29 marriage proposals—which some perverse part of you felt the need to track—you cannot get married because you're adopted? What kind of freakish stupidity is that? And you expect me to sit here and just take it! You think you're going to leave me and you both in this dungeon of depression? No, Susan. As God is my Father and you are my friend and sister, you will not do this to me or to you. Do you hear me?"

But did I say any of it to her? No. No, I didn't. I thought all of it. I even felt my body getting hot from the heat of my anger. But not one word did I speak to stop her. I couldn't. The last time I let fly like that she got so angry that she took 27 extra-strength pain pills. We shared an apartment back then, and I, feeling badly for shouting at her, had knocked on her bedroom door to offer an apology. That's when I found her. I know she took 27, pills because I'd just bought the bottle and had taken two of the pills earlier that day. When I found her, there was hardly any breath left in her, and only one pill rattling around in the bottle.

Dear God, touch my beautiful fragile-china friend. She's Your child. Help her find healing through You, through me, or through whomever. Lord, You see how she needs You and how empty she feels. Lost, dear Lord. That's what she is. Find her a haven of rest.

Susan kissed me on top of my head, rubbing my arms to comfort herself. Then she left me in the dark. I felt the heaviness coming back, and I almost let it come. But I shook my head and got up. *Dear God, what indeed have I started in asking such a simple question?*

I needed to think of something else. Later on I'd give Susan a call, and we'd talk some more. The claim that she could recognize a therapist's voice from across great distances was spot-on. After that extra-strength episode, she'd seen a number of them. The last one provided the biggest breakthrough. She was in no danger right then of harming herself. She'd go home and feel blue for a while, then start working on her next salad creation or do more research on sperm banks.

You realize that I haven't yet changed the subject? Susan's life is like that. You can get consumed within it. The heady days of laughter with her are great, and the dark days are very dark. But she's my best friend, and I will see her through as much as lies within my power.

So what shall we talk about? What can you suggest to take my mind away to something else? Please, let it be something lighter.

Edward! You want to talk about Edward? What about him? You want me to tell you what I think about him? What—*you* like Edward? Never mind, I won't tease you.

Edward? Well . . . let me see. He seems intelligent. Sure of himself. Seems to know his way around the kitchen and is very helpful. Oh yes, it looks like he's quite familiar with the Bible. I liked his calm. If you're asking me if I think he likes Susan, I'd not be surprised. Every guy likes Susan. Even the married ones. But we're not supposed to be talking about Susan—right?

Let me tell you something. This married question is causing me to assess myself in ways I've never done before. I've always thought of myself as Quilla Hazelwood, daughter of Byron and Dru Hazelwood and sister to Michael. Michael is rich and lives in California with his leggy model-type wife, Gabrielle, and their two children. Michael is six years older than I am, so while we love each other, we were just too many years apart to bond well. I know that if I'm sick or in need of anything, all I need to do is call him and he'll be there, mostly financially, for his little sister. But I can't talk to Michael about personal girl stuff. It makes him uncomfortable.

I'm a nurse, now a public health nurse, and a pretty good one. I go to church, practice systematic stewardship, assist with children's ministries, and sing in the choir. I've always assumed marriage was in my future, but now, after only three conversations (with Mara, Stelle, and Susan, and I guess we should count Edward, too), I'm beginning to question my assumption about what my life should have been.

Should I be married? What is God's will for me? If I ask Him, as Wendell advised, will He answer? What if He says no? How would I deal with that?

Unlike Mara, I've never gotten to that place where I stopped speaking with God. I can't say that I talk to Him the way Wendell and Gloria do, but I need God the way fish need water. Years ago I realized that. Yes, there've been times I've willfully gone against His direct instructions, and there have been times I didn't mean to do so but did. But after every slippage from the path I feel the need to run back to the shelter of His presence. It's only there that I feel safe.

One could say that I'm a conservative Christian. I follow the rules and like the comfort of conformity. I very rarely question God or rail against my lot in life. I play the hand that's dealt to me in full belief that if God wanted me to have another hand to play, He'd make it happen. I submit to Him, and He takes care of me. It's that simple.

But while I very rarely question God, I question myself a lot. As I read over what I've written I wonder if what I'm describing is simple faith or habitual Christianity. I mean, Jacob wrestled with God; Moses, the humblest of men, had moments of anger—well, maybe not at God, but at the people. Job demanded an audience with God for all the losses he experienced in life, so against this background of people who railed, my acquiescence seems bordering on passivity.

I don't have the husband and family I assumed would be part of my forty-fourth year of life. I'm not happy about it, but I accept it. This must be God's will. Yet I've never asked Him, never questioned my assumption.

Isn't there a Bible text somewhere that says "You do not have, because you do not ask God"?* And while I'm doing this soul searching, I have to face the fact that I've never really tried to change my circumstances. By that I mean that never have I put myself out to seek eligible men, men I might possibly marry. I've somehow assumed that one day he, sent by God, would walk through the doors of my church, or I'd meet him at another church, or a friend would introduce us, and we'd develop a friendship that would grow into love, and prayerfully we'd commit ourselves to each other and our life together to the Lord.

When did I agree to this submissive role for this area of my life? It's not as if I practice it in other areas. I wanted to come to Toronto after finishing school, and Susan and I together conspired to do so. When my father got sick, I decided, without any invitation from my mother, to move back home to help her look after him. In every area of my work, when I got bored or restless I applied for something else that would challenge and grow me—case in point, the new job I'm going to next week. Then my current quest to find answers to the question of why I'm not married by now, the interviews, the discussions, the willingness (not always) to share bits of my own story with these women—these are not the traits of an acquiescent person. So I ask again, When did I internalize the idea that love should come *find* me, just fall into my lap?

Could it be that I'm hiding behind my so-called unquestioning faith? Is it possible that I'm using it as a crutch for my lack of courage? Poor, poor me! God has not seen fit to send me a husband. Poor little ol' me that has no one to love her.

Now that I'm looking closely, I see that my cowardice is so profound, my fear so intense, that I have opted for the path of loneliness. No, I need a stronger adjective. I've accepted, given over to, taken on, and fervently embraced this assignment of singlehood without so much as a whimper of protest.

I've never applied myself to the finding of a mate the way I've applied myself to the finding of a job or a house or a new project. Had I done that and was still single, I would be able to say I did my best. Had I applied myself, asking God to work with my best efforts, and ended up where I am, then I'd know that this path, this reality, was, for this time in my life, meant to be. But never have I tried. Never have I exerted one iota of effort. Not even with Ken (not that I'm saying he was the one), when he probably just needed some word of encouragement from me to say that he mattered in my life, not even then did I dampen my pinky finger on my tongue and wave it in the air to possibly change the current of my passivity.

It's not the place of the woman. She must be the sought, not the seeker.

Whoa! That just popped right into my head! When did I accept that message? Who told me? And most important, is it true?

Is it true that the woman must always be the "sought," not the seeker? I say the words out loud, noticing how my lips shape them, how they roll off my tongue, and even the shape their sound leaves in the air after I've spoken them. Is that what I truly believe? Does that long-ago-accepted statement still resonate with the woman I now am?

You know, I think not! Now that I can see that statement, test its mass, and examine its properties, well . . . well . . . I reject it. Completely and unequivocally, I reject it! I refuse to be so complacent about my destiny. I simply . . . I . . . I . . . simply refuse!

"So there!" I challenged the universe from my back porch perch. "So there!" As in "take that and see what you do with it."

And in the utterance of that challenge, my heart does a funny flip, causing me to catch my breath and cough. There. It did it again. What's going on? My pulse rate is increasing, and I feel so . . . so . . . exposed. Naked.

"Oh, Lord, help me!"

Some veils, maybe, should remain in place—this being one of them. Because once you remove them you have to deal with what you've exposed. I fill my cheeks with air and slowly blow it out.

"Calm down, Quilla girl. Calm down."

I recognize the feeling. Panic—that's what it is. Right there behind the pulled veil of my former acquiescence, just as I speculated, stands fear.

And why am I afraid, you ask? Don't you see! I'm not beautiful like Susan. I'm not full of personality like Mara. I'm not mysterious like Stelle, and I'm certainly not confident like Gloria. Who is going to love me for me? Mara called me gold, and good wife material. But I think I'm melba toast or plain rice cakes with hardly any taste, substance, spice, or flavor. I am a diet food that no one enjoys snacking on.

Stop it, I tell myself. Susan's melancholy must be getting to me. I lay my head on the table, darkness growing tight around me, and talk to my Father. "Dear God in heaven. What do You want me to do? What am I preventing You from doing through me because I'm too afraid to ask You to bless me? I'm afraid, God. You know that. Fear makes me unable to step out in faith and live the life You desire for me. I see now that I accepted loneliness because it was easier than seeking companionship. I did not have to risk my heart. I did not have to risk rejection.

"I forgot, however, that You love me. Your love defines me. No rejection can completely cripple me, because You love me with an everlasting love. Yet even Your love I'm afraid of. You've called me daughter, adopted me, died for me, redeemed me, sought me, and provided me with a haven of rest in the bosom of Your grace, yet I walk not like a loved child of God.

"You've given me a royal inheritance. I'm a princess of King Jesus, but even Your gift I fail to embrace. My fear makes it difficult for me to be the bold, confident seeker of the path You need me to walk. How can I get stronger, Lord? How do I get past this revealed fear? Please, Father God, show me how. Show me how to trust. Show me how to love, to be hurt, and not become hardened. Teach me how to step out in faith and grasp Your perfect plan for my life. With heart fluttering in my chest, with knees knocking in trepidation, with doubts within and without, brace me, Lord, so that I can be all that You created me to be—with or without a husband.

"Thank You for shining the light on this part of me that needed exposure. Walk with me now, Father God, and show me what to do. Will You talk to me too, as Wendell said You did to him? I want to hear from You, Lord. Speak to my heart."

I paused in the stillness and waited.

Welcome to the heart of God, Quilla.

"God, is that You? You really speak this way?"

I heard a chuckle. How can a voice without sound chuckle?

Are you ready?

"Ready for what, God?" I ask.

This can't be real. I cannot be talking to God like this and He to me. The King of the universe is talking to me. This is the Holy Spirit living in me? speaking to me about my stuff?

A journey of discovery. You took so long to get here, but here you are. Welcome, Quilla, to the heart of God.

Words failed me. But maybe that's one other aspect of prayer I've never explored. The part where words fail and the heart speaks. I just never stopped long enough, and shut up long enough, or waited long enough, or simply invited Him to speak and for me to hear.

Tranquility Victoria Hazelwood has just been welcomed into the heart of God!

---

* James 4:2, NIV.

Chapter 6

B y the time I entered the dark house I felt I'd lived a lifetime on that porch. I couldn't believe it was only 9:30. Weary, but somehow at peace, I checked to make sure Susan had locked the front door behind her. She had. Turning to go up the stairs, I was surprised by the ringing of the doorbell, joined seconds later by the ringing of my phone. I picked up the receiver on my way to get the door, only to be greeted by a strange yet familiar voice.

"Quilla, it's Edward, Wendell's nephew. I'm at your front door."

Opening the door, we both smiled at how silly we looked, talking to each other on the phone with just a screen door between us. I clicked off the phone and let him in, suddenly feeling concerned.

"Is something the matter with Gloria or Wendell?" I asked anxiously.

Edward loomed above me. He certainly was a tall man. "I'm sorry to drop in on you like this, but I accidentally left my Bible here."

"Your Bible? Oh, yes, I didn't give it back to you after you looked up that text for Wendell, did I? Come in; I'm sure it's here somewhere. Oh, here it is," I said, retrieving the Bible from the chair that had been vacant during lunch. I must have placed it there when I was cleaning up my spew of water from the table.

"Great!" Edward said. "Even though I have a few Bibles, I'm attached to this one. It has most of my favorite verses marked for easy reference. I'd hate to lose it."

"I know what you mean. I have a favorite too. So when do you head back to Atlanta?"

"Not till Monday. Gloria was telling me that you're starting a new job soon."

"Yes, Monday. I do my first school visit on Thursday. I'll be doing immunizations. Hopefully I won't get too many kids who are afraid of needles."

"You seem the type to calm them down."

My face must have registered the question in my mind. Edward answered: "You hate discord or any kind of upset. So with the exception of

53

moments like today, when your friend Susan made you gag on your water, I think you can be counted on to keep things under control. Am I wrong?"

"Well, no, but . . ."

"I'm a student of human nature, Quilla. By the way, that's a rather . . ."

"Unusual name?"

"Guess you get that a lot."

"I would be very rich if I charged for the number of times people have said that."

Edward headed for the door. "Well, thanks again for a great lunch. I enjoyed the discussion and the company. Are all your lunch affairs this engrossing?"

I looked at this tall man with the neatly trimmed hair and a well-maintained goatee. Intelligent and honest dark eyes set in a chiseled face looked back at me. *He's not bad looking*, I thought. *Too bad he's a baby. Susan would surely look good on his arm.*

"No. Most of my lunches are regular affairs. But today's created its own page in history, and you, young man, can take a good share of the responsibility."

Edward grinned. "I won't deny it. Guilty as charged. But it was fun to take on your friend. By the way, did you get around to doing your interview with her?"

I thought back to my conversation with Susan, the pain and heaviness that had surfaced and her conclusion that she must be marriage-averse. "I suppose you could say so." The look of desolation on Susan's face when she left made me add, "I have enough material for now."

Edward nodded. "Remind me again what your reasons are for not interviewing men? Don't you think they have a perspective to add to the topic?"

"I'm sure they do, but I just want to hear from women."

"And you're not even curious to hear what I'd have to say?" Edward asked with a twinkle in his eyes.

"On another day, maybe. Tonight I feel mentally exhausted. You wouldn't be getting me at my best. Actually, when you rang I was about to change clothes and go for a walk."

"But it's almost 10:00! You take walks by yourself this late at night?"

I smiled at his astonishment. "All the time."

"Well, tonight I'm coming with you." His look told me arguing would be a waste of breath.

"Only on the condition that we have no heavy-duty conversation. Actually, minimal conversation would be ideal."

He pressed his right hand over his heart. I nodded. "Good. As long as we understand each other. Excuse me for a minute."

When I returned to the living room, Edward stood up from his perch on the arm of the couch. And true to this pledge, conversation was kept to a minimum as we completed five blocks of speed walking. I noticed that Edward kept up with my pace without much effort. Granted his legs were longer than mine, but it seemed he was not a stranger to a cardiac workout. He saw me to the door, refused my offer of a drink, thanked me again for sharing my day with them, and walked in the direction of his car. A few steps down the road he retraced his steps.

"Quilla," he called. I was just closing the door.

"Yes." I hoped my voice didn't sound as clipped as I felt.

"Tonight might not be ideal to have that chat, given you're tired. But would you mind if I kept in touch to find out how things are going? This topic has piqued my curiosity."

"I don't know what I'll be able to tell you, but feel free to keep in touch. Gloria has my contact info."

Edward saluted, turned, and continued his walk to the car. Locking my door and bolting it, I made my second attempt at the stairs to take that much-needed shower. But when I got there, the idea of soaking in a tub of bubbles presented itself, and I did not resist.

Sunday morning, rested and rejuvenated, I rose early, conferred with my Father in heaven, who again welcomed me into His presence, and started a list of the things I needed to get done.

1. Call Susan.
2. Call my parents.
3. Follow up with Gloria regarding her friend Lynn.
4. Review work schedule for the upcoming week.
5. Summarize findings so far.
6. Make a list of the qualities I desire in a husband, including my assumptions.
7. Prioritize desired qualities and revisit my own assumptions to produce a new list.

The last two items had me thoughtfully tapping my pen against my cheek. Again I felt my deep-seated reluctance to go down this path. And yes, the fear. But on the heels of the fear, a soft voice whispered to my heart, "Trust in Me." I made myself breathe out slowly and relaxed.

A half hour later I'd called Susan, who reassured me she was OK; talked to my mother, who sounded a bit tired; and glanced at my work schedule. Knowing it was too early to call Gloria, I contemplated item 5. At this point all I had were unfinished conversations that raised more questions than provided answers. But so far nothing had addressed the reality that for Christian women there seemed to be a paucity of eligible men with whom to establish relationships. Bottom line: there are very few men in my church and most of the churches around. Furthermore, the few who were around were not exactly one's first choice for a mate.

And there it was again. The assumptions. It looks like no matter which angle I approach things from, the assumptions come back to haunt me. So, fine! I'll deal with it. I will lay out on paper right now, while my tummy rumbles for food, what I desire in a husband. I will be honest and unapologetic. And once I'm done with that part of the exercise, I will examine the list and see what comes of that. So here goes.

Quilla's Dream Man List of Credentials

1. He is intelligent. (Do I mean book smarts, or college-educated? I think some kind of postsecondary education would be nice. He must be mentally stimulating without being arrogant.)
2. He is taller than I am.
3. He has nice teeth. (I'm really particular about this.)
4. He is considerate.
5. He loves the Lord and has a secure relationship with God.
6. He understands the importance of servant leadership.
7. He's Black—but not too dark. Somewhere between pale milk chocolate and caramel.

Now, this is interesting! What do I mean by "not too dark"? That's sounds like a racist comment, doesn't it? Could it be that I am a racist of my own race?

Dru Hazelwood's voice was in my head now. "Look at him! Black like sin! Lazy, good for nothing, nappy-headed liar . . ." This said of the man who'd come to fix the bathroom and ended up botching the whole job, which forced us to have to pay someone else to get it done right. Yes, she'd been mad. But even as a young child, way back then, I "knew" that to be really black was not a thing to be desired. Somehow that got included in my list.

Father, help me here. How can I call myself a Christian, a follower of You, and retain such feelings about the beings You've created?

Every February at the celebrations of Black History Month (I make it my duty to attend as many as I can) I stand proudly, hand over my heart, and sing the Black National Anthem, and recite Martin Luther King's "I Have a Dream" speech, especially the part about the day when we will judge people "not by the color of their skin, but by the content of their character." And all the while inside of me, inside this hypocritical heart, lurks prejudice. There is a name for this thing—when we despise our own race—but I cannot recall it now. Is this what being welcomed into the heart of God is about? Seeing with eyes of holiness the things that are unlike God?

The jangle of the telephone interrupts my musings. Mara's voice of sunshine flows through the line.

"Quilla girl, how's your Sunday morning going?"

"Well," I answer, "I just discovered that I'm prejudiced against Black men who are too black."

"There's a discovery to rock one back on her heels! What made you think of that now?"

I recounted yesterday's lunch conversation and the relevant bits of my looking-inward talk with God from the previous night that led to my list of desired qualities.

"I see," replied Mara. Then in her typical swing mode, "Would you marry a White or Asian man?"

"I've never really considered that," I said thoughtfully. "The color and cultural divide always seem too much to heap onto a marriage."

"That's interesting, and I can see the argument from the point of view of someone like me who's new to this country. But you, you were born here. Don't you have any friends of another race, or haven't you ever dated someone?"

"Of course I have friends who aren't Black!"

"But Quilla, how could you have grown up in this country, gone to school with people of all races and ethnicities, and not ever have dated someone of another race? I don't understand."

How indeed? Mara had asked a good question. I had always seen the differences in the races and had not embraced the similarities. I had moved to the city hoping to find more people like me to socialize with. I had assumed there would be more Black men in the church, and assumed that White or "other" was too different for me, so I had never opened up myself to any guy of another race. Assumed, too, that "other" meant that I liked "same," but I had still put boundaries around the degree of "blackness" I'd tolerate. Who then did I have to blame for my current singlehood?

"Quilla! You've gone quiet on me."

"Oh, Mara, whose idea was it anyway to start this 'why am I not married by now' project? It's taking me places I don't want to go! This was supposed to be a straightforward topic. I'd interview a few women and come up with some conclusions to satisfy myself that none of this was about me. But I've done more looking inward within the past few weeks than I've done in a lifetime."

"It's a provocative question that your project is based on, Quilla girl. And you're not the only one going down roads better left untraveled. That's why I called you. Since we talked last week, doors I shut long ago are flying open, and what's behind some of them are, shall I say, somewhat disquieting. You should have left the sleeping dogs sleeping." Mara sighed. "What are you doing today? If you're still interested, I'd like to tell you about guy number two—the one who broke my heart and spoiled me for other men."

Mara and I agreed to meet that afternoon by the park at Harbourfront. When she arrived, we took the ferry across to the central island. There, away from the amusement park area, we found a picnic table in a spot relatively free of bird droppings and talked. Once she got started, Mara could not get the words out fast enough.

"Garry Livingstone visited my church one afternoon and gave a fascinating talk to the young people about believing in yourself. I was youth leader at the time and had heard him speak at camp meeting. He seemed sincere, God-centered, down-to-earth, and even sweet, but still a man's man, so I'd asked him to consider coming to speak at our church. He agreed. After the program I thanked him for coming, and we started talking. We soon realized that we had much in common. Before he left, he gave me his card and asked me to call him soon. That was a Saturday.

"Tuesday of the following week I called the number on his card. It was a work number of an insurance company in town, and he was listed as an adjuster. Needless to say, I was a bit disappointed to find him in this line of work. I admit right now that I don't have a high regard for insurance people. The men who work in that industry always strike me as being a bit—how can I say it?—not quite on the up and up. However, we all need insurance, and they are indeed a necessary evil. He wasn't in the office, so I left both my work number and my home number. He returned my call about 8:00 that evening. It was the first of many conversations to come.

"Garry broke the mold of all my stereotypes of insurance men. Talk about passion for one's work! He saw insurance in the same vein as securing one's soul salvation. He didn't see it as a rip-off, or at least didn't present it that way. For him it was all part of responsible living and ensuring that risks were minimized.

"The same passion that Garry brought to his employment he brought to his work with young people. Did you know, Quilla, that my beautiful island of Jamaica has one of the highest incidents of homicide in the Western world? Garry believed it must be something our society or parents were doing to our young men to cause them to devalue life—theirs and other people's. His quest was to save as many as he could by showing and teaching them how to love and value themselves. He tried to teach young men that despite the circumstances they were born into, God loved them, and their lives could become meaningful if they took time to discover what God created them to be."

"Wow!" I said. "I can see how you'd fall for him."

"Fall? I don't think I did that. But he surely fascinated me. His mind was a beautiful thing. No, 'fall for him' was not what I did. But we talked every night, and the more time we spent talking, the more drawn we were to each other. He challenged me and said that I challenged him, too. It was about three and a half months after we started our nightly conversations that we actually went out together. And without my even knowing when and how it happened, one day it dawned on me that this man completed something missing in me."

"So you proposed to him? How did you get to the engaged state?" I was eager to move the story along to what for me was the really critical part.

Mara's eyes took on a faraway look, her perch on the Toronto picnic bench providing the panoramic screen to life in another country far, far away.

"People will be people. Our friends, our families, everyone told us we were meant for each other. Look how we matched. See how we complemented each other. And what could we say? We agreed. We felt it too. So on the way home from a picnic one day—we'd gotten there late but wanted to enjoy what was left of the festivities—Garry was rather quiet. I asked him if he was OK, and he just said he was thinking. That seemed fine to me. I too had my own thoughts to occupy my mind. We were good together like that. We could be silent in each other's presence and not feel the need to fill it up with talk."

"Mara, how much time are we talking about? You and this Garry had been going out for how long by now?"

"About nine months. Why?"

"And all that time he'd never kissed you? He never showed any interest in you of an intimate nature?"

"Not really. I mean, we talked about it. Garry was very much of the opinion that we should not put ourselves in a position to be tempted in a sexual way. I really respected that about him. We spent time really getting to know each other. I'd invite friends over to my place, and Garry would help me entertain them. Everyone would help with the cleanup, and soon after everyone left he'd kiss me on the cheek and go home himself. Later he'd call me from home, and we'd talk long into the night."

"And even then, didn't he say anything about how he felt about you?"

Mara blushed at my question.

"Well, sometimes he would. Sometimes we would talk about it. I mean, he acknowledged he had feelings for me, and I told him I did for him, too. But our friendship was so special to both of us—he had no siblings and I had no brothers—that we really enjoyed each other. I think we were afraid that if we got intimate it would spoil the beautiful friendship."

"OK," I said. "I can see that. Now tell me what happened that evening on the way back from the picnic."

Mara drew in a deep breath, placed clasped hands between her knees and rocked herself slowly. When the rocking stopped, she said, "The evening of the picnic, as we were getting close to home, Garry asked if I had anything pressing that I had to get home for. I told him no. He then said that he wanted to talk to me about something important, but needed to find a place that was well lit and at the same time quiet. I mentioned a nearby hotel restaurant, so we decided to check it out. Garry asked for and got a table in a fairly secluded section. He must have given the host a good tip, because everyone who came in after us were seated far enough away that we felt we were indeed in our own little world."

"And then?" I could not believe my own impatience.

"And then this man, who up to this point had been my best friend in the whole world, became a stranger. Quilla girl, he took my hands in his (I remember that the index finger of his left hand had a chipped nail, and I wanted to file it down) and looked into my eyes in a way that made my belly button feel as if something had shifted beneath it. He just looked at me for what seemed like forever. And me, I looked back at him, too, feeling my heart fill up with this new thing that was unfolding through our joined hands and locked eyes. Words can't begin to describe that moment.

"That's when we stepped across the great divide, eyes wide open, and entered into intimacy. I stepped into love. Garry looked at me, eyes a bit frightened, it seemed. Tears overcame him. When one full lid threatened to spill its contents down his cheek, I reached across and wiped at it with my finger. This finger, Quilla." She held up her bent index finger. "His grip on my hand tightened even more as I returned my dampened finger to our joined hands.

" 'Mara,' he said, 'tell me you love me and that I am as necessary to your life as you've become to mine. Tell me that to love you like this means that I've gained even more than the beauty our friendship provides.' That's what he said to me, Quilla. And I could only answer 'Yes. Yes. Oh, yes!' "

My own breath caught in my throat. I was there. A fly on the wall, but a fly with emotions. Mara said nothing else for a long time. Again, just as with Susan, I had no words of comfort. But in this case I already knew the ending to her love-of-a-lifetime story. Guy number two, this Garry character, had bailed on her six weeks before the wedding. Using the tip of my runners to kick at some hardened crud on the edge of the picnic bench, I felt a cloud pass under the sun, and in that small moment I caught a glimpse of Mara's pain.

"You're probably wondering how the story went from that special moment to a canceled wedding," Mara finally said.

"If you don't feel like talking about it, it's OK with me. I understand."

"No. I need to talk about it. You see, I never have. Not to my mother, sisters, or his mother. Not even to God. When Garry came by that awful night and asked me to take a walk with him, I hardly had any time to spare. I'd been sorting through ideas for how I wanted the hall decorated, plus I had tons of bonbons to wrap, and I wanted to do it all by myself. Garry had no patience with that kind of detail. He'd say, 'Mara, honey [he'd started to call me honey already], it's not about the wedding. It's about the marriage.'

And I'd agree with him, but I wanted everything to be perfect. Everything!"

Mara's words caught in her throat, so I reached across and took her hand in a gentle grip. At that she jumped off the picnic table, wrenched her hand away, and made quick strides to the edge of the park. There she stopped, back tense with her fight for control. Minutes passed. When she finally turned around to walk in my direction, her beautiful face downcast, watching her slowly moving feet, no sunshine lit the sky. Neither was there any left in her voice as she took her seat beside me and continued.

"So we took that walk. When he took my hand—just as you did mine just now—and turned me to him, his eyes were full of pain. 'Mara,' he said, 'I can't do this to you. I cannot marry you next month.' And stupid me, I stood there clearly not understanding plain spoken English.

"Finally my brain computed: he did not want to marry me. He did not love me. I was not necessary to his life after all. I tried to slip my hands from his, but he grasped them tighter. But I had to get away. Farther away. I wrenched my hands from his grip and ran, and ran, falling down, and running still, getting up and running, running as far away as I could get. I heard him calling my name, but I ran harder, faster, the colored string I'd bought to tie the bonbons in clear plastic streaming out from my pockets.

"He didn't come after me. As fast as I ran, he could have caught me if he'd wanted to. We'd raced each other many times before, and always he'd catch me. When my body brought my headlong flight to a halt, I turned around and limped back home in a daze of confusion. I'm sure people greeted me as I passed—one or two must have seen me race by— but I recall none of that. Just the whimper of a dog in one of the houses I passed—sounding as though someone evil had kicked it."

I wanted to touch her hand again so she'd be reminded that I was right here beside her, but I held back, not certain how she'd react. I too wanted to whimper like that kicked dog. Mara, however, continued to play out the tape that had been wound too long in her mind.

"My phone rang that night at the usual time. I let it ring for the 11 times it took to get the message through to him that I didn't want to talk to him. I had to go lie down. As I passed by the kitchen table, I saw the pair of scissors I'd been using earlier to cut the paper for the bonbons. I took the scissors with me to bed. Lying there on top of the sheets, opening and closing the blades, I started to get angry and cold—you know, the cold kind that can hurt someone real bad."

I nodded. I knew the kind. I'd experienced it once.

"I got up from the bed, reached into the back of the closet, and removed my wedding dress. I'd hidden it from myself way in the back so I wouldn't be tempted to keep trying it on. Carefully I removed it from the white plastic bag. I then dragged the footstool that I kept at the foot of my bed to the middle of the floor so I could climb on it to reach the hook in the ceiling. I hung the dress on that hook, climbed back down, and sat on the edge of my bed just staring at the dress. It was such a beautiful dress, Quilla."

The chill in her voice made goose bumps grow on my arms. I was wishing she'd look at me. Only the occasional mention of my name kept me from shaking her back to the present. She couldn't be too far gone if she remembered she was speaking to me. So I rubbed my palms up and down my arms to warm my skin and waited.

"It seemed logical to do what I did next," she said, looking fully at me for the first time in a long while. "I took the scissors and swiftly cut a slit right up the front of that dress from hem to dropped waist. Then I tossed the scissors aside and ripped the dress apart with my bare hands, ripped it till my hands were sore and the cloth refused to rip anymore.

"When I came to myself, I was surrounded waist-high with the lacy remains of a dead dream—the naked hanger still swaying on its hook and the plastic garment bag half standing where I'd thrown it.

"Sometime in the early-morning hours I wadded all the strips of cloth into a tight bundle the size of a pillow and brought them to bed with me. I fell asleep hugging that bundle.

"The phone calls continued for three days, then stopped. He didn't come see me. Not even once. A letter came two days after that. I took my scissors to it as well, cutting along the folds in half-inch strips, then threw it in the garbage. By the time my rage was spent, and my friends and family were asking what explanation he'd given for canceling the wedding, and finding I had no answer, I went to the garbage and searched for whatever I might find of his letter. But, of course, the garbage had been hauled away by then, and no other letter came. Weeks later I heard that he'd left for an indefinite stay in Florida."

"Mara, this is such a sad story!"

My heart felt almost as broken as if this terrible thing had happened to me. That's the problem with loving somebody like that. When they reject you, it messes you up. I've seen it happen time and time again. Yet we women keep running after this love craziness. What's wrong with us?

But Mara did not allow me to wallow in my angst for long. Her story was not finished.

"His mother eventually came to see me. When I opened the door to find her there, arms open wide and drawing me into the comfort of her ample bosom, all the tears I'd bottled gushed out in a torrent. Turning around with me anchored to her chest, she backed into my apartment and closed the door. She stood there holding me and rocked me back to sanity.

"'Hush now, honey chile,' she said. 'Hush. My boy is a good son, but he's a fool. I know he loves you. Never was he so taken with a woman. But you scared him. Ah mean, the feelings you stirred up in him scared him. Feelings so strong he couldn't deal with them. It made him feel weak, like his heart was hangin' exposed outside his chest. Lotsa men get scared when a woman makes them feel like that.'

"Oh, Quilla, that just made me hurt even more, because I had no clue how to fix what ailed him. I couldn't love him any less and could do nothing to make him feel strong. I wanted him to love me like that. But he could not bear it.

"You know that song that says 'God kept me'?* That's how I got through the days and weeks, and then finally the months. Four years later, when I broke things off with guy number three because I didn't love him—because I was marrying him for the wrong reasons: to have a child and to fulfill the societal expectation that I should be married by a certain age—I made the decision to make a fresh start on life. That's when I moved to Canada, and the rest, as they say, is history."

What could I say! Nothing. I just felt cold. But the song Mara mentioned played in my mind, and before I was even aware, I began to sing it. Sitting there on the park bench as the clouds parted and the sun set, I sang. And then, ever so softly, Mara's lovely alto joined in with mine. Without saying a word, we got up, still singing softly, and walked with the measured steps of companionship side by side to the ferry dock. There the music faded to a hum and as the blast of the horn sounded the call to pull away from land, we rested elbows on the rail and watched the city come into view.

---

*The name of the song is "I Almost Let Go," by Kurt Carr.

Chapter 7

I love my new job. I work in the department that manages vaccinations and treatment programs. Right now we're doing school visits. Even though some of the children are terrified of needles, I can usually calm them enough to administer their shots. A team of three nurses typically do the school visits. If the schools are small, we can, barring no major mishaps, manage two schools per day. I also like being home by 5:00 in the evenings.

Three weeks following my conversation with Mara, I had no other interviewees lined up. Not that I had made any effort to do so. Even though I love the flexibility of my new job, during the first couple of weeks dealing with all those kids' emotions left me exhausted. Now I'd found my rhythm. On the way home, after stopping by my favorite Japanese restaurant to buy myself some sushi for dinner, I decided that tonight would be a good time to get the project back into gear.

Not that in the absence of new interviewees the project had left my mind. On the contrary, I thought about it constantly. My new prayer experiment of conversing with God and actively listening for His voice helped to make peace with my circumstances. The peace involved being open to what God might send my way instead of passively accepting what I thought to be my lot in life. Even though nothing had changed in my circumstances, I had a new relationship with God that I wouldn't have had without this query into my nonmarital status.

During my sushi dinner I noticed my phone message indicator was flashing. Biting into the first sushi—one containing not only the sticky rice I loved, but carrots, avocado, and cucumbers, then further dipped in soy sauce with a measured swipe of wasabi—I pressed the play button and learned I had four messages.

Lo and behold, there was a message from Gloria to tell me that her friend Lynn would talk with me. That surprised me. I'd met Lynn a few times, for she sometimes frequented our church with Gloria and Wendell. She also provided counseling talks to the young people now and then. My surprise, and as I said, I did not know her all that well, was that Lynn seemed to be like a closed book or, more specifically, a locked diary. This interview should prove interesting.

Messenger number two offered me a free, all-expenses-paid, weekend at a fancy resort up north. Yeah, right! Next thing I'd be sitting through daily presentations with someone trying to sell me something I had no interest in purchasing. I'd been taken in once. Never again. I hit the delete button.

Message number three was from Susan, checking in. Said she'd call me later. And message four required three replays. It went like this: "Quilla, it's Edward. How are you doing? Here am I sitting at my desk trying to complete a project due this weekend, and who should pop into my mind but you? So instead of sending you an e-mail, I thought to leave you a message to let you know that I am thinking of you and have prayed for you today. Catch you later." The time of the call was 4:47. I looked at my watch. It was 5:23.

Somebody prayed for me today! How powerful is that? I don't know, but suddenly I felt rejuvenated. Energized. Hearing that Edward not only thought about me but took the time to pray for me, and called to let me know, added a real lift to my day. How many times had I thought of someone and even prayed for that person but never told them? Too many to count! I had never thought to tell them. And even when I did think of telling the person, I'd shied away from doing so. I didn't want them to think I was being too "holy and righteous." Yet Edward's message left me feeling buoyant. Someone thought enough of me to stop and mention my name to God. Again I say, how powerful is that!

After clearing away the remains of my meal, I turned on the computer and sent Edward an e-mail of thanks. For a deed like that maybe I should at least see what he has to say on the "Why am I not married by now?" subject. No harm in asking, and if I don't like what he has to say I don't have to include it in my research report.

Within a minute of sending my e-mail, I had a reply: "You are very welcome. I've prayed for you every day since I left Toronto."

"Really?" I questioned. "Why?" *Send.*

Thirty seconds later: "Does one need a reason to pray for someone?"

I thought about that. Do I pray for people without a reason? No. I pray for people when I think of them, when I worry about them, when they're in pain, distress, facing trials, or when they're on my mind. Why was I on Edward's mind?

"Yes." *Send.*

Another 30 seconds later I refreshed my screen and found this question.

"And what reason do you think would prompt me to pray for you, Quilla?"

This was getting interesting. What reason indeed? OK, two can play this game. "You tell me." *Send.*

"I see you like playing dodgeball. OK. As I said in my message, I prayed for you because I thought of you."

I typed in another question.

"No, erase that, Quilla girl," I told myself.

I typed the same question again. Yikes, do I really want to ask, "Why were you thinking of me, Edward?"

Tell me the truth. That sounds a bit flirtatious, right? Did I want to be flirting with this babe in the woods? No. I think not. Erase message. Ask something else.

Before I could think of another question, a new message came through. "What? Cat got your tongue?"

My self-talk continued. "Ah, live dangerously. This is all in good fun. What could it hurt?"

I shut my eyes tight. *Send.*

New message: "Are you sure you want to hear the answer to that question?"

A giggle popped out of my throat. Oy vey! I haven't heard myself giggle since I was a teen trading boy stories with Susan on the phone. This man was proving pesky. And intriguing.

"As long as the answer will not hurt me." *Send.*

"How will I know if you'll be hurt?"

"I guess you don't. Trust your gut." *Send.*

This time two whole minutes passed. I refreshed the screen. I clicked Send/Receive at least three times. Nothing. Three more minutes passed. Still nothing. Finally a message came through. "I can't put this in writing. I'll call you when I get home. Give me an hour."

I stared at the screen. I did not want him calling me. That would make our little game more personal, more serious. I was just playing. What could he want to say to me? I felt my heart rate increasing. The same feeling I'd had when I'd lifted the lid and looked at my fears a few weeks back.

"Oh, dear God!" I groaned. A prayer.

Then (I kid you not!) I heard a chuckle right before He answered. *Yes, Quilla.*

Stupefied, I asked, "Are You laughing at me, God?"

A loud guffaw broke out in a hollow space occupying the vicinity between my head and my chest. That's the location where I seem to hear the voice of God speaking to me. Not quite in my head or heart, but somewhere in between. The guffaw was followed by a determined attempt to cut the mirth. Finally His voice, containing still some residue of merriment, answered me.

Yes, Quilla, My dear. I am laughing—taking pleasure in the joy you bring Me. You are a work of art.

"I'm doing the Chicken Little thing again, aren't I? I'm ready to run without even asking You if there is reason to fear."

And are you afraid, My daughter?

"I think something about this upcoming conversation with Edward scares me. I want to talk to him, but I don't want to at the same time. Am I making sense, Father?"

Trust in the Lord with all your what, Quilla?

"All my heart."

Trust in Me. Rely on Me. Lean on Me, and I will direct your path. I will give you the words you need to say, and My Spirit will guide you into all truth. Even in your chat with My son Edward, I will be with you both. Both of you bring Me joy.

"But what . . ."

Hush, Quilla, and trust. Hush. I pictured fingers with no hands lifted to mouth with no lips, shushing me. I exhaled, turned off the computer, and went to set myself a soothing bath.

At 6:58 my phone rang that double ring that told me it was long distance. I picked up midway through the third ring.

"Hello." Yikes, my voice sounded breathless, husky. I cleared my throat and perched on the edge of my love seat.

"I'm 10 minutes late. I'm sorry. My mom always tells me never to keep a lady waiting."

"No need to apologize, Edward. I knew you'd call when you could. Plus I got a chance to have a leisurely bath, and I've even started on my laundry."

Keep your tone nonchalant, I told myself.

"Well, I promised to call you to explain why you've been on my mind since I left Toronto, but before I get to it, are you sure you still want to know?"

"Only if you still want to say," I replied, resting my head against the cool wall.

There was a pause. "You'd think this would be an easy question to answer. I assumed it was putting thoughts into writing that was causing the problem, but it's not."

The phone line went quiet except for an occasional click and the soft sound of Edward breathing into the instrument.

"Quilla, what would you say if I told you that I don't know why you've been on my mind, but since I left Toronto I've thought of you every day?"

Why had I forgotten? Like Mara, this man, this baby, does not beat around the bush. He comes straight to the point. What would I say indeed? I'd say that he was crazy or . . . I don't know what. Why would he be thinking of me every day? I'm old enough to be his . . . his . . . at least his oldest sister, if he has one. It was Susan who'd gotten his goat, not I. Susan's the woman guys call to ask me about . . .

"Quilla?" His voice had dropped an octave, bringing with it a kind of intimacy. "Quilla, are you there?"

I cleared my throat of its cowardice and, straightening up, said brightly, "Yes, I'm here. I guess I'm at a loss for words too."

"Have I offended you?"

"No. Of course not. Just surprised me, that's all."

"Why? Why the surprise?"

"Well . . ." I might as well tell him the truth. Taking a cue from him, I got straight to the point. "After most guys meet my friend Susan, when and if they call me it's usually to find out how they can get in touch with her. That's all."

"I see. How about I tell you something else?"

"What's that?"

"I'm not 'most guys,' Quilla. Do you want to know what I think of when I think of you?"

"If I say no, you're going to tell me anyway, aren't you?"

Edward chuckled, and the resonance of his voice warmed my heart. "My estimation is proving true. You are a perceptive woman. Yes, I will tell you anyway. You see, whenever I talk to God, which I try to do as often as I can during the day, He brings your smile to my attention. And when He does that, I ask Him to be with you in whatever activity you're doing at the moment. I also claim for you the prayer of Jabez, that God will bless you indeed and increase your territory. That His hand will always be on you, and that He will keep your hand from evil so that you do not cause pain. I also think of that companionable walk we took together. I felt comfortable being quiet with you, Quilla. Even though I know you'd had a long day and wanted to get to bed, I wanted to stay as long as I could in your presence."

My knees went weak as my voice gained strength. "What are you saying, Edward? You have feelings for me? You can't! I'm years older than you! Years!"

I had to stop him. His words, spoken by a voice with the kind of timbre I'd always loved in a man and by the kind of man I'd love getting to know— had he been older, had he been even only two years younger than me—I could have dealt with it. Welcomed it. But this was wrong!

"Nine years, to be exact," he clarified.

"And you don't think that's a problem?" My voice rose in pitch as I paced the room and sat facing the seat he'd occupied during his visit.

"Nope. It's under my 10-year limit."

"Edward!"

"Quilla, listen to me. I don't know you very well, but I know God. I've chosen to give control of my life over to Him. I ask Him for wisdom, knowledge, anything I want, and when He brings things my way, I know it's for a reason. I did not come to Toronto in August in search of a relationship. I came to see my relatives. At your house I was briefly dazzled by the pretty face of your friend Susan, but by the time I left it was your beauty that stayed with me. Every day God brings a vision of you to my memory, and that vision makes me smile. So I think God is urging me to get to know you, and nothing about your age was mentioned."

I could so see the expression on his face as he talked. My response to the empty chair was adamant. "Well, God has not been speaking to me in any such terms."

"I've not been on your mind? Is that what you're telling me?" he shot back with measured calm.

"Yes. I mean, no. Not really. Not in the way you talk about it."

"How then?"

Beguiling. That's the word for this man. Beguiling as a rare treat. But I must not give in. I must not be beguiled.

"What do you want from me? I'm old enough to be your big sister. I can't go there."

"Would you like to?"

"What?"

"If there wasn't a nine-year gap, would I be the kind of guy you'd give a chance?"

"Of course."

Now we were on solid ground. "Edward, you are an intelligent man who loves the Lord and is passionate about making a difference in the world. Of course I'd give you a chance. But like it or not, we do have a nine-year age gap. If I were just four or five years older than that, I could have mothered you."

"I see," he said quietly. Then: "Tell me something, Quilla, why are you not married yet?"

"Because I haven't found a man who loves me and moves me and loves God and, uh, . . . I haven't found this guy."

"How will you recognize him when he comes? What will he look like? Is he tall, short, fat, thin, Black, White, naked, clothed, working, unemployed, noble, good-looking, plain, simple? Shall I go on? In essence, have you asked God to reveal to you the man He wants in your life?"

"Edward, you can't be that man. I'm 44 years old! I'm too old to have children, too old to give a younger man a family. Get real, Edward. Don't you want these things for yourself?"

"I want what God sees best to give me. And if the woman He blesses me with cannot bear me children, then we can adopt. But you have already decided that I cannot be the man. Already you've worked out the problem of children when all I am asking is for the opportunity to get to know you. I'd like to explore where this might take us, and leave the rest to God. Can't you trust Him to bring to us only those things that are for our best?"

"But why don't you like Susan?" I wailed.

"Is Susan younger than you?"

"Well, no, we're about the same age."

"So other than insulting my intelligence to know whom I like and choose accordingly, why are you recommending her above yourself?"

"I'm sorry. I don't mean to insult you. I'm just used to all the guys going for her. Plus, she listens to you. I saw it with my own two eyes. She doesn't do that to a lot of people."

"You didn't answer my question. Don't you think that you deserve first place in a man's affection? Don't you believe that you can be loved by a man to the exclusion of all other women?"

I looked at the clock through misty eyes. Blinking, I saw it was almost 8:30. I knew the answer to his question—knew it as clearly as anything! No. I did not believe that. At least not by a younger, wonderful, intelligent man like this one. Once the scales fell from his eyes, he'd regret his choice. And then, then where would I be? Where would I be!

So I told him a half-truth. "I don't know what I believe anymore on this subject."

He sighed. "Will you do me a favor? Will you talk to God specifically about me? Will you ask Him that if I'm to be part of your life, He'll give you a sense of rightness about us in spite of our age difference? Will you do that for me, Quilla?"

"But why is this so important to you?"

"You ask a lot of questions! But I'll answer however many you have as truthfully and honestly as lies within me. And my answer to this one is that it's important to me because I want more than anything to do God's will. And if you are meant to be part of my future, it's important that you know it too, for yourself, revealed to you by God."

"You don't ask for much, do you?" I found myself back on the arm of the love seat in my original position. When did I get here?

Edward chuckled. "I do ask for much. But God in His infinite wisdom does not give me everything I ask for. Just the things I need."

"Wow, that's profound!" And it was. He was. But that age gap put him oceans away from me. I'm sure God in His infinite wisdom understood that!

Our conversation wrapped up soon after. Edward prayed with me. It was a prayer eerily similar to the one I'd prayed for Mara, and it left me a trifle miffed. Unlike Mara, I did not have any angst with God. I'd reached out to Him for a deeper intimacy, and He'd welcomed me, Quilla Hazelwood, into His presence. I was on good speaking terms with Him and listening daily to hear His voice. Of that I'm 100 percent confident!

Chapter 8

Lynn

Lynn Swanson was of average height with kind eyes that somehow managed to look all business. She came across as someone who takes care of everyone but let very few people into her world. That's why I was surprised when Gloria told me she had expressed an interest in being interviewed for my project.

We arranged to meet at 6:00 p.m. at her office, located east of the Parkway. Old money and new development mingled in this hybrid community. Her office occupied the second floor of a three-story complex—one of those buildings that have the homey exterior of a house and the professional feel of a business. Perfect ambience for her counseling practice. As I opened the front door to the building I almost collided with Gloria on her way out.

"Kiss, kiss, I gotta run to pick up my godchild," she said, throwing kisses at me as she hurried by. "Go on up. Lynn's expecting you."

I also knew that the godchild being referred to was Lynn's daughter. Taking the stairs to give myself a workout for the one I'd be missing tonight—being Thursday—I felt pleased to find that my body took the stress in stride. No windedness. Good.

Lynn answered my knock and ushered me into her office. I liked it at once. Soft music played in the background, the kind of water falling over rocks string accompaniment you hear when you go for a massage treatment. My body immediately went into relaxation mode. The light from the weakening September sunset filtered through gray mesh blinds. Lynn showed me to a two-seater area to the right of her desk. The scent of raspberry-cinnamon tea wafted from a teapot on a side table, and two white mugs and several digestive biscuits on a white china plate completed my welcome.

"Thanks again for agreeing to talk with me, Lynn. I know how busy your life is."

"Not a problem at all," she responded, lifting the teapot and motioning to my mug. I nodded and she poured for me, then herself, and sat down opposite, facing into the sunlight. "Gloria told me a bit about your lunch conversation a few weeks back and the issues that arose from that discussion. It piqued my interest. Have you observed anything noteworthy from your interviews to date?"

She turned those light-brown eyes on me, face wearing a question mark. I got the feeling she was trying to find a way to get to her story. OK, I could provide her with something.

"Well, my biggest surprise is the unpredictability of the conversations and how deeply personal each one became. You'd think I would have anticipated that, but it's like opening a Pandora's box into people's past. Stuff comes up for them, and for me, that enlightens at the same time that it provokes. You still want to go through with it?"

Lynn cradled the mug in her palms and blew across the rim. I tuned in to the music. What instrument was playing now? Some kind of string-plucking—might it be a harp? Beginning to wonder if this would be one of those occasions when my question was ignored, I was reassured when Lynn took a small sip of her tea and began to speak.

"No." Her gentle voice had a slight rasp to it. "I'm not sure, but I do believe in the adage 'physician, heal thyself.'"

Lynn read the question mark on my brow and went on to explain. "Lately I've been having recurring memories of someone who, at one point in time, meant a lot to me. I don't know what has triggered them, but when Gloria told me about your project and the conversation at your lunch table, my mind suggested a connection. Maybe talking to you will allow me to understand why." She placed the cup on the table and crossed her arms. "I see what you mean by this becoming personal."

"You don't have to do this if you don't want to, Lynn," I reminded her. "However, if you choose to tell your story, I promise you on my nurse's honor that I will not disclose any of your personal information with anyone else. I'm not even sure what I'm going to do with these interviews. My primary reason is to come to some kind of understanding for myself as to why the question, asked so innocently by a complete stranger, unnerved me so. Listening to the stories of other women helps me, and hopefully will help the tellers as well."

Leading by example, I gave Lynn a précis of my own journey to 44-year-old undesired spinsterhood. She listened with the warm acceptance of a caring counselor, and when I'd finished my story she started her own. It took my brain a few minutes to realize that her tale started at the end.

Lynn's Story

"Sometimes in my quiet moments I'd think, *How could such a wonder come out of me?* Everyone says she favors me. I don't see it. She is beautiful. I could stare at her all day long and see something different to admire every time—in the shape of the lips, the turning of the head, the furrow of the brow." She paused. "This is really hard to talk about, but after . . . long ago I promised myself that I would never dodge the truth no matter how uncomfortable it makes me."

Absentmindedly she rubbed one hand against the side of the warm mug. "This past Sunday after being cooped up in the house all morning I decided to go to the park close to the junior high school two streets down from the house. Katie, that's my daughter, pedaled a few feet ahead—not yet comfortable with going too fast on her bike. When we got there, I spread my little folding mat by the base of a sturdy maple and made myself comfortable with a book. Katie dumped her bike and gleefully ran around the tree playing peekaboo with me until she tired of the game. Soon she ventured a bit farther, but I could still hear her somewhere behind me. Minutes later she returned with one of those mangled dandelion love bouquets that only children can pick.

"'Here are some flowers, Mommy. These will cheer you up. And don't let them blow away, 'cause they're special.'

"She skipped off in search of more discoveries before I could say thanks. I wondered why she thought I needed cheering, but as I looked at the wilting dandelion blooms I felt my lips stretch into a smile. *Yes, I* thought, *they are special like you.*

"From my vantage point by the maple tree I had a clear view of the street below. This Sunday was beautiful and quiet. Even the numbers of cars driving by were unusually sporadic. Two squirrels frolicked up and down a tree by the roadside. Suddenly one of them darted toward the street and came to an abrupt stop right in the middle of the road. You know how squirrels do that sometimes. But this time a car was bearing down fast. I watched in horror as the animal froze, not seeming to know what to do. It started to turn back to its mate, but changed its mind. As the car continued speeding toward the panicked animal, my body tensed. This would be close.

"*Run, run run!* I screamed urgently, silently, and the squirrel made a desperate run for the opposite side of the street. I shut my eyes, not wanting to watch it die, and when I opened them there was the little daredevil running up the tree on the opposite side of the road. And just like that—POW—I was blindsided by a bolt of memory so unexpected it made me cry out.

"Oh, God, no! Not here. Not now." I felt my arm gripping my stomach. *Please, no. Not now, not now!* I continued to plead. But my heart kept slamming against my ribs, and the open air became too close. I had to get inside. I called to my daughter. For a moment her serious eyes regarded me with 5-year-old wisdom, then she took my hand and walked us over to her bike, where she got on.

" 'OK, Mommy, I'll take you home.'

"That night, in the quiet of the house after she had gone to sleep, I faced myself. *Why now?* I questioned the unresponsive darkness. *What brought on that, that . . . THAT! It's been years.* But the memories would not stay buried, Quilla. They brought him back to life, this man who does not know he's my child's father."

See what I mean when I say you never can predict where these conversations will take you? I felt the surprise in my body, but dared my face to remain impassive. It had crossed my mind that I'd never seen Lynn with a husband, but I assumed she was divorced. Now I learned that she'd probably never married. This professional woman, so in command of every situation. That's why we should not judge. But here I am doing just that, judging and assuming all kinds of things about her before I hear the rest of her story. I tuned in again.

"We met in a 'breadth requirement' course at university. He was a business major back then, and I was in the social sciences. One day as he passed by my desk he accidentally knocked over my hot chocolate with his bulging knapsack. I jumped out of my seat to avoid the spill, but needless to say, the incident created a bit of commotion. The class had already started, and the professor was not known for his sense of humor. My notebook was soaked, but other than that I was OK. Even though I had worked very hard not to merit the attention of this particular professor, I now had his full attention. His look screamed impatience. As thoughtful classmates sent tissues my way, I sat back down, cheeks aflame, and quietly cleaned up the mess.

"Satisfied that he had his class back under control, the professor resumed his lecture. Needless to say, I was harboring a few resentful thoughts about this big oaf when a note slid in front of me a few minutes later.

" 'I am really sorry,' it read. 'Allow me to buy back your cup of hot chocolate after class. And in case you're going to say no, please accept my apology in writing so I won't have to disturb the class again by coming over to kneel at your feet and beg for it.' It was signed 'Bigfoot.' Despite myself, I had to smile, and after class he was so profusely apologetic I had to forgive him. From there on I called him Bigfoot, especially when he did something I thought stupid."

Lynn looked at me fully for the first time since we had started the conversation, a half smile lifting up one corner of her mouth.

"So the name stuck, and a friendship began that day that was to see us through the next three years. We lunched together at least once per week, compared notes, debated, and celebrated university and life in general. I liked his sense of humor and his wit. He was a kind soul, and while my girlfriends gushed about his good looks, I simply saw him as a really good friend. In my mind intense relationships with the opposite sex were relegated to sometime in the distant future. Plus, my two near brushes with the love bug had left me skittish. He never pursued. I never invited.

"After university I went on to graduate school, and he took a lucrative job as a marketing analyst in the Maritimes. Despite promises to keep in touch, the phone calls became less frequent over time, dwindling to annual birthday and Christmas cards.

"When I finished grad school, I worked in a few agency settings for several years, and then decided to begin my own counseling practice. I was fortunate that at the same time I was contemplating this career change my friend Gloria was looking for something different to do too. She literally browbeat me into a partnership with her, making the case that she could best serve as office manager/business officer, intake counselor, thus freeing my time to spend with our clients. Sceptical at first about mixing friendship with business, things have worked out very well, and our joint venture is what you see today.

"Despite our work relationship, our friendship has grown even stronger over time, and we have learned to separate the business from the social sides of our lives. Wendell adopted me as a sister, encouraging me to join them for worship services at your church. I come from time to time. It gives me a chance to spend time with my friends, understand more about their lives, but that's about all I want to do with religion. I know I should be concerned with saving my soul, but truthfully, I don't think I'm such a bad person—you know, the kind of sinner in need of this salvation you folks keep preaching about.

"Yes, I believe there's Somebody out there looking out for me, but I just don't see the need to have religion consume my life. To me, one should live a moral life, treat people with respect, share what you have with others, and try to do minimal harm to the planet. These are the rules I live by. My mother tells me that she prays daily for my soul, and I suppose Wendell and Gloria do too, but they are less vocal about it. I love them all dearly and could not imagine life without them in it.

"So what does this long, winding tale have to do with your question? Why am I, Lynn Swanson, not married by now? How is all this background information relevant to the topic?

"Before I had my daughter, I would have said that I had everything in life that I needed—a full and engaging career, a few close but wonderful friends, and a loving family. I'm quite content to enjoy my solitude whenever I get the time, so while a husband and children would be nice, it was still someday in the future. Getting involved in a relationship was the last thing on my mind. I liked my independence, was content with life, and saw no need to complicate it.

"I did get the constant harangue from my mother about my single status. She believed her life would be complete once I, the only girl, was happily married with children of my own. Thank heavens my brothers had gone ahead and provided her with grandchildren. That took a bit of the pressure off. So it was a typical busy day at the office when the phone rang. You'll guess it, of course. It was Bigfoot saying that he'd moved back to the city. Without planning to, without meaning to, after a few months of hanging out together and rediscovering each other, we became intimate. I fell really hard for this man, and in a textbook moment of weakness I let my feelings overrule my reason. I got pregnant.

"It was such a stupid teenager thing to do that I could have flogged myself! Here I was, a mature single woman of 29, pregnant. I should know better! I have easy access to birth control, money in my pocket to purchase it even if it wasn't available almost everywhere for free—and I got 'knocked up.' I didn't know what to do. The only thing I knew was that I could not abort the child.

"Did he love me? I didn't know. How could I have become so involved with this guy and not know the answer to this critical question?

"I knew he cared about me. He's just that kind of guy. But love me? If I asked him, what would he tell me? So one day I built up my courage and asked—not quite 'Do you love me?' but how he felt about me. His response? 'You are very special to me, Lynn.'

"What does that mean, Quilla? How do I tell a man to whom I'm 'special' that I'm pregnant with his child?

"Looking back now, I think I started to withdraw, or maybe he lost interest once he'd conquered my defenses sexually. I don't know. Within a couple months, and yes, we continued to see each other up to that time, he told me he'd been offered a chance at a partnership back in Montreal. Even though it took every ounce of control I possessed, I did not cry or beg him to stay. He chose to go, and obviously I did not mean enough to him for him to stay or even ask me to accompany him.

"By sheer force of will I banished the man from my mind and have successfully kept him banished for the past five years. Till this past Sunday. Since then, it's been like he never left! Feelings that should have been expunged from my memory have returned with all the pain and vulnerabilities of those long-ago years. I feel weak. Helpless. I don't like it. But what I hate most is that for the first time in my life I miss how he made me feel and the sense of belonging I had with him. He would have made a great father for Katie, and on top of everything I am starting to doubt the rightness of my decision not to tell him about her.

"To date, I have not even entertained the idea of letting another man in my life. My child and I did not need the complication. I had my daughter. I had my friends. I do work that I love. I needed nothing more. Up until Sunday last, that would have been the answer I'd have given you for why I'm not married by now."

I sensed Lynn's story had ended. The sun had set, and I resisted the urge to look at my watch. The digital clock on the table between us, however, read 6:51. I thought more time had passed. I asked the question. That's what I do. I ask questions.

"And now?"

I don't know what I expected, but when she turned bleak brown eyes darkened with uncertainty on me, I realized that this strong woman needed me to tell her something she did not want to hear. Five years is a long time to let this particular sleeping dog lie, but even I could see that the squirrel is connected to the car, which is connected to the near miss, which is connected to the need for closed spaces, which is connected to the bleakness—which is connected to him. Still.

"You love him." I said. "After all this time, you still love him."

The bleak eyes fell away from mine. Lynn's shoulders slumped. "That's the most ridiculous thing."

I also knew that the comment was not a response to my statement.

"If you were a guy and found out that you had a child out there somewhere, what would you do?"

My question pushed at the borders of our acquaintance, but I really hated the thought of a child growing up without a father figure. Women can't teach boys how to be men. Yes, women can teach their children how to be decent human beings, and many do a superb job of it, but I like to see a family complete. Maybe parents can't always live together or get along, but kids, wherever possible, should know about their heritage. Look at what not knowing is doing to Susan.

Lynn did not answer immediately. She got up, stepped to her desk, opened a drawer, and took out her handbag. "What does that question have to do with your research project?"

There was a slight testiness in her voice.

"Absolutely nothing."

"Then why do you—"

I cut her off. "Because if he's as decent a guy as you say he is, I'm sure he'd do everything in his power to be there for Katie. But you don't need me to tell you that, Lynn. In your heart you already know."

She slowly pushed the desk drawer shut. "What am I going to do?" Pain again leeched through her plea. "If I tell him about her, he'll be livid that I kept it from him all this time. But then he would come. With all the gentleness he's capable of, he'll woo her into his heart. And I, still loving him, would not be able to bear having him so near."

"Is he married?"

"I don't know," Lynn whispered.

"He never kept in touch after he left Toronto?"

"I told him I'd found someone else. What he didn't know was that the 'someone else' was his own daughter."

"So Google him!" My earnestness put a smile on Lynn's tired face. She came around the desk and gave me a hug.

"You're a good sort, Quilla. Your friends must love having you in their corner, watching their backs. Thanks for listening to my story, and I hope that something from it will help you find your own answers. I'll let you know if I ever find the courage to do what needs to be done."

That was the end of that. The interview was over. But I could not just leave her like this—so hopeless and despondent. "Will you be offended if I pray with you?"

"Since I don't pray myself, Quilla, others' prayers never offend me."

I beamed at her. "Then it's my pleasure to mention you specifically to God in prayer, and I promise to do this as often as you come into my thoughts."

Taking her hand, I presented this daughter, who was not yet a child of God by second birth, to her heavenly Father. I asked God to grant her the request of Solomon for wisdom, knowledge, and understanding to raise her daughter well, to meet the needs of her clients, and the courage to do the things that had to be done when the time was right. Then I waited as she got her bag from her desktop and together we walked out into the September night.

Quilla's Notes

1. Lynn is not married because she's still in love with the father of her child.
2. This father does not know he's a dad.
3. Past baggage comes in many forms.
4. Sometimes people do not know they have baggage from the past until something simple triggers a response.
5. Sometimes we are not married because we intentionally or unintentionally give off negative vibes to men who might have approached us.
6. There are those who were formerly content with not being married, but with time and age discover they want the companionship of marriage, only to find no one available.

Chapter 9

Sometimes stuff is just in the air. You think of something, speak it out loud, and like the blowing of dandelion puffs, the wind takes your thoughts and seeds the atmosphere. I never noticed gray Mazdas with spoilers until I purchased one. Then I saw them everywhere. Pregnant women talk about noticing lots of other pregnant women and wonder where they'd been before. I start interviewing women with the question "Why aren't you married by now?" and weird things begin to happen. So I think it all has to do with my "seeding the air" theory. Sometimes the planet aligns with our thoughts. We might call it serendipity, but when I get to heaven this will be an area of research for me. How much of what we now call coincidences really are?

It's Sunday, October 12. Tomorrow is Canada's Thanksgiving Day, and I'm having my typical "bring all your friends" dinner. Mara is coming too. Actually she's already here. She and Susan have been here since last night. This Jamaican sunshine of a woman is a wreck.

Since our last talk Mara and I have bonded, and lately she's been sitting in church with Susan and me. Susan's attendance is more sporadic than her nursing schedule warrants. I try not to harp to her about it.

This day in particular I was really into the music for the praise segment of the service. Come to think of it, the whole church was. People sang lustily, greedily, unashamedly. Some days church just whets your appetite for heaven. We all had much to be thankful for.

When the songs ended, the appeal was made for us to offer our thanks, needs, hurts to God by faith. Come to the altar. The aisle streamed with worshippers. After the prayer of consecration Mara went to the washroom, and by the time she returned, the congregation was again singing as a prelude to the invocation. Mara slipped in between Susan and me and bowed her head. *Looks like she's made things up with God.*

A dignified man in a frock robe stepped to the microphone and began to pray. The guest speaker, I assumed. At his first words I felt the air around me change—become charged with electricity. I felt more than saw Mara's head, her whole body, snap to attention. So I fully looked at her, at her eyes, and I kid you not, they goggled out of their sockets.

The prayer ended, and we all sat. All but Mara. She stood, frozen as a statue, staring at the podium. Something must have communicated itself to the preacher, because on his way back to his seat he turned, probably feeling eyes burning through his frock into his back, and looked around. For a moment time stood still. He stared. Mara stared back. Then she uttered a sound like a moan and plopped into the cushioned pew, breathing as if she'd just run a marathon. The thread that had connected her to the preacher snapped, and he too sat, looking distracted.

I took her hand. It was hot. "Mara, what is it? What's the matter?"

She just shook her head from side to side, making that soft moaning sound.

Someone announced special music. While the woman sang, Mara made whispering noises to herself. Susan and I looked at each other over Mara's bowed head.

Susan tried. "Are you OK, Mar?" she breathed.

Mara grabbed up her purse and Bible. "I have to go."

And she went.

I took off after her, and Susan after me. Heads turned at our quiet commotion, but I didn't care. In the foyer I pulled Mara to a screeching halt. "What is going on, Mara? I can't let you leave like this. Something's upset you."

She tried to work her hand free, but I held firm. "Let me go, Quilla. I have to get out of here. He's here. Why didn't you guys tell me he was here?"

My eyes met Susan's. She looked as confused as I felt.

"Tell you what?" I asked. "Who's here?"

Her eyes squeezed shut. "Him."

"Who?"

A deep bass voice answered from behind me. "Hello, Mara."

Her eyes popped open. She gripped my hand painfully, but her voice, when she acknowledged the greeting, sounded as cool as refrigerated watermelon. "Garry."

Then everything fell into place. Oy vey! This is guy number two.

He started toward her but stopped himself. "How have you been?" he asked.

"Garry," Mara said again.

Light clapping from inside the church penetrated through to the foyer. The special music had ended.

"Don't go, Mara. Please. I must talk to you. It's so good to see you. What are the probabilities that you would be here?"

The Scripture reading was announced.

Divided loyalties warred.

"I have to go back," he said, "and preach."

"Garry, I . . ."

"Give me one hour. After church, give me one hour, just one hour. I'm scheduled to go to the pastor's house for lunch, but I'll get out of it. One hour, Mara. If after that you don't want to see me again, I promise in front of your friends here that I will leave you alone. Please."

Silence. The man turned to me. "Please get her to stay. It's—"

The door opened to let a child out, and we heard a voice ask for God to bless the reading of the Word.

"Amen!" the congregation chorused.

Garry grabbed my free hand in entreaty. "Please," he hissed as he hurried off.

Susan looked at me. "What was that all about? Who's this . . ." she reached for her bulletin. "Who is G. David Livingstone?"

I looked at Mara. She remained silent. I didn't want to betray any confidences, but I knew Susan would not let it go without some kind of explanation, so I supplied a morsel. "I guess he's someone Mara knew from before."

"OK, fine!" Mara snapped. "One hour! I can do that. I'm a big girl and will not let this man drive me out of my church. Come on, ladies. Let's go face down this devil God has sent to preach the Word."

She stormed toward the door of the sanctuary, not looking back to see if we followed.

The senior pastor had just begun his introduction when we took our seats. G. David Livingstone hailed from somewhere in Florida (sorry, I don't recall the name). He had a Ph.D. in theology plus a master's degree in adult education and counseling. He's the head of an active men's ministry department within his church, and so on.

When G. David rose and walked to the pulpit, he looked straight at Mara and gave us a slight nod. It communicated thanks. He thanked our pastor for sharing his pulpit, commended the congregation on their warmth and exuberant praise, then bowed his head and waited until the place grew quiet.

Into the stillness his deep resonant voice beseeched the throne room of heaven, asking God to hide him behind Calvary's cross, to use him as a medium through which His Spirit could communicate what this waiting congregation needed. He asked God to focus him, to remove from his mind anything that would distract from the message, and then he claimed all he'd asked for in the name of the Father, the Son and the Holy Spirit. The congregation said amen.

G. David's head remained bowed a moment longer, then with a nod he too said, "Amen, so let it be."

My heart picked up his prayer. *So let it be, Lord. Bear up the preacher, sustain Your child Mara, and grant us all a special measure of Your blessing today. Amen.*

During the next hour God answered all our prayers.

There are sermons that work on your emotions and get you all fired up but by the end of the day you can't recall even the topic. Then there are sermons—preached with such power, packed with such substance, that you are forever changed. You notice not the clock on the wall, the groaning of your belly, or the passage of time. These sermons represent a spiritual oasis to a soul lost in the desert. They get you reaching for your notepad to record key texts and messages for later exploration. These kinds of sermons, preached by those not only gifted in elocution but touched especially by the Spirit, usher you into the presence of the Almighty.

G. David's sermon, titled "Defying All Reason," took us through 2 Chronicles 33 and showed us the life of Manasseh, king of Judah. Read his story. The atrocities this man performed are simply unbelievable. This king, who should represent God to his people, consulted with mediums, practiced witchcraft, built altars, and sacrificed his own sons to appease pagan gods. He then made a carved image of one of these gods and placed it in the temple of God. As the record describes in verse 9: "Manasseh led Judah and the people of Jerusalem astray, so that they did more evil than the nations the Lord had destroyed before the Israelites" (NIV). Imagine that!

So God fixed him. He brought the king of Assyria to fight against King Manasseh. Captured, a hook placed in his nose and shackles binding on his feet, Manasseh was thrown into a Babylonian prison, a fitting place for one who had committed such atrocities. My blood boiled when I digested all the evil that King Manasseh did. I wanted to be the one pulling the chain attached to his nose hook. But the story continues to the part that defies all reason.

There in the darkness and dank of the dungeon that miserable, indescribably evil king had time to think about how he got to be where he was, and he started to experience remorse. Great distress overtook him. As we all tend to do when we get backed by our own willfulness into a tight corner, he remembered God. So what did he do? Verse 12: King Manasseh "humbled himself greatly before the God of his fathers" (NIV) and repented of his sins. Imagine that! He begged the God of heaven (not any of his many other gods!), *the* God in whose face he'd spat, the God whose children he'd sacrificed, for mercy.

And our unbelievably merciful, compassionate Father, on hearing the prayer of this notorious greater-than-Hitler evildoer, was moved by Manasseh's entreaty, and He listened to his plea.

He forgave him. Not only did God forgive him, but He restored to him his kingdom. "Then Manasseh knew that the Lord is God" (verse 13, NIV).

Blow me away! Can you imagine that! God forgave him. I must have read this story before, but I'd missed so much. Here was the God of the Israelites, who sometimes came across as a stern disciplinarian raining down fire and brimstone on anyone who stood in His way. And here He was showing mercy to this warped man.

Next, G. David Livingstone, wrapped up in the robe of Christ's righteousness, spelled the word G.R.A.C.E. "That's what God gave to Manasseh, ladies and gentlemen—undeserved, unearned kindness! The most evil person we can think of, if they truly repent of their sin, if they in essence tell God that they're sorry, our God, the reader of hearts who desires a love relationship with every one of us, will apply the blood of His Son Christ Jesus, cover their abominations, and forgive them."

Seriously, people. Think of the most notorious killer or child molester of our time. If that person sincerely confesses their sin before God, grace and mercy is provided for them? I had reason for pause. Would I welcome that forgiven brother or sister into the fellowship of my church?

But the sermon did not end there. Pastor Livingstone went further. "There is no good we can do for God that will cause Him to love us any more than He already does," he said. Then he made this corollary. "There is nothing bad we can do that will cause God to love us any less." I wrote this down word for word, because he repeated it three times.

Do you get that? I, who consider myself a good person, am no more important to God because of my goodness than someone I'd consider the worst of offenders, but who has repented of their sin. It's enough to boggle the mind. Why would a God of justice do that? Justice demands a sentence, payment for wrongs done.

I'm convinced the pastor heard the question in my mind, because immediately he asked this one: "Why would a God of justice countenance such a soft landing for Manasseh? How could He forgive evil—the antithesis of all that He represents? You see, there is big evil and small evil, but all evil is abhorrent to God. Neither your sins, be they large or small in your eyes, nor Manasseh's sins, which we would describe as enormous, can exist within the presence of God. But God can do something remarkable with sins—confessed sins, repented sins, the 'Oh, I'm so sorry' sins, real contrition, real confessions, real desire to turn away, real submission—God, through the atonement of His Son Jesus Christ, covers all the yuck in our lives and allows us to experience His G.R.A.C.E. Amazing grace!"

G. David Livingstone stepped away from the pulpit, down the four steps to the congregation level, and began to sing.

"Jesus paid it all,
All to Him I owe;
Sin had left a crimson stain;
He washed it white as snow."*

He invited the congregation to sing with him. Two, three, four times we sang the chorus and then he raised his hand to hush the singing.

"Every time we sin, justice demands payment. But all we need to do is cry out to God and say, 'Lord, I'm sorry, I'm sorry—oh, God, please forgive me,' and quick as you can say Savior, mercy will be extended and grace applied to cover all your transgressions. Amazing grace, mind-boggling grace, incredible grace, how sweet the sound."

The organist started to play softly, and still speaking to the congregation, Pastor Livingstone walked toward the organ and stood beside the organist. Few saw the light tap he put on her shoulder to stop playing. That took finesse and a heart of compassion. Then he sat beside her on the organ bench and continued his message.

"I've asked the organist to stop playing because, although when we consider the goodness and love of God we cannot help becoming emotional, for the next few minutes I want to engage your minds. In the cold reality of

your own consciousness turn your mind to what God wants you to know—
He loves you, He loves me. I know the word 'love' is overused today, but
who loves you enough to die for you? Who loves you enough to give you the
ability not to love Him back? Who will go through hell itself just to rescue
you?

"Look in your Bible. It holds many illustrations of God's love for us.
The woman with the lost coin; the shepherd with 99 obedient sheep in his
pasture but who could not rest until all 100 were safe inside the sheepfold;
the father of the prodigal. You don't need to wait to be good enough to
come to Him. You will never be good enough. If we've been walking the
'straight and narrow path' but one day slip—be it a large or small slip—and
we fall, it is not our past goodness that counts in our favor. It is only the
goodness of God and His amazing grace.

"Give up trying to be good enough. No office, position, series of good
deeds—none of those things—can qualify you to be deserving of God's
favor. He already loves you. You don't have to beg Him to love you back!
Like the prodigal's father, He's already looking out for you, straining for the
slightest sign of your homecoming, desperately desiring fellowship with
you. So what are you waiting for?"

"Run!" he urged.

"Run to your Father! Run and claim your inheritance."

Stepping down from the organist, he came back to the center of the
church directly in front of the congregation. "Who would like to take hold
of Christ today? Whether for the first time or as an act of rededication, who
wants to experience this amazing grace, this undeserved kindness of God?
If you do, then come. Stand with me, and let us claim it together."

That's all it took. People swarmed the aisles. Mara took my hand in
hers and pulled me along with her. But she need not have pulled. My heart
had already taken wing and was at that moment bowed before the Father.
Then the man of God prayed for us and for himself.

And the church said amen.

You can imagine that after such a powerful message people wanted to
thank him and shake his hand. That took time. Finally I approached him,
Mara by my side. Again the world stopped.

"You have your hour," she told him.

He looked at her, and such a smile lit his face that I had to catch my breath.
"Thank you."

I gave him my phone number and told him to call us when he had finished all he needed to do. I said that Mara would be with me. He put the paper on which I'd written the number in a small breast pocket of his robe and turned to greet the next person waiting to speak to him.

At lunch at my house no one was in the mood to do justice to Susan's salad. Mara jumped every time the telephone rang, and we with her. Then at 2:17 the doorbell rang. I answered it.

G. David Livingstone stood in the doorway, and our pastor's car was pulling away from the curb. He greeted me in a subdued tone and asked with his eyes if Mara was here. I nodded, opened the door wide, and stood aside so he could enter. He was not a tall man, maybe no more than 5 feet 10 inches, but he felt larger than life. Susan called from the dining room.

"Who's at the door, Quilla?"

G. David and I walked the few steps to the dining room, and I answered the obvious. "It's the pastor."

Mara stood. "Garry."

"I'm here."

Again the air grew thick with unspoken feelings. Taking Susan by the hand, I dragged us away from what needed to be a private conversation. Mara cast desperate eyes in my direction but quickly regained her bearing.

"Don't leave, guys. Whatever Garry came to speak to me about will be heard in the presence of my friends." She sat down and motioned G. David to a chair in front of her and to the left and right of where Susan and I had been seated at the dining table.

"Mara," I appealed, "this really should be between you both. We can . . ." I stopped, cast pleading eyes at G. David, but he had eyes only for Mara. He must have sensed my desperation, however, because he took the proffered seat and sat.

"It's OK, ladies," he interrupted. "Mara promised me an hour, and I will take it however I can have it."

Susan and I backtracked and lowered ourselves in our chairs, but we might as well have been absent.

Mara spoke first. "That was a powerful sermon you preached today, Garry. You're good."

"Thank you," he said. "But I don't want to talk about me. How have *you* been, Mara? I heard that you had immigrated to Canada, but I came close to losing my focus when I saw you in the congregation this morning."

Mara smiled. Her smile, even at half its wattage, caused the man of God to inhale sharply. "Yeah, it was a bit of a shocker for me, too. How's your mom? I heard she'd moved to Florida too."

"She's well. Daily she calls me every kind of fool for running away from you."

G. David (you notice that's my new name for him) looked steadily at Mara. "I was a fool and a coward, and I'm sorry. Sorry for everything, but mostly for waiting so late to let you know how I felt and then leaving you alone to deal with the cleanup. As God is my witness, I am profoundly sorry and wish above all else earthly that you will find it in your heart to forgive me, if not today, then maybe one day."

He looked so earnest sitting there with his heart in his eyes that I was ready to forgive him on the spot, and he'd done me no wrong. But Susan's eyes narrowed. I could see her mind furiously piecing the story together.

"You left her at the altar!"

G. David did not back down from the accusation. "Not quite. But pretty close."

"Oh, wow! That's terrible! And you a preacher?"

"I wasn't a preacher then, but that does not make it any less cowardly."

"What did I do, Garry? What was it about me that became so objectionable that you could not marry me? I thought you loved me. I was sure you did."

The pain in her voice pulled at my tear ducts.

"It had nothing to do with you, Mara. It's that my feelings for you were too consuming. I felt overcome, and I didn't know how to deal with it except by buying myself some time. I tried to put it all in the letter I sent to you. Wasn't it clear?"

"I didn't read the letter."

"Didn't you get it?"

"I did. I did get it. I cut it up."

G. David's eyes widened. His shoulders slumped. "I'm sorry. I assumed you had at least my paltry explanation to help you deal with things."

"Well, it's never too late to offer an explanation," Susan prompted. "Why don't you tell her now?"

A look of irritation flitted across G. David's face, but in the blink of an eye it was gone. Psychologically blocking Susan and me out of his mind, he leaned in to Mara and took her hands in his. "Are you seeing anyone at the moment, Mara?"

She turned startled eyes on him as she shook her head. "You're not married?" she asked.

"No. I'm not married. Yes, there are pressures on a minister of my age to be married, but I have not been able to find anyone who holds the place in my heart that you still do. No one, Mara. No one. Last time we were together I ran because I felt too much for you. I'm a different person now, but I know enough about human nature to know that trust broken takes time to be rebuilt. I hurt you, Mara. It was the last thing I wanted to do, but I did anyway. So unless you tell me there is some other guy who holds a special place in your heart, I would like your permission to regain your trust and maybe, one day, your love—if this is what God desires for us. I miss your friendship. I miss our talks. I miss our debates and our easy companionship, and no one, even when I tried to make it so, has been such a soul mate to me as you were. But despite all that I miss in you—and this is where the change has been most profound in my life—I refuse to take one step without asking God to order it according to His will."

How beautifully put! I could tell he wanted this woman back in his life. I could also tell that he was prepared to give her up if God, or she, said no. A love like that, which puts God first in everything, would be worth receiving, wouldn't it? I'd surely say yes to it.

I've learned that if we're not prepared to seek first the kingdom of heaven, if we do not believe that God in His wisdom knows what's best for us and that once we submit our lives to Him He will bring us only those problems, those people and situations, that will fit us for heaven *and* bring us into the fullness for which we were designed, then we might as well throw in the towel of our faith.

I heard the soft swipe of a chair being pushed back from the table and glanced toward Susan. With a slight shifting of her eyes she indicated we should leave. The shuffle of my feet communicated my reluctance. I wanted to hear Mara's response. But I left anyway, eyes apologizing to Mara. This time she did not stop us. I don't think she even noticed our leaving, because her head was bowed and shaking, from tears or denial I knew not which.

Urging me up the stairs to my room, Susan closed the door and flopped down on the bed, I beside her.

"Now, *that's* what you'd call a heavy conversation," she said. "But I have to hand it to the guy. He seems to be the real goods. I must say that when he started on all the things he missed about her, I wanted to yell, 'It's not about *you,* bro!' But he turned it right back to God. That's not easy to do, you know—to want something badly and still say 'not my will,' and mean it. I don't think I could do it. Not for things that really, really matter. But this preacher guy seems to be ready to walk his talk. I have to respect that. I just don't think I have that kind of chutzpah!"

I opened my mouth to argue with Susan, but closed it again. Why argue with her honesty? At least she's up front about it. Many times we say we want to do the will of the Lord but don't begin to understand that it means the submission of our will to His, whether it is convenient, or palatable, or preferred. We submit eagerly only if His leading fits in with our plans. So no, I couldn't argue with Susan. You see, my mind had jumped to Edward. He'd asked me a question, but I had already made up my mind that there was no way God could want what, in my opinion, was inappropriate. And what's even more telling is that even knowing this, I still hold on to my position, not prepared to cede even a millimeter to God's will.

And that's basically the gist of it.

Susan fell asleep, and I distracted myself from the questions in my head by focusing on other growth areas in my life. Eventually a tired Mara came to summon me, and I watched in appreciation as G. David did due justice to the lentil-chickpea salad Susan had brought.

Later I woke Susan, and together we returned to church. Mara remained behind, pleading a headache. G. David again held her hand in his and without words communicated his resolve to stay in touch. Then he left with us. The evening service blessed us with another inspired talk. It was mostly for the men, but edifying for us all. What did Mara do, you ask? She promised to think and pray on the matter. I can understand that. I'd probably have done the same.

---

* *The Seventh-day Adventist Hymnal* (Hagerstown, Md.: Review and Herald Pub. Assn., 1985), hymn 184.

Chapter 10

There I go again. How I ramble sometimes. I started last time talking about my plans for Thanksgiving and got caught up in the retelling of Mara's story. But you have to admit it was worth the digression. So help me get back on track here. So many stories and all the pain and drama accompanying them . . . stories that are turning out to be full-length feature films with enough plots and dramatic twists to mess with my mind. I need to find my way back to the pure objectivity of my initial commission. Am I getting at the root of my original question?

So before the house fills with Thanksgiving scents and hilarity, I've got to get out. Walk. Think. Do a mental checkup. The dinner menu is all planned. My contributions are taken care of, and the others will bring the rest of the meal so worry not, everything is under control.

I'm going to the park. Yes, I know it's a bit nippy right now, but the sun is shining, and the weather report calls for a high of at least 63°F (17°C).

Besides myself, there are a few other solitary wanderers at Moss Park. Muffled against the slight chill in the air, I head toward my favorite thinking spot, only to notice that one of the benches is occupied. I turn to find another when I hear my name.

"It is Quilla, isn't it?" says the figure, sporting a black headscarf and coat.

Recognition dawns. "Natasha!" I hurry toward her. "How have you been?"

"Ah, so-so. You know how it is," she replies with a shrug and in that soft accented voice I'd almost forgotten. "What brings you to the park on your Thanksgiving holiday? You should be at home cooking supper for yourself and a nice young man. Did you find one yet?"

I sit opposite her and grin. "You're a romantic one, aren't you? No. I did not find a nice young man, but I have quite a few people coming by later for dinner. It's a 'bring your own Thanksgiving favorite' potluck. What about you?"

"I wish I did. But the nice young men I meet only open doors for me and help me cross the street." There's a twinkle in her eyes.

I give her a comic eye roll. "You know I was talking about dinner plans. What are you doing for Thanksgiving?"

"I'm here at the park counting my blessings. When that is done, I will go home and do it again."

"If you had your wish, what would you rather be doing today, Natasha?"

She looks away from me, and I recall our first meeting and how much I'd admired her face in repose.

"Oh, Quilla. What would do this old woman's heart a world of good cannot be easily put in words. What I wish for and what I have are two very different things, and I've taught myself to no longer wish for the impossible. Just accept what is, and make the best of it."

"Do you know the song from *Man of La Mancha* about dreaming impossible dreams?" I ask.

"Do I know it! I used to sing it for audiences. Not in English, of course . . ."

She sings the familiar tune in a language I do not immediately recognize. Polish? Her voice holds the slightest of quavers, but the richness and clarity of tone can still be heard. Mesmerized, I listen as the song builds along the quest toward the determination to persevere, no matter how seemingly foolhardy—to reach the unreachable.

She finishes and I stand to my feet letting my hands join in the cheering. "Bravo! Bravo! That was simply marvelous."

Natasha beams, eyes shiny with tears. "Look at you making an old woman cry on Thanksgiving." She dabs at her eyes. "You're a good woman. You bring out the good in people. For a minute there I wanted to be able to dream again and wish for things impossible."

I want to invite her for dinner, but somehow I know my offer will be refused. She will construe my invitation as pity. But no one should be alone on Thanksgiving unless they choose to be. How could I return home and enjoy a meal with all my friends while Natasha dined alone? Already I'd spoken to my parents, who also were having guests to their house. It has always been part of our family tradition to include others in Thanksgivings and Christmases. But how to get this woman with a seemingly fascinating history to come mix and mingle with my motley crew—none of whom she knew? What would entice her to come? And then it comes to me. She might do it if she could contribute in some way.

Checking my watch, I see I have another hour or so before I need to head back, so before I can change my mind, I dive in. "Natasha, I need a big favor. If you could help me out, I would be eternally grateful." As quickly as I can, I sketch out the situation with my interviews to date and the hope that my walk in the park will help me put them all in perspective. "I can't tell you who the women are, but at least three of them will be at dinner tonight. If my instincts are right, you with your artistic temperament might be able to identify who is who. The problem is, Natasha, these women have begun to look to me for support, and I don't know how to help them. I hadn't banked on this part. Can you come to dinner and be my helper and observer? See if you notice anything that will give me a clue or two about how to proceed."

"Quilla, I can't. I don't know your friends."

"I know you don't, but you know me. You know I wouldn't ask unless I needed you. This is only our third meeting, but I feel I've known you forever. I came to the park today because I needed to think—to figure out what to do next. Instead God allowed me to meet you. You have no dinner plans, and I have. I have no solution to my problem, but I think you can be part of that solution. Say you'll help me, Natasha." I hold her mittened hand in mine and make my best puppy dog eyes.

She vacillates. "I don't know. I don't even know how to get to your house."

"I'd come and get you. If I leave now I could get my car and pick you up, or better yet, you could just walk back with me now. I don't live too far from here."

Her countenance reveals her ambivalence.

"Please, Natasha. Please do this for me," I beg.

Still she wavers.

I try my second last incentive. The last would involve dropping to the grass and begging like a dog. "Do you know how to make pierogies?"

I have said magic words.

She grins at me.

"I am the diva of pierogies. I will show you how to make pierogies that will get that young man of yours kneeling at your feet, yes."

As simple as that. Food and favors, and we are on our way.

True to her word, once we get to my house Natasha asks to be provided with potatoes, flour, cheese, and olive oil. Fortunately, I have all those ingredients on hand. As I mentioned before, I like my cheese.

In no time she has pots boiling, dough rolling, and a lively conversation going on as I blend the ingredients for my famous cherries jubilee crepes— dubbed thus by sated consumers.

The ringing of the telephone interrupts our chatter. It's Edward calling to wish me a happy Thanksgiving. Guilt assaults me. Since our last deep talk I have not given him much airtime—not even in my mind. He'd persevered in his correspondence, however, never failing to remind me that I was in his prayers. I hang up the phone feeling like a heel. Natasha is looking at me.

"That's the young man who wants to get to know you better?"

I nod.

"And you do not want him because he is younger than you?"

I nod again, turning on the blender, hoping she will let it go.

She waits till I finish the batter and turn off the machine. "Quilla, sometimes we say we want things, but we have so many conditions attached to the thing we want that it becomes next to impossible to get it. Then we need to ask ourselves why we're unhappy. Do you not think that?"

"What are we talking about now?"

"You like this man. I can tell. But you've already decided that he cannot be for you because he does not fit—how do you say?—some cri . . . What the word?"

"Criteria?"

"That's it. Some criteria you set up. Don't be stupid like Natasha, Quilla. There is still time for you. Me? What I would pay to undo some of my stupid mistakes. I too had a nice man. He loved me and would have married me if only I give him the time of day. I loved him, but I wanted life on stage. Not such a bad thing. He waited for me. I took him for granted. One day I had a big performance, and he came all that way to see me play Aldonza, that's Dulcinea, in *Man of La Mancha*. I was magnificent. The audience loved me. That night after I received two standing ovations Michal came backstage to give me flowers and ask me to dinner. Of course, the whole cast was going out to celebrate."

She nimbly manipulates the dough as she talks. "Even though I asked him to come along, there was no room for him at that party. Many men wanted to dance with me and kiss my hand, and I fell heels over head with success and all the attention. I didn't even know when Michal left. He did not say goodbye, but a week later I got letter from him to wish me all his love. I kissed the letter, but did not take the time to write back.

"Two weeks after that he was back with flowers and a ring. He proposed to me that night, but I told him no. My music must be my priority. How could he want me to give that up to become housewife? He looked at me in shock. 'Did I ever ask you to give up your music, Natasha? How could I do that when it is part of who you are?'"

She rolls the dough out on my clean countertop and, improvising with a cereal bowl turned upside down, begins to cut neat circles with practiced hands. When she runs out of cutting options, she balls the scraps and begins rolling again. I start to say something, but she lifts a floured finger and stops me.

"Listen. Don't talk. What Michal said, I could not believe him. My own mother had dreamed of the stage, but my father did not want wife whose life *his* had to revolve around. She gave up her dream, but made me promise on her deathbed that I should do what mattered to me. So with that lesson in my head, I refused to believe Michal. I let him go."

Throughout her story I watch her hands. They move in a rhythm all their own. She rolls and shapes the dough, seasons the potatoes, wraps, crimps, and drops. In no time fluffy pierogies are dancing atop the boiling water.

"I don't know, Natasha. Looking back on life through the lens of hindsight always gives one a better perspective. But at the time, with the information you had, you made what for you was the best decision. Nothing's wrong with going for your dream." I paused. Took a deep breath. "At least your Michal was not a whole decade younger than you."

"I'm speaking of regrets, Quilla. I regret not trying to have it all. Now in my old age I regret not having someone to share my pillow. I regret not having a little grandson to bring me sticky candy. Nowhere in my mind did I allow for being alone and old."

I want to tell her that even if she'd married her Michal, there would have been no guarantee that it would have lasted or that they would have had children. That the road not taken will always keep us wondering "what if." Edward would have to be a road not taken. That road, even in my most cursory of deliberations, has too many potholes.

"So you became a popular diva of the stage then?"

Natasha scoops up a floating pierogi that's split and leaking potatoes, and places it on a plate. "If you freeze pierogies before cooking, this will not happen. As for the stage, I had good run for three years. Then one day it was all over. I caught bad cold that became pneumonia. I had such awful coughs every time I tried to sing. The manager brought another singer to take my place so show could go on, but when I got better my voice was never the same. So I gambled for my music and lost. Even though Michal kept in touch—I don't know how he kept track of me— he never proposed again. And my pride! Pride is terrible thing, Quilla. My pride would not let me tell him that my dream had been lost. I never told him I had left the stage. I did not tell him that I filled my evenings teaching hardheaded children of tone-deaf mothers to sing."

She adjusts the burner controls to a lower setting. Then she gives me her full attention.

"One Christmas I got letter from Michal with picture of his family. They looked so happy, him and his wife. Her cheekbone looking like it could cut cheese, and his two boys. I put picture on my dresser mirror to remind me about choices and regrets. Every time I looked at that picture, something in me died. Every time I saw it, the face looking back at me from dresser mirror, my face, was that of a lonely, childless fool getting sourer every day than bad pickle.

"There were days, there still are days, that the music burns deep inside me. I feel the power of the gift and the urge to . . . to . . . (She searches for what must be an appropriate English word, but comes up short.) "put my pain in song. The music would float me away to some happy place, and then I hit a note which tickle the back of my throat, and the coughing . . ." (She closes her eyes as if the memory pains her.) "The coughing would come again, reminding me of my imperfection.

"One day after such an episode"—I notice that as she talks and becomes more emotional, her accent gets more pronounced and her English less certain—"I took paper and wrote down all things I would never have. No children. No husband. No grandchildren. No more opera. No being a bride. None of these would be mine. So I threw a big piece of wood on fireplace and made a big blaze. First I burned my lost dreams. Then I burned photo of Michal and his family."

"And you never had another proposal? No other man ever sought you?"

Natasha sighs. "One, maybe two. But I could not let them know me. Music was thing what made me special. Without music I am ordinary. An almost-walk."

"Almost-ran," I correct her.

She does not seem to hear me. "After my father died, I came to Canada. Got job in factory making costumes for opera company. Last year I retired. Now I collect pension and count blessings. I made my choice and will live with cost. I not bitter, but wish I could go back to past with wisdom of today and choose again. I would have give Michal a chance to show me he was different from my father. I would gamble to have it all—the family and the stage. Who knows if it would work? But that's what I would do."

Before I can respond, the doorbell rings. Thanksgiving greetings, laughter, and food fills my house. And in the middle of it all, Natasha, hanging back at first, allows herself to be engulfed in the hilarity. When the time comes for us to gather around the table and do our traditional go-around statement of what we are thankful for, she joins in, giving thanks for beautiful smiles and beautiful hearts. Jason, a friend of Susan's, pronounces a grand blessing on whoever made the pierogies (he'd stolen one), and when I jerk my head toward Natasha, he breaks away from the circle and goes to kneel at her feet, declaring his undying love.

And as he kneels there, Natasha sings to him the first line of "The Impossible Dream" to the howls and cheers of everyone. Then she raises him up, eyes shining with mischief, and gives him an exuberant hug to show she too can jest.

I feel it. Right now I feel it. Deep in my bones. This is going to be one of our best Thanksgiving dinners yet!

It's minutes to midnight. I lie in bed, every part of my body giving thanks for this respite. I sigh with contentment. A day well spent. Savoring every part of it, I close my eyes and breathe deeply from the diaphragm.

"Thank You, Father, for this gift today. Thank You for laughter, for pleasures experienced on my palate, for satisfaction, for a clean kitchen, for fellowship, for friendship, for love, and joy, and You. Thank You for this bed that cradles my tired body, for a new friend who can still find her music, and for old friends with big hearts. For these blessings and more . . . thank You, giver of all life's bounties. Thank You."

I let my mind revisit each section of the day. From Mara's gorgeous smile of triumph when her ackee contribution was declared the best ever tasted, Susan's flush of satisfaction at the exclamations her salad received, Wendell's waltz with Gloria, Lynn's daughter's glee at the piggyback ride Jason provided, and so on, and so on. And yes! My crepes again produced moans of pleasure from people who should have been too full to have dessert. Oh, the singing, the joy—did I say that before? Sorry. It really has been a great day.

Susan and Jason volunteered to drive Natasha home, and all the while as they readied to leave and even on the walk down the short driveway and onto the street, Jason kept at Natasha—what did he have to do for her to make pierogies for him at Christmas? And Natasha, the diva side of her coming out, flirting with him unmercifully.

Ah! What a lovely day.

The ringing of my telephone makes me jump. I look at the clock. Who could be calling at this hour?

It's Edward.

"Don't be mad at me," his husky voice greets my anxious hello. "I couldn't get back to sleep. When Wendell and Gloria got home, they called to tell me about your great dinner and how much they wished I'd been there. They were even singing on the phone! Something about Dulcinea."

He sounds so put out—not only for missing the occasion, I guess, but at his "evil" uncle, who had the temerity to wake him up to tell him so.

"I agree. Your aunt and uncle are two mischief makers, but it truly was a fun evening. All of it. I couldn't have planned it, and wouldn't change one iota of it. Perfect joy!"

A groan across the miles. "Not you too!"

I laugh out loud. "Don't sound so upset. We took many pictures. I'll send you some."

"Not good enough," he replies. "I wish I'd been there. All I had to comfort me was a mandarin salad from the fast-food store down the road and a glass of water."

"Stop whining. You'll get your Thanksgiving in another five weeks. You can celebrate all you want then and call us to brag about it."

The prospect cheers him. "That's right. My mother still puts together a mean feast. Pumpkin pie, roasts, fresh bread . . . I'm salivating just thinking about it."

"See! Something to look forward to. Do you think you'll be able to sleep now? I have work tomorrow."

"Only if you'll pray with me."

I like this man. Nothing is too simple or difficult for him to talk to God about. Oh, that he was older!

"I never turn down the offer of a prayer, Edward."

"You go first."

Yikes! He wants me, I mean us . . . to pray together. Why does this request suddenly feel so intimate? Always before he'd pray or tell me he's been praying for me. But now he wants *us* to pray. Duh! That's what he'd said. But that's not what I thought I'd agreed to.

I recall my earlier prayer of Thanksgiving to God, and with the memory, praying for a fellow believer becomes as natural as saying my name. I send a prayer thought to God. *Give me the right words, Father.*

"Heavenly Father," I say, "today You gave us a gift of joy so precious it whets my appetite even more for heaven. If eye has not seen, nor ear heard, and nothing we can conceive compares to what You have in store for us in heaven, then my God, what can I say? We wait eagerly to be dazzled by Your majesty. Till then, Lord, You've left us in this preparatory school here on earth, and our sole responsibility is to become fully equipped through our tenure here for life with You in heaven. Here You will test us and re-test us, train us, intern us, inform us, and educate us about the God that You are and about what we can become, shaped by the discipline of Your specialization for us. So we yield again to Your lessons, Father. Hard as they may be at times, we know that You are using them to bring us as close as we can come on this side of heaven to Your holiness.

"As we submit ourselves, despite ourselves, against our want, but according to Your will, as we yield and trust and trust and trust, even when we don't feel like it, even when the trusting makes no sense to our minds, as we submit to Your lordship, let the glory of You that You implanted in each one of us, the image of You that You made in us, emerge so that we can clearly be recognized as Your children.

"Hold my friend Edward in the palm of Your hand and continue to do for him all that which will bring him into the personhood of Your design. Help us to be relentless in our pursuit of holiness, Father, with eyes fixed on You. And even when our steps falter and we lose sight of You, help us up to continue willing our minds and hearts to pursue You no matter what. This is our quest, Lord, and we know that by Your dying and even more so by Your resurrection, our quest, our dream, is not an impossible one. Hold us as only You can. In the name of Jesus I ask this, and in the name of the Spirit we claim it. Amen."

At some point during the prayer my mind had taken flight. I had forgotten Edward. Yes, I'd prayed for him, but I'd forgotten myself, my consciousness of me. This prayer had come from deep within me. So when I hear, "Oh, Quilla," it startles me.

His voice whispers with a "full of wonder" kind of breathlessness.

"Is it possible to fall in love with someone during prayer? Quilla, woman of my heart, you have lifted me up to a place I never knew I needed to be. Through your prayer you did that. And yet you will not let me pursue you because of a simple issue of years? If you can pray like this, woman, can you not put this thing that hums between us, this tangible, palpable, quivering resonance of our souls, in God's hands and ask for His will to be done? I will yield to God on this if He says no. But surely you feel it too."

In the quiet of my mind I acknowledge it. I dare not lie to myself. It is there, and I do not want it. I do not want this impossible dream.

O God, help me not to encourage this man whom I could so easily love. I must not love him like that, Lord. I must not hurt Your child. I must not feel anything that will tempt me to deviate from what must be Your decided will on this topic. Too many years between us, Lord. This cannot work. Let me not go there.

Quilla. The voice now in my ear has no sound.

Yes, Father.

"*My thoughts are not your thoughts, neither are your ways my ways.*[1] *Nothing is impossible for Me.*"

What are You saying, Lord? You want me to allow myself to love this man, to encourage a relationship with him? It will not work! Don't You see? I'm old enough to be—

Do you believe that I know all things?

Of course I believe that, Lord.

Do you believe I love you with an everlasting love?

Yes. I believe that.

Do you believe that people come into your life for a purpose? That when you gave Me permission to be Lord of your life, My covenant with you include not letting anything that is not in My plans for you happen to you?

Yes, Lord.

Then trust Me. Now will you please answer the young man whom I sent to you with a question. He's still waiting for you.

"Are you there, Quilla?"

I sigh. "I will talk to God about it, Edward. But my mind is against this. Totally against this."

"What of your heart? Is your heart against it too?"

"My heart does not matter. It has proved unreliable in the past."

"Then trust in the heart of God. I will do that too. And my prayer for you is that God will continue to open you up to all the potential He wants to fulfill in and through you—just as you prayed for me. God bless you, my friend. I will call again."

On that note he bids me good night. More like good morning. My joy is gone. Behind it remains a soft anger—at Edward, at God, and at me. Mostly at me.

Why? Because I hate finding out that rebellion still thrives in me and that despite my prayer for God to use me I want it on my terms and with my approval.

"Trust in the Lord with all your heart, and lean not on your own understanding; in all your ways acknowledge Him, and He shall direct your paths."[2]

All my heart! That's what God desires. Trust with all my heart. I know that it is not only my heart that is appealed to here, but my mind. My emotions and intellect.

Oh, for a heart like God's!

Then it comes back to me: "the welcome to the heart of God." But the rebellion in me remains entrenched. No budging or yielding.

Not this time. Not Your will this one time, God. It makes no sense. Please see it from my perspective.

Yet even as I argue, I hate the "me" that still insists on my way. I want so much to be at the place when God's way is my joy and delight. Why must I continue to rebel against the very thing that I trust to be good for me? Oh, that God did not give me this power to choose!

Program me to obedience, Lord. Let me do Your will because it's the only option!

The phone in my hand beeps me back to the present. I had not said goodbye to Edward. Not even replied to his "good night."

---

[1] Isa. 55:8, NIV.

[2] Prov. 3:5, 6, NKJV.

Chapter 11

So many times I've tried to summarize the various stories that comprise my project thus far, but every single time something gets in the way. I need to do it. I need to take stock. So what have I learned to answer the question Why am I not married by now?

From Mara I learned that it's because she still has feelings for Garry. Lynn's story is pretty much the same except for the complication of a child the father knows nothing about. Susan isn't married because she thinks she's got nothing to offer a husband, and Natasha lost her one opportunity and feels that without her music she too has nothing of equal value to offer. Stelle has not yet found her soul mate and is content with life the way it is.

Five women—four of whom had proposals that did not come to fruition. Is that all there is? Uncapitalized opportunities, low self-esteem, and fear? And what about me? I have no stellar record of plentiful proposals. I don't even have a good proposal under my belt. I know there are many other women like me who've completely missed out. We've all attended the weddings of our friends. Some of them married the wrong person just to be married, while the love of others shone so brightly on their wedding day that when we returned to our lonely houses we wept for this glimpse of bliss we cannot seem to grasp for ourselves.

And with every harvest, every marriage season, the prospects get fewer, the pickings get slimmer. You know you've turned a critical corner when younger brides start asking you to be their wedding organizer or matron of honor. Worse yet is when you start receiving invitations to the weddings of your friends' children—the friends who married young. That happened to me last summer.

In all those seasons of coupling and decisions to have and hold, how did I get missed every single time? Why have I been the one overlooked?

Less-attractive, less-educated, less-personable women than I (and I'm not being a braggart, just honest) have gotten married. Many happily so! I have no identity issues (as Susan does), no leftover feelings for a guy from my past (as Mara and Lynn do), and certainly no seeming ease with singlehood (as Stelle demonstrates). I would leap at marriage to the right guy. I want this shared intimacy marriage offers. Why have I been overlooked again and again?

Yes, I know that the number of single women in the church is way higher than the number of men. But why is God denying me this thing that I want so badly, this precious union He created and blessed? Dare I conclude that marriage is not in God's plans for me? I have never considered marrying outside my faith, and I won't now. So do I close this chapter in my life? give it up? Or should I go down the road of considering a younger man—a wonderful younger man such as Edward? Am I that desperate?

But why do I label it desperation to consider marriage to a younger man? Could it possibly be what God wants for me?

No. Completely out of the question! I just can't go there.

But I will pray, since I promised Edward I would, for God to speak to me. What He will have to do to get me to listen, much less take that road, I don't know. Perhaps as Mara demanded, He'll have to send an angel three times with specific signs, the way He did for Gideon.

Crystal, Danesha, and Mia

Last week three of the younger single women in church accosted me in the parking lot. They'd heard about my project and wondered why I wasn't seeking their opinions. They had questions too.

I looked at them, so full of promise and possibilities. They had many good years and many more marriage seasons ahead of them. But they would not be silenced or reasoned out of their need for an audience, so I gave in. They came this afternoon, and in preparation I invited Susan and Mara to join us. This proved to be an interesting meeting. I provided finger snacks and comfy couches.

All three arrived together. Crystal, a vivacious leggy brunet; Mia, a petite Filipino woman of about 28, and Danesha, athlete-turned-scholar who just completed her Ph.D. in microbiology and is now ready to turn attention to marriage and family. First, however, she has to find the man.

After taking their coats, I showed them the powder room, and all three traipsed in together to wash their hands. I had set out our light repast in the living room, and soon a healthy buzz filled the air. Exclamations abounded over the warm artichoke-parmesan dip served in the large pumpernickel loaf. Improvising on Mara's recipe, I'd even risked serving my version of a mango punch. That too received its share of accolades.

Mara arrived next, looking more chipper than I've seen her in a while, and Susan eventually made her appearance. She looked naked and apologetic without her customary salad fixings.

"Sorry I didn't get around to making anything, Quill. I was kinda busy today," she whispered in my ear as soon as I opened the door.

"Get in here," I scolded, "and stop apologizing for something so silly. Plus, today we're just doing finger foods, and there's a whole veggie platter that you can nibble from to your heart's content. "

Following introductions, I prayed, inviting God to join our discussion. Then I briefly outlined my project and the reason I was doing it.

"So what have you learned so far?" asked Danesha, the young scientist.

"I've learned that the reasons for still being single are as varied as each woman's story and that I now have more questions than I do answers."

"Like what?" Danesha asked.

"Are all women who desire marriage meant to be married? Is that the best thing for a woman to do with her life? Could it be that we need to revise our predetermined criteria for husband material? Do we communicate by our words or actions that we are above certain men, or not interested? Are there things from our past that prevent us from experiencing intimacy with men? Are there—"

"Whoa! Hold on a minute." Crystal's hand was raised as if to stem a tide. "Back up to predetermined criteria. Are you implying we shouldn't have expectations of the qualities we want in a husband?"

"No. I'm not implying any such thing. But have you ever sat down and put to paper all the 'qualities' you want Mr. Right to possess?"

"Well, he'd better have a job, and a good one to boot!" Crystal shot back. "He should be decent-looking, treat me with respect, have eyes for no other woman but me, want kids—"

"What color is he?" I asked her.

"White, of course!"

"And how old is he?"

"My age, or a couple years older," she quickly replied. "I'd say between 29 and 33."

"Crystal, do you believe that God has a plan for your life?"

"Let's not bring the religion issue into the discussion at this point in time," Danesha retorted. "It makes people feel guilty for wanting things that they don't have. Let's apply reason and logic to this discussion."

I caught an indulgent smile on Mara's face before she spoke. "By all means, Danesha, let's leave out religion. But let's certainly include God. I assume that all of us here are Christians. We believe in a God who invites us to come and reason with Him. We believe that the same extender of that invitation is our Creator, and that He wants to give us the very best gifts."

(Yes, Mara was definitely, solidly back on speaking terms with God.)

"And that's why I say park the 'God's will' issue for a holy minute," Danesha retorted. "Too many times during discussions of this nature we end up blaming the victim. We don't have what we need or desire because we don't have enough faith, God doesn't want it for us, or some such nonsense. Truth is, sometimes we don't have things because we haven't applied ourselves to getting it. We hide behind some silly God's-will excuse and use it as a crutch for our situation!"

"Then how do we know the difference?" soft-spoken Mia asked.

Susan leaned forward in her chair. "Maybe sometimes God needs for us to meet Him halfway. Pray, and then take action, asking Him to bless our decisions."

"Certainly not, if those decisions fly in the face of His expressed commandments!" I countered.

"Of course," agreed Susan. "However, with some decisions we need to make, no amount of looking in the Bible is going to provide the answer. So we pray to God and take action. We make the best decision we can based on what we know."

"But what if it turns out to be the wrong thing?" Mia asked cautiously.

"God will strike you dead!" Danesha said so emphatically that Mia's face blanched.

"Mia!" Danesha objected. "Don't take everything I say so literally. I'm just kidding. But just so you know, that's what some people believe."

Mara answered Mia's question. "I think that if our decision turns out to be wrong, God still loves us and waits for us with open arms to recognize our need of Him. Just as the prodigal's father did for his son."

Ignoring Mara, Crystal turned back to me. "Why did you ask me if I believed God had a plan for my life?"

"Instead of answering your question, Crystal, what if I give you an illustration?"

"OK."

"Let's say, for argument's sake, that all of us here have in our heads a list of criteria for our version of Mr. Right. Now, what if the person God sends you has all the qualifications you want except for one. Let's say, if I use Crystal's criteria, this really terrific guy God sends you is Black. Would you consider him?"

Crystal pursed her lips and looked at me fiercely. Then she said, "Don't take this the wrong way, guys, but I think marriages are hard enough to navigate without adding a racial element."

"But how do you know that the so-called racial element is going to be a big issue in your marriage?" Susan asked.

Crystal rolled her eyes. "Obviously you do not really know my family, and before you point out the obvious, I am quite aware that Mia and Danesha, two of my very best friends, are not White. Having girlfriends of other races is not the problem. But within my family there is an unwritten rule hanging over our bedroom doors: Thou shall not get involved with someone from another race. Why would I want to expose myself and my children to that kind of intolerance? My older sister dated a Black guy for a little while, and boy, did she get grief over it! Every time the poor guy came by to pick her up or to drop her off, my usually warm parents gave him such a frosty greeting that he became a stuttering fool in their presence. I know for a fact he doesn't have a stutter, but that's the effect they had on him. None of the White guys got that degree of frostbite."

"I think your story helps to illustrate my point, Crystal," I replied. "Sometimes our singleness has less to do with God and more to do with the obstacles we put in His way. It doesn't have to be a race issue. It could be a situation in which the guy is much older or younger than us, or has children from a former relationship. Whatever the reason, somehow we will not let our minds go beyond our preformed fantasies."

My little speech quieted the room. I didn't mean for it to, but I wouldn't take it back. This message was for me too.

After an awkward pause, Mara looked in my direction. "When Quilla interviewed me for my views on this topic, one of the issues I raised was how to deal with our sexual feelings."

I nodded for her to continue.

"What are your opinions, ladies?"

Danesha spoke up. "Obviously you're not asking us if we should have sexual feelings. You're really asking how we handle—or should handle—our sexual urges, aren't you?"

"More or less."

"Don't focus on it," Susan said dismissively. "This sex thing is all overrated anyway. Just as any other urge, if left unappeased it will pass."

I didn't ask the first or second question that came to my mind at that. No, I really didn't need to know.

"But what if it doesn't?" Danesha brought my attention back from the land of speculation.

"Take a cold shower. Trust me, if you refocus your mind, the urge will go away," Susan stated emphatically. "It works."

"I hate it when people give me simplified answers like that," Danesha challenged. "As if all life is that cut-and-dried. If your prescription was so easy, Susan, so many people would not find themselves in compromising situations, and so many of our sisters would not end up with unwanted pregnancies."

"They just don't have the mental discipline, that's all. The mind does what we focus on. I'm sorry to make it that simple, but it *is* that simple. Take your mind off the sexual urge, and eventually it goes away."

Mara chimed in. "I don't know that it is all mental discipline. Hormones play a huge role in our sexuality, at least for women. Men, I don't know."

"They are always hormonal, no question!" said Crystal.

"You remember that old woman who used to do the Sunday night sex show on the radio? Occasionally I would listen in, and one of the things she kept telling her audience is that the more sex you have, the more you want to have it. I presume the opposite is also true: the less you have, the less you want it."

"Starve it with neglect, then?" Mia asked

"Either that or do the lust-run-to-the-altar-thing," replied Susan.

"Or you can do the deed, and confess later."

All eyes turned on Mara.

"*You* are going straight to hell!" Susan pretended shock.

Mara held up her hands as if to ward off an assault. "Hey, I'm not saying I'd do that, but some of my sisters see it that way. That's all I'm saying."

"Come on, people; be real! We are talking as if our sexual urge is stronger than the God we serve. It's not!"

"Hello!" Crystal exclaimed. "Did those words just come out of Danesha's mouth? The very same woman who wanted to park the God involvement for a holy minute?"

Danesha didn't bat an eye. "Look at your watch, my friend. A minute, holy or not, has long passed."

"Touché!" Crystal conceded.

"Speaking of time, I have to go get some shut-eye. I have early rounds in the morning," said Mia, sounding reluctant.

I checked my watch. Yikes! A whole evening wasted, and I had no additional information from these three younger women as to why they're not married. What had this discussion about dealing with sexual feelings accomplished?

Nothing! Yes, I know it's a part of the singlehood reality, but . . .

God had to be laughing right then. If only I could have foreseen where my question would take me! I must admit, though, that the learning has been mind-boggling, to say the least. Awesome, even. More dendrites than I ever wanted have embedded themselves within my brain.

"Sorry our discussion got sidetracked," Mia told me. "It's already late, and none of us have told our own stories." She leaned toward me. "Can we come back another time?"

"Of course."

I'm not sure she even heard me, because she went on without taking a breath. "But more than that, I really enjoyed myself. We need more honest discussions like this, don't you think? Maybe a by-product of your project, Quilla, could be forming a women's group to talk about the issues that occupy our minds and impact our spirituality. Listen, it's a good thing you're doing."

"I second that," Danesha added. "This was fascinating and mentally stimulating. And thanks for keeping God in the picture, even though I kinda wanted Him out. I'm looking forward to next time. Who knows? Maybe Crystal will have found a tall and really dark love of her life by then. I can just see him . . . He's basking under a coconut tree in the Bahamas . . ."

Crystal flung a piece of carrot at Danesha. The aim was true, and it hit her cheek. "That's for being cheeky!"

"You little worm! But I won't retaliate. It's not my style. Reason devoid of passion is my mantra."

Crystal didn't miss a beat. "Well, that would explain why *you're* not married by now. Who wants to hug a brain?"

"Only a person who can recognize one!"

"Ouch! You guys can zing!" Susan laughed. "How long have you two been friends?

"Since sixth grade," Danesha said.

"Fifth," Crystal corrected.

"Come, children," said the quiet-spoken Mia. "Let's go home. It's way past your bedtime, and I can see you're both getting cranky. Thanks for everything, Quilla, and please let us come again and share like this."

I prayed with them, and another unpredictable conversational evening ended.

Chapter 12

As I pull into the driveway, thick snow clinging to my wipers, my cell phone rings. I flip it open.

"Quilla, Quilla, tell me you're home!"

It's Susan. "Just pulling into the drive. What's up?"

"I'm coming over!"

"I don't know about the roads, Sue. It took me forever to get home. They're predicting more snow later tonight."

"Forget about the snow! I've got news. I'll be there in five minutes. I'm just around the corner."

"Susan, listen to me . . ." The phone goes dead. I sigh and heave my tired body out of the car and into the house. What a long day this has been. Since the recent influenza outbreak, I've done more talks about handwashing and sneezing into your sleeve or in a tissue than I dreamed possible. The news media is not helping with the recent hype about the latest flu virus. The last thing I need right now is a dose of my best friend's excitement. Typically what excites her stresses me.

As soon as I take off my coat and boots the doorbell starts ringing insistently, accompanied by an impatient rapping on the door. With a great deal of deliberate forbearance I open the door, and there stands Susan, coat open, hair speckled with snowflakes, excitedly moving from one foot to the other.

Rattling the screen door handle, she yells, "Come on, Quilla! Open the door!"

I flick the lock, unaware I'd locked it after I entered. Yep. The tired old body is on autopilot.

Susan erupts into the house, pulls me into her arms, and dances me around the foyer and into my living room. She then plants a loud smack on my cheek and exclaims: "Congratulations, Quilla! You're going to be an auntie! Yippee!" She performs a perfect pirouette. "I'm so excited! I didn't expect it to happen this quickly. I thought it would take eons and eons, but just one try, and voilà!" She turns sideways. "Do you see anything? Does it show a little? I think so. Pinch me. Go ahead. Pinch me!"

I pinch her. Hard.

"Ow! Not that hard. What are you trying to do?"

"Pinching some sense into you, that's what I'm doing. Could you at least back up and tell me what exactly you're so excited about that has me being an auntie? What pet have you taken in this time? I will not babysit any more of them! No smelly hamster, cute rabbit, abandoned puppy, or broken-wing bird."

I give her my hardest, meanest stare. Susan stops her excited jitterbug dance, and at her stillness I feel a weird movement in the vicinity of my belly. A foreboding.

"Quill, I'm going to have a baby. A real live baby!"

I gape. What else can I do? I stare at her with my mouth hanging open and with what I'm sure is an uncomprehendingly stupid look on my face.

"Aren't you excited for me?"

Her question focuses me. "Whose baby is it, Sue? Michael's?"

"Michael! Why would I do something so silly? The guy is besotted with me! Don't you listen to anything I tell you? I told you I wanted a child. I specifically told you I was researching sperm bank parenthood. If I recall correctly, I got a long litany from the 'voice of doom' regarding the matter. But see, I found a way to have a baby. No sex. No father in the picture. Just me and my baby!"

I sit down and cup my face in my hands. She's done it again. Her audacity, gall, and . . . excitement leave me breathless.

"I guess I've shocked you. I didn't mean to, but I'm so excited. Never mind, Quill, I'll make it up to you. Please tell me you're happy for me. I can't do this without your help."

I hear her rattling speech and cannot look up to give her the reassurance she's begging for.

"I'll make us both some tea. No. Hot cocoa! Just sit and take things easy, Quill. I'll be right back. Everything's under control."

She flutters off to the kitchen, but I can still see behind my closed eyelids lingering flecks of her happiness. I hear my cupboard doors opening and closing. I can tell that she's opened the can of cocoa and has spooned three teaspoons of cocoa into a mug. I hear the pouring of hot water from the kettle into the mug, then the mug pouring into the pot on the stovetop. How many times have we done this ritual together during moments of celebration, crisis, pain, comfort, and just because? I hear her place my jar of whole nutmegs on the counter and grate a light dusting into the pot of cocoa. Next she'll search for the sweetened condensed milk to add to it with a pinch of salt. Any minute now she'll be back after she's turned the stove to medium low, leaving the pot to come to a gentle boil.

I reach deep inside me for the love that has seen us through so many life circumstances, and it's there. Still intact. *Give me the right words, please, Father. Tell me what to say to my friend.* As she reenters the room I look up. I can do this.

"You OK now, Quill? Did you have a bad day at work, or is it just my news that's knocked you for six?"

I feel my mouth smiling. "Make that a yes."

She pulls up a chair so we're sitting knee to knee, then she takes my hands into hers. "Please tell me you're not too, too mad at me, Quill. I'm sorry for not telling you before. I just wanted to wait, you know, to make sure it would work. And since you were so against the idea, well . . ."

"Are you ready for this, Sue?"

She nods her head vigorously and emphatically. "Readier than I've ever been for anything else in my life. I want this so much. A child of my very own."

"And I get to be an aunt."

She nods again, this time spilling a few tears. "The best aunt a kid will ever have."

My own eyes begin to tear up too. And all my words of wisdom, all my worry words and damnation words, and 'how stupid can you get' words, they all fall away in the face of the raw need of a friend who so much wants a baby of her very own to love. Like it or not, circumstances ideal or not, this moment marks the beginning of letting go and setting out to welcome this life in the making who chose neither the circumstances of their birth nor the perfection of their parentage.

I squeeze Sue's hand and pull her to her feet. "Then let me be the first to congratulate you, Mommy. I'll pray every day for God to watch over you and this little one."

I enclose her in a hug that only God could have put in my arms. And this simple giving of love breaks her heart. She clings to me and cries. With the wind howling outside I rock her and coo nonsensical words of comfort because I know the crying contains more than just relief at my acceptance of her news. It also contains great big gobs of regret, shame, rejection, and abandonment, along with an attempt, through this child, to right a perceived wrong.

A hissing sound from the kitchen sends Susan flying out of my arms. "Oh, no! Your cocoa is boiling over!"

And indeed it had. Susan grabs the pot and, in her hurry to move it to the adjacent burner, bangs it against the lip of that burner, spilling the contents over the whole stovetop. She turns wet eyes to mine in a look of supreme stupefaction.

I button my lips tightly, but laughter gurgles at the back of my throat. Taking the pot from Susan's hand, I place it in the sink, running the cold water loudly to hide my mirth. When that proves futile, I grab the steel wool and begin a furious scrubbing of the pot. But the laughter will not be turned back. My shoulders shake with it. I sneak a peek at my friend, only to find her standing still by the stove with that same look of bewilderment on her face. Then my laughter erupts for good. It unfreezes her. She spears me with an evil look.

"I don't like you very much, Quilla Hazelwood. You have absolutely no sense of honor."

"Of course you love me," I reply, reining in my mirth. "You have to. I'm to be aunt to your child."

"Be that as it may, you still have no honor."

"I still have no hot cocoa, and I'm absolutely starving. Now please get over here and help me find us something to eat for dinner. Before you do that, take a look outside. Chances are you're not going back across the city tonight. I hope you have clothes upstairs."

"I always keep a change of clothes in my car. Plus what are friends for if you can't borrow their clothes?"

"Sorry, I have no maternity clothes in my closet."

"Ha! Ha! I'm so laughing at your joke. As if I'm showing yet! Oh, Quill, I'm going to be a mom! What am I going to do?"

"First thing? Help me make us some dinner. Please. I cannot think anymore on this empty stomach."

Forty minutes later we are seated at the kitchen table, remnants of a hurriedly-put-together chili smearing our bowls. I feel a burp making its way toward the back of my throat and stifle it.

"How pregnant are you?" I ask even though a part of me does not want to know.

"Nine weeks."

"How long have you known?"

"About five weeks or so. Why?"

A pain briefly constricts my tummy. It's hurt feelings. For five weeks she's lived with this secret and not one word to me. But then again, this is not the first thing she's kept from me. And if I'm honest, I don't tell her everything that happens in my life. I guess all of us need a little private space to do our own thing, at least sometimes. I can respect that.

It still hurts, though. This thing that she's done is big, but when I answer her "why," all I say is, "No particular reason. Just wondered, that's all."

We sit, each immersed in our own internal conversations, the slight smell of burnt chocolate milk mingled with chili powder and onions perfuming the air. I get up to open the front door, and as I do, the phone rings. It's Gloria.

"Hey, Glo, what's up?"

"Wendell and I just want to be reassured that you're home and out of this horrid weather. I tried Susan's house, but got no answer."

"She's here. Safe and sound. I just told her she's going to have to stay the night. The weather is awful, and more snow's expected later tonight. To tell the truth, I wouldn't mind a blizzard. I could do with an early weekend. Listen, Glo, talk to Sue while I go cover my car. I was too tired to do it when I got home."

I hand the phone to Susan, grab a hooded jacket from the closet, haul on my boots, and step outside.

Amazing!

How do I describe the white blanket of snow against the green of the pine trees? The silence. The untouched look. The falling flakes doing a spiral dance in the air. I want to stick out my tongue so it can be tickled by fluffy droplets of cold. The words of that childhood prayer by the poet Browning comes to my mind.

"God's in His heaven—
All's right with the world."

Here in this moment of stillness where conversations with God come as naturally as the urge to breathe, I talk to Him softly about the stuff on my mind.

"Dear Lord, my best friend is pregnant. Soon to be a mommy, and I know I must not yell at her even though I so much want to! This feels so wrong. And I'm afraid. I don't know why I'm afraid, but I just am. I think I'm afraid because here comes another child into the world to be born under less-than-ideal circumstances, to grow up without a sense of fatherhood, and who will have to learn to navigate life without this most important role model. I know that not all fathers are good ones and that many children have been wounded by life, but still, Father, how do we help this child who I've already decided is a girl?

"But whether Sue has a girl or boy, please help her remember all the wonderful qualities of her adoptive father and to lean on the love of her heavenly Father. When You look at us, Father, I know You see behind our foolish actions to the child within who is motivated by fear or hurt or anger or pain. And You love us despite our selfishly made decisions, because You understand the underlying reasons we do the things we do. Help me to continue to love her despite our differences and to love her in spite of her choices. Help me to be an extension of Your heart, Your hands, Your beneficence, and Your mercy. And please, Lord! Help me not to yell at her. I still want to. I do. I do."

To channel my pent-up anger I race like mad to the end of the street, skidding in the snow, forcing my legs to pump, my lungs to gasp, and my urge to cause pain to turn inward for the good of my muscles. At the end of the block I run just as furiously back to my driveway, puffing warm steam into the night's perfection. But the one run is not sufficient, so I do it three more times. Back and forth, back and forth . . . back . . . and . . . forth till most of the fury is spent and I am in control again. Only then, mouth wide open to expel the accumulation of CO_2, am I able to reach in my pocket for the car keys and remove the cover and snowbrush.

I brush the snow, disturbing its nestling, realizing even as I do it that my work is partially futile. No sooner do I brush one area than it becomes a new nesting for the steadily falling flakes. So settling for doing the best I can, I cover the car. I can't stop what's already under the cover, but I can minimize the work I'll have to do the next day.

When I reenter the house, Susan is still on the phone. Her animated face makes me think she's told Gloria the news. I remove my coat and boots, curious to learn how Gloria is taking the glad tidings. Then I hear her say:

"It's all your doing, you know. You got me so riled when you were last here, forcing me to deal with things I would've kept on dodging. So I took matters into my own hands. No more being a patsy to fate, waiting for life to happen to me. And for that you will have to be made an honorable uncle."

I guess Wendell's on the phone offering congratulations. Leaving them to their talk, I head up the stairs for a nice hot shower. Later I'll turn on the TV to get the weather update.

The warm water cascading down my back feels so good that I want to stay there forever. Reluctantly I turn off the tap and dry myself, and continue to will my mind to a place of thoughtlessness. God's in His heaven, and truly, in the best sense, all is right with the world.

When I emerge from the bathroom I feel restored, capable, and renewed—until Susan greets me.

"So Quilla, my friend," she says as I enter my bedroom, "you've been holding out on me, eh? There I was talking to Gloria when the line buzzed. Like the good person that I am, not wanting my best friend to miss out on her calls, I put Gloria on hold and answer the incoming call. And what greeted my ear, you might be wondering? A sexy baritone saying, 'Hello, woman of my heart!' For a moment I was speechless. And then . . .'"

I don't need to hear the rest of what she says, for my flipping heart starts doing its thing. Oh, no! The caller could only have been Edward.

Eyes dancing with mischief, my "gray-hair-making" friend, who's lying across my bed, beckons me with a crooked finger to enter my own room. I feel the restorative the shower provided swiftly leaving and walk like one condemned to a punishment I wish to avoid.

"Since when did you become the woman of Edward's heart, Quilla dear?"

Without saying a word, I fluff my three pillows, remove my robe, and drape it at the foot of *my* bed half across Susan. I then peel back the covers and slip into my bed, 'accidentally' kicking Susan off in the process. She gets up slowly. I'm in trouble.

Grabbing a pillow from under my head, she flays me with it, ignoring my pleas for mercy as I burrow even further, pulling the bedcovers over my head. She waits till I poke my head out and gives me a final thump. "Now are you ready to talk?"

"No, I'm not. There's nothing to talk about."

"This guy likes you, Quilla?"

"So he seems to think."

"And do you like him back?"

"That's irrelevant. Nothing's going to come of it."

Susan looms over me. "Why's that?"

"How can you ask? The man's a baby! Trust me when I say nothing is going to come of it."

"He's at least 32 years old, unless I miss my guess. Should be—"

"Thirty-five."

"—of an age to know his own mind," she glares at my interruption, "and based on my limited knowledge of him, he is very mentally mature as well. Did you say 35?"

"Yes, 35."

She drops the pillow on my head and sits on the edge of my bed. "You still want to be married, Quill?

I give her the look. "What kind of question is that? Of course I want to get married!"

"And this guy wants to get to know you better. Probably already has feelings for you? Has he been calling you since summer, when he was last here?"

I'm not going to answer. Any answer will give her more ammunition to tease me. I don't want to be teased about Edward. I just want to make my decision that he's wrong for me and live with the decision. Is that too much to ask?

The bed gives as my friend makes herself more comfortable, and I realize that I've indeed asked for too much.

"Talk to me, girl."

I turn my back on her. "Go to bed, Susan. It's late."

She gets up, and before I can say boo she's in front of my face. "How do you feel about Edward, Quill? Do you like him?"

I must give her something or she'll never go away, so I do my best matter-of-fact voice intonation. "Of course I like him. What's there not to like? He's a very nice man and will make some woman a wonderful husband."

"*Grrrrrgh!* I hate it when you get like this. Stop stonewalling! Do you or do you not have feelings for this man, Tranquility Victoria Adeline Hazelwood? Just answer the question! When he calls you on the phone, sends you an e-mail, when he calls you 'woman of my heart,' or whatever else he does, do you find yourself looking forward to hearing more, wanting more of him? The truth, Quilla!"

"Susan," I say in measured tones, "the man is nine whole years younger than I am. A relationship between us just won't work."

"How do you know that?"

"I just know. Older woman-younger man matches do not work. Not when the age gap is so wide."

"And since when did you become an expert on the subject? I like Edward. He's a man's man, and if I was in the running for a mate I'd take him on. He could be good for you, Quill. Why don't you give it a try? He seems the real goods, plus Gloria and Wendell really like him."

"They have to. He's their relative."

"No, they don't. They speak very highly of him and really enjoy his visits. They even talk regularly on the phone."

"How do you know all this stuff?"

She ignores my question. "Do you like him, Quill, even just a little bit? He's good-looking, spiritual, intelligent, tall. He clears the table, seems to be able to cook, is a good conversationalist, and can hold his own in an argument. So what if he's a few years younger? It's not a big deal!"

"It's a big deal to me. The guy might want children one day, Sue. I've lost my chance for that. Can you just picture me pregnant at the ripe old age of 45 or 46?"

As soon as the words leave my mouth I realize my mistake. Susan, however, is unfazed. "There you go. Imagining all the worst impossible scenarios. Does the guy want children? Does he even want to marry you? You haven't even gone on a date, and already you have questions about marriage and children. It's reasoning like yours that gives older single women the bad name of desperate. Go out with the man. Allow yourself to get to know him and him to get to know you. See how his friends and family relate to you and how you feel being around him. Discover each other's minds and then make a decision. No, before you do that, ask God for help. *Then* make a decision. You owe yourself that much. And so help me, Quilla Hazelwood, if you do not give this thing an honest try, I do not want to hear any more laments from you about no good men around. Do you hear me? Sometimes they come in packages we'd not anticipated."

"Look who's talking!" I mutter.

"I heard that! But I've made the decision to be a single mother, and for now that will require all my middle-aged attention. I'm one of those who will be having a child in my ripe old age."

"I'm sorry. I wasn't meaning to cast judgment on you. I was talking for myself."

"I know that." She rose from the bed. "Oh, look at the time! I need to get my bag from the car." At the doorway she paused. "Give the guy a chance, Quill. You never know."

I pull the pillows over my head, but the phone is ringing again. I briefly consider ignoring it, but knowing it might be my mother, harassed by my dad to call me to make sure I'm OK, I reach across for the instrument.

"Hey, Quilla!"

It's the sexy baritone, and indeed my heart does a bit of a flutter at the sound.

Dear God, I must not have feelings for this man.

I pray, but there is no divine intervention to rescue me. And when he inquires so caringly about how I am, tells me I sound tired, then proceeds to give me words of cheer, I feel so buoyed. This is nice. To have someone concerned about me and wanting to make my day better. This is very nice.

"Thank you, Edward. How did you know I had a tough day?"

"Well, I've been on the phone to Toronto a lot this evening. I talked to Uncle Wendell and Aunt Glo earlier. They told me about the weather. Then I called you to make sure you'd made it home safely, and I got Susan. She told me her news. How are you taking it?"

"Well, God and a good run helped me not to yell at her. But tell me, Edward, have you ever heard of such a thing? What do you think the church's position is for something like this? I mean, technically she hasn't committed a sin of immorality, so how will it be viewed?"

"Before I tell you my opinion, why didn't you yell at her?"

"I just couldn't. It would be the worst possible thing to do. Having this baby is so very important to Susan. She needs, or thinks she needs, this baby. By having it on her own and not abandoning it, as she was abandoned, she thinks she'll get a chance to make up for the fact that she was rejected by her own birth mom. That's why she's doing it. I don't agree with her decision, but like the rest of us, she is a wounded soul trying to make peace with her past. And more than that, she's my best friend whom I love very much." An overwhelming feeling of sadness joins the tiredness in my body.

"Then whatever the church's position is on the matter is not critical," Edward says. "What we are required to do first and foremost as Christians is to love people—those who are well people and those who are wounded. Every day God looks beyond our faults and sees into the heart of us, and even when we make poor choices, He's ready with open arms to greet returning prodigals—male or female."

"So you're saying I shouldn't stress myself about how she got pregnant?"

"The deed is done, Quill. Stressing will not undo it. Focus on how to be there for her and her child. She's going to need you."

"I know. She's already told me she can't do it without me. I only wish she'd at least informed me before she did it."

"And you would have tried to talk her out of it, wouldn't you?"

I acknowledge the truth he speaks. "Yes, I would. No need to say more; you've made your point, and I plead guilty."

"I'm coming up to Toronto weekend after next."

My heart does the flip-flop thing again. I pretend mild curiosity. "Oh? For how long?"

"Four days. I promised Mom I'd be home for Christmas, so that's all the time I can afford right now. I'd like to spend a good chunk of that visit with you. Will you let me? No strings attached."

"Oh, Edward, I'm not sure that's a good idea."

"You don't think I should come to Toronto?"

"You know that's not what I mean."

"So you don't want to spend time with me. You find my company offensive, is that it?"

I hope he's teasing, but I'm not sure. "Now you're trying to put words in my mouth. I do not find your company offensive. We talk almost every day. Obviously I enjoy your company, but—"

"Say no more, woman of my heart. Let's start there, and the rest we'll see. Now promise me you'll take care of yourself and stay home tomorrow if the weather is really bad. I don't want to spend the day worrying about you."

"I promise not to put myself in unnecessary danger. How's that?"

I hear him sigh. "The best I can hope for, it seems. Good night, Quilla."

" 'Night, Edward."

I hang up the phone, shout good night to Susan, and reach to turn off my light. The phone rings again. I grab it before it rings twice. "Hello?"

"Woman, why didn't you remind me that we hadn't prayed? I love praying with you. As soon as I hung up I knew what I'd missed. So since you're tired, I will pray for both of us tonight. Ready?"

I turn off the light. "Ready."

"I'll make it short. Father in heaven, thank You for bringing all of us safely home. Thank You for the constancy of Your love. Please watch over Susan and her developing child. Help us to be extenders of Your grace to her. And please give Quilla a peaceful rest. She's had a long and emotionally draining day. Sustain her and guide her to the path wherein lies her happiness and spiritual development. Help me to continue trusting in You, and thanks again, Lord, for allowing me to experience the friendship of this very special woman. Amen."

I say amen too.

"Now snuggle down and go to sleep. I'll talk to you soon."

He hangs up after I bid him a husky goodbye.

Lord, I continue, *You have to help me not to love him. Please. He's just too wonderful, and way too young for me.*

I do, however, as Edward asked. I snuggle down in bed and for just one moment allow myself to entertain the possibility that our nine-year age gap does not matter in the least.

Chapter 13

Friday morning's brightness wakes me before my alarm could. There is an eerie quietness to the day. Rising from the bed, I pad to the window, open the blinds, and have to close my eyes. Pure white, blindingly beautiful snow is piled all the way to my windowsill. Not even footprints of squirrels mar its surface.

Intent on getting a weather update, I hurry to the kitchen to turn on the TV I have in there. But Susan has beaten me to it.

"The news is not good," she informs me. "Roads are closed all over the city, and they're saying that if we don't absolutely need to go out, we should stay off the streets, because the plows haven't been able to do any clearing yet."

I call in to work anyway. For once, no one is there to answer the phone. I leave a message to say I'd not be coming in and then contact the school I'm due to visit and leave a similar message. Two minutes later the news station announces that all schools in the GTA are closed for the day, so I get my wish. A snow day . . . yaaaay!

"Sue, I'm going to get some more shut-eye. I feel weary down to my very toenails."

Susan mumbles something. I look at her. She does not look great at all. "What's the matter?"

"Nothing I won't survive," she says tiredly. "Just plain old morning sickness. It's been waking me up for the past few weeks. I feel like there's a hollow space in my tummy that must be filled with food, but the only food that it will accept this time of day is water crackers and weak tea."

She turns sheepish eyes on me. "Yeah, it's one of the costs I didn't count when I decided to do this. Then I'm so sensitive to smells. Yesterday at breaktime I went to the caf to grab a bite, and a woman sitting at my table had some kind of caramel- or butterscotch-flavored coffee. When she opened the lid and the smell wafted over to me, I almost lost my breakfast."

She rests her head on the table, looking more dejected than I've ever seen her.

"You sure it's OK to leave you like this?" I ask, torn between my own need for sleep and the urge to assist her any way I could. Without raising her head, she shooes me away with her fingers. I reluctantly obey.

No sooner have I settled in my bed than I hear Susan go to her room next to mine. Seconds later she dashes to the bathroom. The splash followed by groans tells me the water crackers and weak tea have been rejected. I get up from my bed and search my bag for something to give her, but nothing I have is recommended for pregnant women. The bathroom door opens again, and a pale-face ghost waves to me.

"I'm not OK, but trust me, Quill, I'll be fine in about a half hour. Get your sleep. I'm slowly getting the hang of this." She disappears into the bedroom again.

The bed creaks, informing me that she is at least sitting on it. Residue of leftover adrenaline chases the sleep I want so badly. So stacking three pillows against the headboard, I pick up my Bible and continue my study about women in the Bible.

After I talk with God, I decide to call Mom and Dad. It's surprising that I hadn't heard from them last evening. Mom picks up the phone.

Yes, they're snowed in, but she'd heard the forecast and had gotten the cupboards and refrigerator stocked with food. Logs are by the fireplace in case of a blackout, and they have a gas stove, so not to worry. Daddy is fine.

"Mom, can I ask you something?"

I know what I'm going to ask her and I call myself every kind of fool for broaching the subject, but maybe I just need the matter-of-fact wisdom of Dru Hazelwood today. All right?

"Of course, you can ask me anything," she replies in a brusque manner. "What's on your mind?"

With Mom I must not prevaricate, so I get straight to the point. "There's this really nice man who's interested in me—"

"It's about time!" she interrupts. "What's the problem? He's got kids?"

"No, Mom."

"Intimacy issues?"

"What?" What was I thinking to raise this subject with her!

"Is he a religious fanatic?"

"Mom, can you let me talk?"

Willing myself not to lose my cool, I tell her as calmly as I can about Edward. "He's really a great guy, but he's much younger than I am."

Dru Hazelwood pauses. I can hear her thinking. "You mean like the older woman in that movie who was trying to get her groovy back. Tell me you're not interested in a 20-year-old baby."

I implore God for patience. "Groove, Mom. The word is 'groove,' and he's 35."

"Whatever! Groove or groovy doesn't matter. That was just wrong! So your guy is not a baby then. A man old enough to know his own mind. How come some other woman hasn't snatched him up by now? Does he have buck teeth?"

Absolutely my fault! I walked into this one eyes wide open. Yes, I did. I started this conversation and for good or for ill, I'm going to see it through. "No, Mother. He does not have buck teeth. He's Gloria and Wendell's nephew. You remember Gloria and Wendell?"

"Yes, I do. I like them."

"So what do you think?"

"You're asking me if I have a problem with you dating a man seven years younger than you?"

"Nine years, Mom."

"You're 44? When did *that* happen?" I can hear her mumbling calculations from the date of my birth to now, but this time I'm right and she's wrong.

"Never mind," she finally says. "Seven or nine years is neither here nor there. I'm four years older than your father, and in my day that was considered scandalous. What I have a problem with is you not being married. I could have done with a couple grandkids closer to home. Michael's once-a-year visit is not enough time for me to bond with his children. That being said, however, I would prefer to have you single and happy than married and miserable, so this young man's age is not really my issue. My issue would be whether or not he will make my only daughter's life hell, or treasure her like a good husband should. I would like to see for myself what caliber of man he is."

I take the phone from my ear and stare at it. Every time I think I have this woman pegged, she flips on me. For someone who was such a stickler for protocol when I was growing up, I would have wagered my last loonie (that's a Canadian dollar coin; it has a loon on its tail side) that she would have come down strongly against the age gap. But it's my happiness that is uppermost in her mind. What do you know!

Realizing that I'd stopped paying attention, I quickly return the phone to my ear.

". . . bring him by for a visit?"

"Say that again, Mom? Bring who by for a visit?"

"That young man of yours! Isn't he the one we're discussing? I want to meet him. I've been praying for you, you know, asking God to send you someone who will love you and take care of you. You're the type of woman who needs a husband."

Now even my eyebrows are paying attention. "What do you mean I'm the type who needs a husband? Haven't I been on my own all these years? I've worked, made friends, bought a car and house on my own, and live a very busy and fulfilling life! What do you mean I need a man?"

"Now, don't go putting words in my mouth, child. I didn't say you needed a man. I said you need a husband. Big difference."

"I don't see it."

"Tranquility!" (She must have heard my puff of exasperation). "I mean, Quilla . . . by the way, I hate that short form you use for your perfectly fine name. It reminds me of a feather pen . . . Anyway, ever since you came of age you have latched on to a pet, your dad, a needy friend, or some kind of project. You need to love something or someone. I also know that you're not the type to go shacking up with some guy or have casual relationships. It's just not your style. So where does that leave you? Despite what I said earlier about waiting for you to have children, I'm not holding my breath. While it's not impossible at your age, somehow I suspect you've come to terms with not birthing any. I'm not happy about that, but it's your body! What you need, however, is a husband. Someone to lavish all the love you have stored up in you."

"Mom, you make it sound like it's—"

"Let me talk, child," she says, cutting me off. "You need to find a man who is worthy of all that love you have to give, honey. That's why I want to meet this young man. It's the first guy I've heard you talk about in that tone of voice for a long time, not since what's-his-name. Come to think of it, this is the first guy you've asked my opinion about. You have feelings for him. I can tell."

I picture her nodding her head in agreement with her own analysis.

"I don't really. I . . . I . . . I mean . . . it's . . . not anything really serious. He's the one who . . . never mind. I'll just shut up."

"You do that, love, but bring him by for a visit one of these days. Something tells me I'm going to like this not too, too young baby who's going to help my daughter get her groovy back. Now, do you want to talk to your father?"

She does not wait for me to answer or discuss what she just said. Dru Hazelwood is having the last word again. I shake my head. In this, at least, she's consistent. I speak with my dad for a few minutes and then say goodbye.

Nothing about anything in my life these days is making any sense.

Four days after the big snowfall Toronto experienced an eastern Canada version of a chinook. The temperature soared to double digits, and the streets went from massive snow to massive flooding. Even the trees looked confused—not sure whether to droop and sag or say hello to the sunshine. For 24 hours the dream of a white Christmas seemed just that. Reality set in soon, however, and within a day we were back to the natural order of things—weatherwise that is.

If only that was true for my crazy project and my mixed-messages life.

Following that fascinating conversation with my mother, I temporarily suspended further discussion of my life or my "Why am I not married?" project. What I had not counted on were actions set in motion that had nothing to do with me and everything to do with the situational enzyme my questions had released in the lives of the other women.

It started with Mara. Mind you, we were long overdue for a heart-to-heart since I'd not heard much from her for a few weeks. Then I got a call from Lynn. Remember her? She's Gloria's business partner and the therapist who has the child that the father knows nothing about. And if that wasn't enough, Mia called back to say that she and the girls wanted to put a proposal to me. You realize I've not mentioned a word about Susan. That is its own story. So before I confuse you and myself any further, let me start with Mara.

Mara agreed that she would at least give G. David a fighting chance. Saying it and doing it, however, proved to be two different things. "Once bitten, twice shy" is the perfect idiom to describe her timidity. She and G. David had been conversing regularly via telephone, and he'd asked her to come to Florida for a visit during the U.S. Thanksgiving weekend. Her initial yes became no as the date grew near. From what I understand, not only is he extremely disappointed, though understanding, so is his mother, who had been over the moon with happiness at the prospect of an imminent reconciliation between the two. Mara needed to talk. Guess to whom? Yep, you got it.

"It just feels too rushed, Quilla," she told me. "I feel that once I visit Garry in Florida, wedding bells will start ringing, and I will not be able to assess if this is what I truly want."

"But I thought you still loved him," I said. "Have you discovered you don't after all?"

We were sitting in a downtown restaurant, having ordered a light meal in order to splurge on one of their signature desserts.

Mara drained her water glass, face frowning in concentration. "I wish I had a simple answer to that, Quilla girl. When I saw Garry at church that day, and when he came by your place later for the one-hour talk I promised, just looking at him turned my knees to jelly. He is even more handsome than I remembered, and has matured into a very fine preacher. Since then we've spent hours on the telephone talking, repairing our relationship, and laying the foundation for the reconstruction of mostly my trust in him."

She sighed hard. "But I've changed, Quilla. I don't know when it happened, but something's shifted in me."

I could see where she was coming from. "Isn't it ironic that we often yearn for something that we supposedly lost or missed out on, but when it's offered, we find ourselves backing away from it? We don't factor in the intervening years during which we were still growing in most every which way. Voilà! We're not the same."

My comment, however, only increased Mara's confusion.

"So what does that mean for me and Garry, Quill? For so long I kept malice with God because He wouldn't give me a man I could love. Then He drops the perfect one literally on my doorstep, and here I am, wanting to run. He must be calling me all kinds of idiotic names."

"Do you still want to be married?"

Mara's face became a study of mixed emotions. "I think so . . . I don't know. I think I want to get married one day but . . . but . . . I don't know . . ."

She seemed discombobulated by her sudden lack of certainty. (Don't you just love that word? Discombobulated! I found it in my thesaurus a few weeks ago and have been waiting for the perfect moment to use it. I just love the sounds of words—don't you? Anyway, back to Mara.) I decided to try a different line of questioning. Having Susan for a friend makes one extremely proficient in questioning strategies.

"What have you gained in the past few years that you think might be lost if you allow yourself to get involved with Garry?"

The answer shot out of Mara's mouth. "My freedom!" Shocked at her own response, she questioned, "Now, why did I say that?"

"Would it have anything to do with being the wife of a pastor?"

She thought about that for a minute, and then her head started to nod before any words came out of her mouth. "I think so. Yes, that's a factor indeed. Can you picture me, the wife of a pastor?" At the acknowledgment her words gained momentum. "I like my independence. I like having my own income, making my own decisions, and living life on my own terms. I like to speak my mind and not play politics. I am my own person, Quilla, and I cannot see myself kowtowing to people's expectations of what a preacher's wife ought to be or how she ought to act. I would die from suffocation if I had to be that proper."

"So it's not that you don't love Garry. You're just not sure you want to be married to a preacher?"

Oh, boy! That set Mara off.

"Marrying a preacher is just not in my plans, Quilla. Not by a long shot. Who would have thought Garry would become a preacher, of all things? Of course, he was quite effective when I knew him before—a lay preacher. But now he's a bona fide preacher, and what's worse, he's good at it! If the preaching he did at our church is any example of his capabilities, the man is called, Quilla. I cannot compete with his calling. And if I cannot complement it, then now is as good a time as any to back out."

I waited till her breathing got as close as it was going to get to normal.

"So he's asked you again to marry him?"

Silence.

"Well, not really. You think I'm jumping the gun? Making mountains out of anthills?"

"I can't say, Mara. Right now, though, I think he's just asking you to come for a visit. Maybe just to see how you are together. To see if there's still some synergy happening. You should go. Going is not an acceptance of marriage. It's a checking-things-out visit. A testing of the waters."

"I'm panicking for nothing, aren't I? But I'm so afraid, Quill. I just can't go through another heartbreak. I'm sure I wouldn't survive it." The emotions drew out her Jamaican accent.

Reaching for her hand, I told her what I hope someone would tell me if ever I found myself in a similar situation. "Trust God with this, too, Mar. He wants what's best for both of you. Trust Him and see where He leads. If it's right to go ahead, He will make it clear—not just to Garry but to you, too. If not, then He'll make that clear too. You'll sense what to do when the time is right."

She nodded. "You're right. I'll talk to God about it. But I'm glad He used you to talk to me, too." Dinner arrived, and we put all intense conversations aside, focusing on our food and the heavenly chocolate volcano dessert that followed.

Later as I reviewed my conversation with Mara, recording her thanks to me for allowing God to use me to speak with her, my conscience smote me. For when I looked into my own heart I found that I did not believe one single word I'd said. Because how could I believe it when I could not bring myself to practice it?

The evening after my heart-to-heart with Mara, Lynn called. She'd just put her daughter to bed and wondered if I could spare a few minutes for her to "think aloud in my hearing." I told her to give me a half hour to get some overdue ironing done, and she would have my undivided attention.

Did I mention that I hate ironing? With a passion! So once I build myself up to do it I prefer not to be interrupted, or else the urge goes, not to return for a long while.

I also need to do a shopping list for Christmas. It's only weeks away, and I'm way behind.

Three "scrubs," four blouses, and one skirt later I gather the rest of the unironed clothes and stuff them back into the hamper. That's the beauty of winter weather—a coat can cover a multitude of wrinkles, and sweaters do not need to be ironed.

My glance at the clock told me I had exactly five minutes before Lynn would call. Just enough time to do a speed shower and teeth brushing. I had finished toweling myself off and was in the process of applying lotion to my especially dry feet when the phone rang. It was 9:00 on the dot.

Hastily donning my comfy flannel nightgown, the one with the Christmas bells, snowflakes, and angels, the very one Susan dubs appropriate for single women with no prospects, I grabbed the phone on the third ring. It was indeed Lynn.

"So how's everything, Lynn? How's that cutie pie of a daughter doing? Considering she was the only child at our Thanksgiving dinner, she certainly had no problem mixing and mingling with the adult guests."

"That's Katie for you. She's doing fine. Just getting over a cold, so she needs her sleep. Tonight I had no problem getting her off to bed."

"And you?" I asked as I peeled back the covers and settled myself in bed, propped up by my three pillow partners.

"Me? Well, that's the reason for my call. I've been thinking about David and about what you said—that if I were in his position, I'd want to know if I had a child out there somewhere."

Had I said that? And to a woman I didn't know that well? I told myself I'd better start watching more closely what came out of my mouth. Playing the hand I'd been dealt, however, I asked,

"And?"

"And despite my fears, I don't think I'm doing the right thing by not telling him. Both of them, Katie and David, have a right to know each other. This is less about me and more about doing right by my child, and, well, David too."

"But?"

There followed the proverbial pause, a clue I've come to recognize as a precursor to the disclosing of sensitive information.

"Lately I've been dreaming about him almost every night. Things I thought I'd repressed are even visiting my daydreams. Uncomfortable as it is, the dreams make sense. I've opened the door to the past, and these things are part of the working-through process."

Lynn, too, was analyzing her own stuff. "But?"

"But I'm terrified. How do I find him? Well, to be honest, I put his name into Google, and I think I've located the office where he works. But how do I broach the subject? 'Hello, David, this is Lynn. Long time no see. By the way, I have a daughter for you. Want to meet her?' Quilla, what am I to do?"

"What does Gloria have to say about this?" I asked. "She's your good friend."

"Oh, Gloria will have nothing good to say about him," Lynn replied dismissively. "Plus Katie is her baby. She's been there for her since her birth, and especially now that Christopher is living on the other side of the world, she doesn't have anyone but Wendell, Katie, and me to lavish her love on. She'll see David as a threat! Plus her opinion of him isn't high to begin with."

Her answer surprised me. "Why's that? Gloria's typically a pretty fair person."

"Well, it's kinda complicated, but the crux of the matter is that most of what Glo knows about David she's heard from me. She's never met him. Of course, when he left Toronto I was devastated. That's what Gloria saw. That and the fact that I soon started to grow a tummy. You know how she feels about fathers who abandon their children."

"Yep! That I know. So how can I help you?"

"Do you think my wanting to contact David is stupid? I don't know if my motives are as pure as they should be. When I think about him, at least the person I used to know, I wonder if meeting him will put me in an emotionally vulnerable position. If I don't contact him, however, one of these days when Katie starts questioning again why she doesn't have a daddy like other kids, I need to be able to give her some kind of substantial answer. Put clothes on the man, if you will."

I thought about her question. It was indeed complicated, but I didn't think there was a simple way to do it.

"If I were in your position, I think I'd write him a letter," I said at last.

"A letter?"

"Yes. A good old-fashioned handwritten letter. That way you can control the content and your emotional response and say exactly what you want to say. I think people still enjoy receiving the occasional letter, even if we don't like writing them. So my thinking is that he would get this letter, react to it, and have time to digest the news before he comes—if he does come—to see you and Katie."

"But what if he's married? What if he wants nothing to do with her?" Lynn's fear came through loud and clear.

"Then you'll be no worse off than you are now," I said. "You'll have proved him to be a no-good deadbeat guy, not deserving of your precious child's love, and a man you've been well and truly delivered from."

Lynn defended him. "He's not like that! Not unless something has significantly altered his personality. But yes, he could be married, and my news would complicate things for him and his family."

"It's still his right to know," I said. "I know I'm stating the obvious, but sometimes we forget the simple rules of life. When men and women have sex, a potential pregnancy is always a possibility. That's the risk we take. In this case, all you're doing is making David aware of the consequence that resulted from his action five years ago."

I pictured Lynn sifting through the information. "A letter, eh? I think I could do a letter. That's certainly better than telling him in person or over the phone. Plus, as you said, it will give him time to digest the news in private."

I nodded, something I have a bad habit of doing on the phone, as if the person can see me.

"Do you mind if I show you the letter before I mail it?" Lynn asked. "I wouldn't mind having a second opinion, and I'd appreciate your input. I can trust you. I don't know what it is, but something about you invites confidences. Please say yes!"

I said yes. "I'd be honored to look over your letter, Lynn, but I think you're the brave one. I sit here with my emotional distance and dole out advice, but who knows if I could do what I'm suggesting that you do. I'll pray for you to find the right words and that everything will work out for the best."

"Thanks, Quilla. I could do with all the prayers I can get. I might even offer up a couple myself. This is a big step, and I'm not sure I'm ready for it."

"Another growth opportunity."

"That it is. Thanks, Quilla. I'll be in touch when I have a draft ready for you to look at. And thanks for providing a much-needed ear tonight."

So there you have it. Lynn's update. Had I not started this silly project I would not be playing therapist to people's life complications. But don't take my complaints too seriously. This seems to be an open door from God, and I'm not going to flinch from it. I will let Him guide me in how best to help these women He's placed within my sphere of influence.

That leaves the trio of younger women and Susan. Since that's another story in and of itself, I need a break before I continue.

Chapter 14

In addition to Mara, Susan, Lynn, Natasha, and I guess Edward—Mia, Crystal, and Danesha have also decided I'm their new best friend. I use the term lightly of course. In truth, they want more conversations with me about singlehood, claiming that I have not sufficiently tackled the issues head-on. Can you imagine that? Suddenly everyone has an opinion on the topic. It's not like I'm going to be writing a book with the information I've been collecting! Exactly when my project became about them, I don't know.

"Why am I not married by now?" as far as I can see, contains a first-person personal pronoun: "I." The point of the exercise is . . . *was* to help *me* (another first-person pronoun) get clarity on the issue. Never was it to be a thesis addressing every single, wanna-be-married sister's issue.

I'm grousing again, aren't I? All right, I'll try to rein it in. Obviously the topic has touched a few nerves—mine included.

True to their word, the threesome arrived at my house on a Saturday afternoon after calling ahead to tell me that if I had plans to go out, I should cancel them. They were bringing dessert and dialogue. My job was to supply hot drinks and to document their points.

How could I say no?

Minutes past 3:30 the doorbell rang. This was immediately followed by vigorous poundings on the door. When I opened it, I saw all three women huddled together inside the screen door shivering. As one entity they poured into the house, almost knocking me over.

"That's it!" shouted Mia, shivering even more in the warmth of the house. "I'm moving back to the Philippines!"

"I'm coming with you," Crystal said.

"Here we go again," said Danesha, rubbing her gloved hands together. "One cold winter day and the complaints begin. Where exactly in the Philippines would you go? Weren't you born right here in Toronto?"

"What does that have to do with anything?" Mia argued. "I'm Filipino, and my body tells me it doesn't have the right constitution for this degree of cold weather. Rain I can tolerate, snow even, but this cutting-through-your-bones cold is not right. Quilla, are my ears still on? They feel like they're on fire."

I glanced at her ears as I helped her off with her coat. "Looks a trifle pink, but I think they still work. Serves you right for commandeering my company and not dressing appropriately for the weather! Now, let's get some hot cocoa into you. It's already made. Where's the promised dessert?"

All three women looked at the other.

"Oh, no!" cried Danesha. "The dessert is still in the car!"

Mia sat down at the table. "Sorry, guys, but I'm not going back out there."

"How come you're all so cold? How far away did you park?" I asked

"Too far," replied Crystal, joining Mia at the table. "With that apology for a driveway that can fit only your car, plus all the snow on your street, there was no place nearby to park. We had to park two streets up the road and trek back through that biting nastiness outside to your house. You need to move out to the suburbs, Quill. Houses with garages and long driveways are available so your guests don't have to experience pain in order to visit you."

If I didn't know better, I'd say she was baring her teeth at me. Impossible!

"If I move far enough away, does it mean I'll see less of you three?"

Danesha, who was in the process of removing her boots, pulled them back on and grabbed her coat. "Give me the keys, Crystal. I'm sensing a slight drop in the temperature of our host's welcome. If we don't deliver on dessert, our visit might be shorter than anticipated."

"Neesh, don't go back out there," pleaded Mia. "I'm sure Quilla will understand that we didn't mean to leave the dessert in the car."

Not even glancing in my direction, Danesha grabbed the proffered keys from Crystal's outstretched hand and dashed out the door before I could stop her. Five minutes later she was back, puffing like a blowfish. (By the way, does a blowfish puff?)

Crystal rushed to help her off with her coat and boots. "I keep telling you to try out for the Olympic team. There must be a category for women in their early 30s. With speed like this you are wasted in academia."

I locked the door, shaking my head at their antics, and turned my attention to the hot cocoa. When they'd gone to wash up, I poured them heaping mugs full, allowing myself a half mug. Much as I liked the drink, my waistline was starting to give me signs of early-onset thickening.

When Crystal opened the dessert box, however, I knew no amount of telling myself to "yield not to temptation" was going to prevent me from having a slice, maybe two, of the delicious-looking cheesecake. Did I mention that I like my cheese?

I licked my lips in anticipation. "Yum-yum!"

Mia gave Danesha a high five. "My friend! You saved the day!"

Later, warm and replete, some regretting their calorie-filled indulgence (I call no names!), we moved to the living room. Mia commandeered the love seat along with the blanket resting on its arm and buried herself in it.

"Ahh!" she purred. "This is the good life. Food in your belly, good friends by your side, and a warm place to be."

I grinned at her. She reminded me of a kitten. "So, ladies, speak to me. What aspect of singlehood do you feel I'm not addressing?"

Crystal cleared her throat. "Well, personally . . ."

"Let's not go there, Crystal," Danesha cut her off. "No more using our discussion time to provide therapy for either you or Mia. This meeting is for us to honestly and factually address the issue of singleness in the church. Our singleness included."

Crystal made a face at her, and Mia looked too blissful to care.

Danesha continued. "Quilla, we believe that while your interviews so far have dealt with individual women and how they come not to be married at their age—whatever the age might be—the fact of the matter is that there is a significant deficit of men in our churches. Somehow religion seems to appeal to women more than to men. To complicate things further, our church strongly discourages the 'yoking of believers with unbelievers,' and even frowns on the marriage of believers to other believers if those believers are not of our 'faith'—interpret that as our denomination. What recourse, therefore, is left for single women in our churches who desire to be married?"

All eyes turned in my direction. "You're looking for me to answer that question?"

"Well, yes!" Crystal replied.

"Well, no!" I shot back. "Do I look like I'm some kind of Buddhist sage?"

"Quilla, how can you be a Buddhist sage? You're a Christian," Crystal corrected.

My sarcasm had gone right over her head.

"We just want to hear your opinion," Danesha added.

"Well, for what it's worth, I don't know what recourse is left for single women. Personally, I hope not to ever get to the place where I'd seriously consider marrying someone outside or inside the church just to be married. As for having children, I've never felt strongly about having kids of my own, so that is not as much of a hardship. Being alone, however, is what I struggle with the most."

"But if God created marriage, why does He not provide the opportunity for everyone to be married?"

"I don't know the answer to that either, Danesha. To date, one thing I've discovered in my interviews is that the more I dig beneath the surface, the more I discover that most of the women had an opportunity at one point or another to marry. And for reasons within or outside of their control, they lost or gave up that opportunity."

"Were they involved with guys in the church?" asked Danesha.

"No. Not all the women I've interviewed are in the church. And the ones who are not struggle just as much as we do with being alone, not having children, and not having the security of a loving married relationship."

Crystal looked as though she wanted to say something, so I stopped talking.

"Lately I've been thinking that maybe marriage isn't for everyone."

Danesha shot her a surprised look, but Crystal didn't catch it, so focused was she on what she had to say.

"I've always expected that I'd be married by now, but here I am—33 years old, and you know what? I kinda like my life the way it is. I come and go as I please. Next summer I'm going on a mission trip to Rwanda, and I am so looking forward to it. If I was married, I'm not saying I couldn't go, but it would be more complicated. Also, if I had kids, I'm not sure I'd be taking them there with me. I'd be too worried about them getting malaria or some other disease."

"Why do you assume that they'd get a disease in Africa?" Mia piped up, "That's discrimination."

"Shush with your discrimination," cried Crystal. "That's not the issue. The point I'm making is that marriage ties your feet. If you want to be tied and you're happy being married, that's fine. But you do not have the freedom to come and go as you please. You have to take someone else's feelings into consideration and consider how your action will impact him."

Danesha finally gave voice to the incredibility her friend was causing her to experience. "Are you saying you don't want to get married, Crystal? When did you start thinking this way?"

"Not long," replied Crystal. "But when I decided to go on this mission trip, it hit me how easy it is just to pick up and go somewhere when it's just you. Sure my folks care what happens to me and will no doubt worry, but I have no husband to consult or kids to fret over. I go where I want to go, and when I want to do so. I like the freedom to do things like that. And because one should never say 'never,' I won't go on record saying I will never get married, but for now, I'm OK being single and unfettered."

Danesha's look of surprise remained. "Did you know about this, Mia?"

"First I'm hearing of it. That just leaves the two of us in the running—the imminent professor and the newly minted family doctor."

I then asked the first question that popped into my mind. "Do you think your professional status or your education is a turnoff for men?"

Danesha sat up straighter. "It better not be," she retorted. "I worked too hard to get here. I don't have time to pander to some guy's fragile ego!"

"Has it ever come up?"

Mia responded first. "Who's had time to look at men properly? Med school took all my attention. Trust me, after a 14-hour day, sleep would win out every time to even a Brad Pitt."

"Not even Denzel stood a chance?" Crystal teased. "You usually can't get enough of his movies. I don't think you even know the plot of any of them. You spend the whole time staring at that specimen of manhood."

"That's right! On the screen, far away and hopefully happily married, Denzel poses no threat to my concentration," Mia replied calmly. "In answer to your question, however, I think it's best that professionals marry within their own circle."

"So in essence, then, you will have to marry a doctor or another professional within that league," I said.

Mia pursed her lips. "Most likely."

Wow! That was sobering. I couldn't help the next question. "Come on, Mia! What if there's this real sweetheart of a guy who loves you, and let's say he has a blue-collar job—maybe he's a mechanic or a construction worker. Are you telling me that you wouldn't marry him if he wanted to marry you?"

"I wouldn't," Mia said without a hint of guile. "Too great a divide. Plus my family would have major hysterics."

Crystal exploded. "Mia, you're 31 years old. Who cares what your family thinks?"

"I do," replied Mia with some heat. "It's important that they like the person I marry. We are a big and close family. It would be extremely difficult to have a husband they couldn't stomach. It just wouldn't work. Plus look who's talking. Wasn't it just a few weeks ago—before you got your new 'singlehood is great' conversion experience—who was saying you wouldn't marry someone from another race? I recall you making mention of family acceptance being important!"

Danesha, who I could tell had been doing internal mental exercises all this time, shook her head in despair. "No wonder none of us is married. The guy has to be a certain color, be from a certain background, belong to our denomination, have a job equal or greater in status to ours, be our age or older, plus he has to be the proverbial tall, dark, and handsome. He's gotta love children, make us feel like a woman while still being a man, get along with our families . . ."

"Don't forget romantic, sensitive, and buffed," supplied Crystal.

"*Your* opinion doesn't count," replied Danesha, scowling at her friend. "Remember, you're not getting married at all."

"I never said that. And even if I did, I still have eyes to appreciate a man who is a stunning reminder of God's creative genius."

Sensing the need for a conversational diversion, I posed a new question. "OK, guys, I have to ask this. Have any of you ever received a marriage proposal—a serious one?"

Crystal's hand shot up. "Two for me."

Danesha's scowl deepened.

"Does a tired, drunk med student count?" Mia asked. "One whose head I bathed and whose stomach I filled with coffee to sober him up in time for rounds?"

"Did he ask again after he sobered up?" I asked.

"No, but he brought me flowers."

"Then the answer is no," I replied.

"Well," shrugged Mia, "that was my only one. Too bad! He was cute and had the nicest eyes."

"Danesha?"

Danesha looked uncomfortable. "Geoff asked me last year."

"Why, you little sneak!" cried Crystal.

Mia flung off her blanket. "Nesha! You cannot be serious! Geoff asked you? When?"

"It doesn't matter now, so why bother talking about it?"

Mia walked toward Danesha. She meant business. "When, Nesha?"

Crystal joined her.

It seemed my tongue had gotten someone in trouble.

Tears sprang to Danesha's eyes as she reluctantly admitted, "Last April."

"April? You and Geoff broke up in May. What happened?" Mia sat down on one side of Danesha and Crystal on the other. "I'm sorry, Neesh. I know you hate crying in front of people, but you're going to have to tell us what happened. I can't believe you kept this from us!"

Danesha brushed impatiently at her tears. "What happened? Nothing happened. He took me out one evening for dinner, and then we went for a walk along Queen Street, but I didn't really feel like walking. I was two weeks behind schedule with my dissertation. When we got back to the car, he opened the door for me, but before I could sit down, he held my hands and asked me to marry him. But my mind was on the work I still had to do."

"You turned him down, didn't you?" Crystal said.

"Well, not really. I told him I'd think about it. He said that I'd been thinking about it for a long time and asked me how much more time I needed."

"You mean he'd asked you before?" Mia asked.

Danesha didn't even hear the question. "I told him to stop pressuring me. I had to focus on my writing, since I was due to defend in the fall. But he wouldn't hear of it, and I couldn't deal with the pressure, so I said that if he could not give me the time to get through my stuff, then it didn't make sense for us to continue to see each other and blah, blah, blah. The whole evening spun out of control just like that." She snapped her fingers to indicate how quickly.

"Do you miss him?" Crystal prodded gently.

"I miss having him around. I don't know if we should have been married or not. I just never had the time to really concentrate on him properly. Now that I'm done and have a job offer locked up, I'm ready to deal with this area of my life, but now there's no Geoff or anyone else."

None of us had a response to that. It described our mutual situations to a tee. Sloughing off her despondency, Danesha stood. "Enough feeling sorry for myself. I need some sugar," she said, and cut herself a healthy wedge of the cheesecake.

"I hate you," Crystal said. "You know that, don't you?"

"I know."

"You hate your friend?" I asked.

Mia answered instead. "She doesn't really hate her hate her. She just hates the fact that Nesha eats all the sweets she wants and never puts on an ounce."

My taste buds started to remember the texture of the cheesecake on my tongue, but this time I had to resist. Watching the studious Danesha enjoying her third slice of decadence, however, made me appreciate Crystal's sentiment. I could hate her, too, and with Christmas just around the corner, the culinary temptations would be everywhere. To distract my thoughts, I selected a Christmas CD and cued it to play softly in the background. Barbara Streisand was singing "Ave Maria." I love that melody.

"Turn that up, Quilla," said Mia. "It sounds pretty."

I turned it up, and we all enjoyed the beautiful rendition. Danesha finished her cake and, thus fortified, turned up the complexity of her questioning.

"Do you think it's God's will for every woman to be married? And if it's not, how do we know that our lack of a husband is our doing and not His will for us?"

Three pairs of eyes turned in my direction. "Listen, you three, I'm going to boot you out of my house into that 'balmy' night air outside if you don't stop doing this."

"Doing what?" asked a perplexed Crystal.

"Looking to me for answers to all your questions. Why do you assume I know these things? I started this project to find answers for myself! I have no answers to give to you. I know nothing!"

Mia took me on. "You know nothing! Are you kidding? Quilla, people come to you for answers to questions. Even at church last week I heard a young woman telling her friend to go talk to you about whatever she couldn't help her with. You know more than you think. Plus, you just look like you know stuff. Now tell us what you think."

"About what?"

"About what Nesha asked," Mia patiently replied.

"I just told you! I don't know!" Obviously the cheesecake had clogged their ears instead of their arteries.

Mia's pesky response was "Yeah. We heard. Give us your best guess anyway. That's better than most people's certainty."

"Guys, you don't understand. I am not . . ."

"I'll take a stab at it," Crystal said. "I would like to think that since God created man and woman, male and female, He must have intended for them to come together and procreate in order to populate the earth. So yes, I'd say ideally it is God's will for each woman to have her own husband."

"Crystal, that's absolutely faulty reasoning," I countered, forgetting that

I knew nothing. "It's like saying that because God created music, everyone should sing, or since He created the stars, everyone should go to the moon. Yes, I know the Bible says that a man should leave his father and mother and cleave unto his wife and that the two should become one flesh, but the fact of the matter is that there isn't always a man for every woman, or a woman for every man. There are wars that decimate populations of men, what then of those women? Lot's own daughters had no husbands after the destruction of Sodom and Gomorrah and Lot ended up fathering their children. How sick is that? We cannot have women go around believing that they are only half a person until they get married. That's ridiculous! You yourself just said a few moments ago that you might not want that life for yourself. Do you think the apostle Paul was speaking only to men when he said that he'd prefer that more people would be like he was—single?"

"And you don't have an opinion on the subject?" Crystal commented dryly.

I had the grace to look sheepish. "I don't know what made me go off like that. I really didn't know I had an opinion. Most likely I was just reacting to what you said. It stuck in my craw somehow."

"So what are we all to do?" Danesha persisted with the difficult questions. "The odds of us all finding husbands within the church are slim to nonexistent. Of the four of us sitting here, maybe one or, if we're lucky, two of us might still find a husband. That's the finding part. The odds are equally good that of the two of us who marry, one of those marriages will end in divorce before the marriage is 10 years old. So not only is there a dearth of men, there is an appalling percentage of marriages that do not last. Why then bother at all?"

"I hear what you're saying, Nesha," I said, "but there is something in me that craves the kind of companionship that marriage represents. It feels right. I cannot go to a wedding and watch a couple repeat their vows without wishing it was me that a guy was looking at with such tenderness. Despite the odds of breakups, people keep getting married. Somehow we still believe, or foolishly hope, that this time, with this man, or for the guys, with this woman, happily ever after will be ours. It's what our spirits crave—this cleaving and becoming one."

Danesha nodded her head in agreement. Warming to my topic, I was about to continue my discourse when Mia began to wag her index finger.

"I don't know if I totally buy into your statement, Quilla, that marriage is what our spirits crave. There are people who are perfectly contented being single. No desire to get married. And I personally know of a few women who are no longer married and have no desire to repeat the deed. For them, once was enough."

"I know that, Mia. I'm talking about women like us who want or wanted to be married. Don't you feel the need to emotionally bond with someone?"

Mia thought about the question. "I suppose. Some days, however, especially when I'm in a crabby mood, I'm glad I'm not married. I'd probably bite the poor guy's head off."

I could so relate to that. "Yeah, me too. But over and above this longing I have for companionship, the bigger challenge is—will I trust God to direct my path whether or not it involves marriage? Instead of bemoaning the fact that I don't have a husband, I should be asking God to lead me in the way He wants me to go."

"But why does it always have to come back to God?" Danesha protested. "If it's His will for us to be married, why do we need to constantly pray, asking Him for what He already plans to give us?"

Crystal's answer surprised me.

"Because prayer is not about getting God to do what we want Him to do. It's about putting us in a place where we can hear His voice. The other day when I told you that I wouldn't ever marry someone from a different race, it was the first time I had said that out loud. And you know something? I'm not comfortable with the color barrier I've imposed on what could be God's plans for my life. I think that sometimes God wants to bless us beyond our wildest expectations, but we insist in putting conditions on the blessings. 'It needs to look like this, Lord,' or 'Our friends must be impressed by Your blessings, Father,' or 'We must not be uncomfortable with Your blessings.'

"Do I believe that God cares about somebody's color, race, age, maturity, or social status? No, I don't. But my friends, my family's, society, me . . . I care about these things. Where, then, is there room for God's will to be done when I've imposed a lockout to certain areas of my life, even though He promises that His plans for me are so much better than any I could make outside His will? But still I resist. I impose conditions. I tell Him that His will is wrong—that He doesn't know what He's doing. And all the time it's me. I'm the idiot and the imbecile! Yet I insist on fooling myself that I trust God and want His will for my life. Pure lies and self-deception!"

Crystal's face flushed from the passion with which she spoke. Then she said in a voice so quiet I had to learn forward to hear her.

"So that's partially why I want to go on this mission trip. I prayed about it, and everything has fallen into place. I need to learn to put God first, not because of what I can gain, but because of how I can best bring Him glory."

Her speech just about shut us up. All of us. Forced us to look inward. Soon after that very moving testimony from the "airhead" of the bunch, the evening came to an end. Crystal had, indeed, given us much to think about.

The question is: Are we willing to offer up our will to God? That's what Jesus did. That was His sacrifice. Not His will, but that of the Father's. And so it comes right back to the sacrifice of the self, the ceding of our will to that of God's.

Already my spirit is rebelling. I do not always want what God wants. I don't want to live by His rules—especially when it inconveniences my own agenda and prejudgment. But it is what I must do, or I might as well throw in the towel of my so-called Christianity, because then it is no Christianity at all. It's a sham, and I know how God views tepid Christians. He'd rather spew them out of His mouth. I either walk my faith or give it up. There is no middle ground.

So the fact that I am not married by now is not the critical issue. If God knows and understands the texture of my loneliness, and in order to perfect my character for the life to come (as opposed to the life I have here) He will do whatever it takes, should I give Him all the permission He needs to work with and through me, to ensure I get to my heavenly home? And no matter what Susan does or doesn't do, or Mara or Lynn or Gloria or Wendell, the three musketeers, or whoever, it is about *me* and *my* relationship with God.

Will I grant Him complete lordship over my life? Do I believe that He will do what He said and bless me abundantly more than I could ask or think? Am I prepared for Him to determine the nature and form the blessings will take—that it might be peace in the storm instead of a piece of the pie, contentment with little instead of preoccupation with the much? Am I serious about my discipleship and prepared to count the cost of serving God *and*, after tallying the count, serve Him anyway—married or single?

Chapter 15

I never gave you that update on Susan, did I? She's all right. The morning sickness is all but gone. Typical of her, she's been researching methods of childbirth and has decided that she wants to do this birth as drug-free as possible. She's retained a midwife, plans to birth the child at home, and has signed me up to accompany her to birthing classes run by this group of midwives.

She's also finally broken the news to her parents. Needless to say, that did not go down so well, but I think they are reconciled to not having any control over the situation. Being the wonderful parents they are, they will continue to support her even as they keep wishing things could be different. Susan's mom called and told me all this, hoping to hear that I had been consulted and could have averted the situation. I had to disabuse her of the hope idea right away.

Then she started asking me questions I couldn't answer. "What of the child's father? Is he supportive of Susan? How will the church handle her pregnancy—will she be removed from membership?"

What could I say? That their imminent grandchild's father is a nameless sperm donor from who knows where? If Susan chose not to tell them that little detail, it was not my place to do so.

That brings me to another new development in my project that has convinced me more than ever how little I know anymore about anything. Let me tell you what happened last Monday. (By the way, don't even think of asking what decision I made regarding Edward following the last conversation with the three musketeers and my own reflections. Knowing to do God's will and actually doing it are two different things. I'll have to work things out with God, but for right now, I just need to distract myself for a while, OK?)

So as I was saying, this weird thing happened last Monday. Immediately after work I rushed to the mall, hoping to get my Christmas shopping done. Actually, I'd left work a bit early in order to get a head start before the after-work rush descended on the mall. I knew what I wanted to buy and for whom, so I was able to make good progress on my list. About 7:00 my tummy began to complain for food, so I dumped my bags in the car and went back to the food court for a meal—something healthy. I'm trying to be good.

I got a nice steaming plate of mixed vegetables with a side serving of pita and hummus. I even ordered a bottle of water, which I drank before eating. And the food was good too. When one is hungry, any food tastes good. (Maybe that's why we should eat only when we're hungry.)

While I ate, I checked my cell phone for messages. There were several, and I proceeded to answer them while I continued eating. Just as I was finishing the last one, I felt someone join me at my table. I looked up in surprise, wondering, as in the meeting with Natasha, if I'd again been selected to be the companion to someone seeking company.

An older woman, with the signature green trays of the food court, smiled at me. She then proceeded to unwrap a sandwich she'd obviously brought from home and arranged it on the tray atop its foil wrapper between a McDonald's apple pie and a bottle of apple juice.

Then she did something I rarely see in public these days. She bowed her head and closed her eyes. After a few minutes she opened her eyes and caught me staring at her.

"Amen," I said.

She flashed me a smile of pure delight. "Thank God!" Her reaction was emphatic and strong.

I must have raised a brow in question, because she began to speak.

"You see, I asked God this morning to direct me to a believer. All day long no one approached me, so I thought He was not planning to answer my prayer today. But here you are right at the end of the day when I'd about given up."

"Wow!" I said, closing my phone. "But why did you ask God to do that? Direct you to a believer?"

"I don't quite know," she told me. "Sometimes I'm just impressed to ask God for things, and what I ask for is sometimes for me, and sometimes it's for somebody else."

Her hand hovered over the cheese and lettuce sandwich, but then she picked up the pie. She eagerly opened up the package and took a bite. Before I could say "Watch it, they can be hot" she had bitten into it, dainty nibbles at one end to let out the steam. Here sat a professional pie eater!

"Is there something you're wrestling with God about?"

I snapped to attention. "You're talking to me?"

She nodded, continuing to nibble at the corner of her pie. Who was this woman? She looked slightly past retirement age—my guess would be about 67. She had silver-gray hair and the mannerisms of someone who'd lived alone for a while, mannerisms I'm probably developing even as we speak.

Was there something I was wrestling with God about? Edward's face came to mind. So did his imminent visit. What would I do with him when he came? He wanted to spend a good part of his four-day visit with me. That's what he wanted. What did I want?

God, is this You? Sending this woman, this stranger, to ask me such a personal question? And what do You expect me to tell her? The truth? I don't know her from Adam!

Just as I knew He would, He did not answer me. Never does He answer me when I want straight answers. My table guest, when I returned my attention to her, had a look of expectancy, as if she had all the time in the world to wait for my reply.

"Aren't we always wrestling with God about one thing or another?" I countered.

"You're right about that," she replied thoughtfully. "It's the sin in us. Every time we think we've crucified the flesh, when we least expect it the thing we thought we'd surrendered is back, tripping us up."

She took another nibble at her pie. She had the smallest teeth I'd ever seen on an adult. "But there is something else, isn't there?"

I prayed for patience. I did not want to be rude, but no way was I going to bare my soul to this perfect stranger. She'd better wipe that expectant look off her face.

Treat the stranger right. You might be entertaining an angel without knowing it.

See what I mean? Now He speaks! However, my seatmate had more to say.

"I'm impressed to tell you to trust God. No matter how foolish or weird things might seem, He wants you to trust Him." Then she added for emphasis, "with everything." She might as well have underlined the last two words.

With everything!

Why won't God just let this go? It's Edward He's talking about, of course. I know it is. It's the one single thing that is standing between me and God. Yes, I have other sin stuff to work through, but with Edward I don't want to hear about it. Yet God keeps bringing it back. It's got to be that. And what makes things even more difficult is that it wouldn't take much for me to fall hard for this younger man. But I cannot risk the hurt and pain that will result when he comes to his senses. For that reason and that reason alone I must not go there.

The stranger began talking again and I was about to tune her out—to focus on my own stuff—when she mentioned something about loneliness. At that, my entire mind became ears.

Martha's Story

"... me was loneliness. As a young girl, I always dreamed of the day I'd get married and have a family of my own. You see, we lived in a small town, my dad, mom, my sister Jeanie, and me, but Daddy died soon after I finished college, and Mom, who was always a needy person, couldn't deal with life without him. I had to go back home and take care of her. Jeanie already had three kids and was expecting a fourth. Between them and her husband, she had her hands full. It had to be me looking after Mother.

"Our little country church had no young men. As soon as the boys came of age they hiked their way out of town. They couldn't get out fast enough. So feeling that life was going to pass me right by in that backwoods we called home, I decided to do something about it. I tried to talk Mother into moving closer to the city, but she wouldn't even entertain the thought. This was her home, and that was the end of it.

"I wanted to be married. I prayed every day for a husband. 'God,' I said, 'You see I have to stay here with my mother. I'm trying to do the right thing by her and honor her, but You know what I want more than anything. Since I can't leave here, could You send me someone to love?'

"Every evening I'd pray that prayer in faith. I trusted God to do for me what I could not do for myself. Every knock on the door could be the answer to my prayer. At every church picnic I somehow expected the relative of a member to be the man who'd come and discover me—wasting away in that backwater place. But no one came.

"Then Mom began to get more and more confused. I took her to the doctor, and the eventual diagnosis was senility. Nowadays I guess it would be called Alzheimer's. She needed someone with her 24 hours a day and, of course, the only one available was me. Even though Jeanie would come by from time to time and give me a hand, the burden of mothering Mom fell completely on me."

My seatmate adjusted the position of her juice bottle. "One day Mother mistook me for someone else, and as I tried to help her on with her clothes she spat in my face with all the venom she could muster. I hit my lowest point that evening. All my loneliness and anger boiled to the surface. Out of the corner of my eye I saw my hand rising up to strike her—my own pitiful mother!

"I ran. I flew out the back of the house in the middle of winter. I remember yelling and cursing God as I ran, and when I could run no more, I turned back. When I entered the house, I found Mama herself again, and she said, 'Is that you, dear? I could do with a bowl of porridge.' I made her the porridge, of course. She died five years later. She was 84. I was 63.

"Only days after we buried her I put the house up for sale, packed my bags, and moved here, to Toronto. First thing I did after finding a place to live was locate a church with a large congregation. That was eight years ago. But there are no men in this church full of nice and some not so nice people, no men who want to love an ordinary-looking old woman who is decades past her prime.

"No men!

"And to illustrate how ironic life can get, my period didn't stop until I was 62. Up until then I might have been able to mother a child from frail old eggs—probably a child with some chromosome abnormality, but I would have loved that child, disabled or not, because it would have been God's answer to part of my dream. When my period finally stopped, though, I had to let it go, reminding myself that God, with infinite resources at His disposal, could still find a way to give me a marriage partner to ease my loneliness."

You might be wondering why I stayed so silent during this rather bizarre encounter. Words had failed me and continued to be inaccessible as she spun out the rest of her tale.

"I have this list," she continued. "On it I write down all the things in life that make no sense to me. I plan to discuss them with God when I get to heaven. One of the things on my list is this. I want to ask God why, when He put within me such a heart to love, why, considering He did not bless me with other gifts to compensate, He did not see fit to give me a husband and even one child. It's not like I had a choice about Mother. I had to take care of her. But He's the God of the impossible! What was so bad about what I wanted that He thought it best not to give it to me?"

Her pie lay uneaten, congealed apple syrup sticking to the opened flap of the red box with the golden arch. She picked up the pie, tested it for warmth, and seemed surprised that it was cool to the touch. Then she ate all of it like the holy wafer of Communion. *Do this in remembrance of Me.*

When she'd finished her pie, she ate the sandwich, then drank her apple juice. By then the tears that had started running down my cheeks in the middle of her story—the part where she'd almost hit her mother and had to run from herself—had been spent. I normally have better emotional control than that, but somehow in her presence it felt OK. Then she talked to me as only a kind angel could, about the meaning of surrender and trust. I had no words again. Here in my very presence sat a true disciple, fashioned in the kiln of loneliness and pain, yet stalwart in her faith as few people I've ever met.

She arranged her garbage neatly on the tray. Then she reached across and touched my hand ever so lightly.

"I'll be praying for you," she said with quiet assurance. "Just remember to trust God, especially when things make no sense at all. Because if we don't trust Him, what's the point of it all?"

She walked over to the waste bins where she took the time to read how to appropriately discard the items on her tray. The bottle, the food scraps, and the paper. Then she looked over at me one last time, gave a little flutter finger wave, and merged into the thinning crowd of mall shoppers.

The fog lifted from my brain. Leaving my own tray with its garbage, I grabbed my bag and ran after her.

"I'm Quilla," I said when I caught up to her, running a bit past her and walking backward so I could talk to her face to face. "Thanks for sharing your story with me."

She stopped walking. "I'm Martha," she said. "God bless you."

I offered to drive her home, but she wanted to walk. It was her exercise. I asked if I could call her sometime, pray with her, and she looked past me for what felt like a long moment before saying OK. I gave her my card, leaving it up to her to call me. She promised she would.

I hope I've captured her story. Not exactly word for word, but the meat and potatoes of it. I went home and wrote until my index finger flattened from the pressure of pressing the pen to paper.

That's what I meant when I said that I don't know anything anymore about anything. Martha! A child of God sent to provide me with a message and another story for "Why am I not married?" Am I so self-absorbed, or just plain stupid? These lonely women who missed out on their dreams of family and are left in old age with no one! They don't even have the consolation of having had a part of their dream fulfilled. I had never thought about them. These who sacrifice their dreams for the good of another—why were they totally off my radar? How could I have failed to consider their stories?

What's even more astounding is that this woman still believes and trusts in what some would label "the God who disappoints." Why?

Wait. What is it she'd said? Yes, here it is: "If we don't trust Him, what's the point of it all?"

Dear Martha had no opportunities. No man came to her door or appeared at her church picnics. What can I even suggest to women today who are in similar circumstances? I suppose my younger friends would tell me that they should get online. Join a dating service. I hear there are several Christian dating services and that people have been successful in finding partners through them.

And me, what's *my* excuse? I've been complaining all this time about my single status when I've never even started to explore the options available to meeting Christian men who quite possibly, might become my husband. They could be waiting online, living in another city, or attending another church! But no. The guy of my dreams should just come to me! But there was Martha at 63 years old, packing her bags to go search, with God's help, for her dream. I am humbled at her bravery.

Is marriage for everyone?
Absolutely not!
I'm not even sure anymore if it's for me.

So what do I do with Edward when he comes?

My own voice comes back to me. Words that I'd spoken to Mara. I need to just let the man come and get to know him. There ought to be nothing too threatening in that.

Who am I kidding? There's a lot that's threatening. I might enjoy his company as much as I enjoy our phone and online conversations. What if he . . .

No, it's not Edward that's the problem. It's me. I am afraid of me. And I'm afraid that my loneliness will drive me into his arms.

Oh, God, help me be strong.

Remember at the beginning of this project I'd written down 10 questions I thought might contribute to the reason I'm not married by now? They were . . .

1. Was there something or a set of somethings I *did* to end up still single?
2. Was there something or a set of somethings I *didn't* do to end up single?
3. Is there something I *can* do about my single state, and if so, how badly do I want to get married?
4. Can I live with being a never-married woman?
5. Where does God fit into my current unwed state, and if my being married would have been good for me, wouldn't He have sent someone my way by now?
6. How do I deal with the pain of loneliness and lack of sexual fulfillment?
7. Is there a defect in me that turns men off?
8. Are my expectations about the qualities I want in a husband too high, not grounded in reality? And if so, how do I know that for sure?
9. What am I prepared to do about my single status?
10. Am I marriage material?

Why am I bringing these questions up at the moment? Here's why. Every time I need to deal with the Edward issue, I seek a distraction. Don't think I've not noticed my own avoidance technique.

The fact is that I don't know what to do with Edward. He makes me nervous. I feel drawn to him, and I've begun to wonder if my imposed age barrier is legitimate. My own mother! For sure, I thought she'd have something to say about it, but she's more concerned about a man who will contribute to her daughter's happiness. Susan doesn't see it as a problem. And God keeps telling me to trust Him.

So can you see why I must not focus on Edward? In that path lies confusion and second guessing. I don't like gray patches when it comes to decision-making. It is necessary, therefore, for me to go back to my questions. They might help me find my way to solid footing.

I think I've tackled questions one and two. The answer to both questions is the same. I did nothing to advance my desire to be married.

Maybe I could coin a whole new meaning to the term "lady in waiting." That's me. Waiting, expecting, complaining, and doing nothing.

Can I live with never being married? Now, that's a tough one. I'm rubbing my forehead as I try to come up with an answer. It's Martha's face, however, that comes to me, and Natasha's. They're living with it. What choice do they have? There they are in their upper years and coming to terms with the cards they've been dealt. So I suppose that just like them, I'd have to, if it comes to that. But I sure hope God has another plan for me. A special someone still in the wings who . . .

Don't say it, please. Don't think of saying one solitary word about Edward. Who came up with these stupid questions, anyway?

Next question: I'm skipping ahead to question 7, OK. "Is there a defect in me that turns men off?" Yes, I know it's a really personal question, but that's the way I feel sometimes. On bad days I wonder. On really hellish days when I'd be approached by some dream of a guy who saw me as a way to get to Susan, I'd really wonder. I knew she'd eventually turn them down or cast them off. Couldn't even one of her rejects discover me, the "pure gold" that Mara sees? But neither them nor the guys I'd encounter on my own, none of them with the exception of kindhearted Ken and now this child-man Edward (here comes his name again—there seems to be no getting away from it).

What does he see in me, anyway?

(Yes, I'm talking about Edward.)

How could he have missed the defect (there must be one) that other men saw? The guy is decent-looking. He's intelligent. He's spiritual. He's got a sense of humor, and he has a job. What's wrong with him that he's lighting on me, an older woman, as the "woman of his heart"?

God, do help me!

What are you saying, Quilla? That I made a mistake? That you're not deserving of the love of a good man?

Yes! I mean . . . no! I know You love me, Lord, but You love everybody. You have to! You're God. But people love some people more than others. A lot of people love the same person, and then there's nobody left to love people like me.

What do you mean by "people like me"? Spell it out.

Plain ordinary people. I'm not ugly. I'm just plain and nice and ordinary. Men's hearts don't race when I walk into a room. Drivers don't get whiplash when I pass by on the street. I leave no one asking "Who's that girl?" My legs are too short, my lips are too thick. My eyes are just ordinary brown—not even a fleck of gold. I have a crooked tooth and spider veins showing at the back of one knee. I don't have the killer smile that Mara does, the presence that Stelle and Lynn have, and certainly Susan's beauty. I'm just blah! Plus now I'm getting old, so there's not even the dew of youth on my cheeks.

So is it Edward's age that's really the issue, or is that just an excuse?

"Excuse for what?"

For not allowing yourself to believe that finally someone, even a younger someone, having met Susan, chose you? You don't know what to do with that!

I so wish I had a slice of double chocolate cheesecake right now.

Quilla.

"Yes, Father."

You are blessed and highly favored by Me. I love you. Could you try to believe that? try to internalize what that might mean?

I hear myself sigh. "Yes, Father."

I need for you to believe, because once you do, you will understand how truly precious you are to Me. That this part of you that will not allow others, even a good man, to love you, this part of you that's so afraid that men will find a defect, is all wrapped up in the whole of you. I make no mistakes, My daughter. I created you and want no other person to be you. None! You're unique and precious, and I will love you all the days of your life. Believe it, My daughter. Believe it.

I sit with wrapping paper and shopping bags piled around me as the CD plays Christmas favorites. None of the gifts are yet wrapped, because I picked up the journal I'd left on the couch after detailing my conversation with Martha, and my mind has been preoccupied since then. And now to top it off, God has spoken the longest speech I've ever heard from Him. Telling me that He loves me—visible and invisible defects alike.

I close the book. I can't deal with any more questions tonight. Except this—do I personally believe that I, Tranquility Victoria Hazelwood, am precious in God's eyes?

God, please help me! Help me yield to You!

Chapter 16

Christmas is now two weeks away, and I'm feeling a bit more in control of my life, at least the Christmas shopping part of it. The gifts I planned for my loved ones are on hand, half of them already wrapped. Also, Edward is coming this weekend. As he reminded me again last night when he called, he wants to spend a chunk of this visit with me. He cannot be dissuaded. What am I going to do with this young man?

You might wonder why I keep referring to him as a young man or a child. Obviously, he's neither by anyone's standard. If he was just an ordinary guy not interested in getting to know me, I'd simply think of him as a man. But every chance I get I must keep reminding myself of our age difference—that I'll be nine years into retirement before he starts his.

Susan tells me I'm being silly. That this obsession I have with the guy's age is pure ridiculousness. That's exactly the descriptor she used, and she's roped in Mara to join forces with her. But thankfully, Mara is dealing with her own stuff, and while she took time just before she went off to Florida (yes, she decided to go—to see how things are, no commitments) to return a piece of my own advice, she's left me alone. She's due back on Sunday. Edward should be gone by Monday. Friday to Monday. Four days to get through without making a fool of myself.

Last weekend our pastor preached a powerful sermon about prayer. Using the analogy of a car key, he showed us that we need to be plugged into the power of the Holy Spirit. He pointed out that the car key would not, and cannot, serve the purpose for which it's made if it is not connected to the ignition, and that prayer is like the key in the ignition. Prayer gets the engine of our souls turned and started so that we can access the power and get to places God wants to take us.

What does that have to do with this situation with Edward?

It's like this. I promised him that I'd pray about us. Ask God what He wants me to do. I mean, I gave him my word. But so far I haven't done it. Every time his name comes up I tell God why my way makes perfect sense. Imagine that! Me insisting to the Creator of the universe that I know best!

The pastor reminded us that one critical aspect of prayer is confession. So before Edward comes this weekend I need to face up to myself. Not because of Edward, but because of this part of me that's not willing to let God lead. I know a big part of my unwillingness is tied up with fear. Yes, the age gap is a concern, but is it a totally insurmountable obstacle? Probably not.

But I have to go further. Whether or not Edward is to be part of my life, God will always be there. So now that the situation with Edward has revealed this place in me where insecurities exist, will I trust God enough to say "Your will be done"?

Every time I've asked myself that question, I refuse to answer it. I see where it leads, and I refuse to hand this situation over to God.

I need to let go of this willfulness. I must. Today. Now. 'Cause if I don't, I think I'll be starting a slippery slide toward letting go of God. This thing that I will not give up, this area of my life that I won't let Him into, will always be there between us. How then can He do what He wants with me for my good, when I've put conditions—"You can have this part of my life, Lord, and this, but not *this*"?

It's wrong! So I gotta deal with this revealed sin.

But even now, I don't want to. I think it was C. S. Lewis, in his book *Mere Christianity,* who talked about what happens when we let God into our lives. God is not content to do a patch job; He wants to do an extreme makeover. We might have called Him in to fix just one thing, but by our calling on Him, He's not satisfied till all the things that need fixing are attended to.

So how do I pray this prayer that I must pray, when my will and want are at war with each other?

I'm writing all this down, you know. I'm documenting it for my own education. Sitting in my living room, bath taken, avoiding my bed that invites the sleep of avoidance, lamps burning bright, I write down my thoughts.

Now there's nothing left to say but to talk to my God about what I don't want to deal with.

"Please, God. Help me."

His answer is swift and clear.

Keep writing!

OK! I will write what I cannot verbalize in prayer.

"*God . . . ,*" I begin.

But I cannot go on. Voices from the past. Voices that I did not know lived in my head start saying things.

Ignoring them, I begin again.

"God, I'm so afraid to accept the fact that I can be loved for me. I'm so frightened by my defects. I fear that if someone should be allowed to see them, they'd not want to be around me. I'm not bright like my brother, Michael. I'm not . . . but I'm not going into this defect list again, Lord. I've already said these things.

"I want to give my fear to You, but I'm afraid. I know You want to expose these secret places—not to the world, but to me. But I'm owning up to the truth now, Lord. I can't deal with them. That's why I've hidden them, Father, locked them up in dark secret places so not even I can find them. But You keep exposing them, wanting me to deal with them. I want to trust You, Lord, I really do, but like an unearthed worm, I lie exposed, writhing in Your light, wanting desperately to return to my dark underground.

"I'm not a pretty sight, am I? Can You not see how unlovely I am? Yet You persist in reminding me that You love me, warts and all. You want me to give this exposed and miserable side of me to You—to allow You to place your kiss of love on this oozing wart of my soul. Do You understand why I want to run away? I don't even want to see this side of me. I don't want to look."

For how long I locked my eyes and stopped writing, I don't know. The ringing of my doorbell calls me back. Closing the journal and placing it on the sofa, I get up to answer the door, glancing at the clock as I do: 8:37. It should have read midnight of my soul.

I check through the peephole to see who is there. This looking inward makes me feel vulnerable. I can't make out who it is. Someone tall.

"Who is it?" I ask.

The reply is muffled.

Confident that the locked screen door will act as a barrier, I crack open the door.

Suddenly I want to run. Shock does that to me sometimes. It's Edward! Edward, who is supposed to be coming tomorrow night. And he's not even appropriately dressed for winter weather. All he's wearing is a light windbreaker on top of his clothes. Not even a pair of gloves.

His rapping on the screen door brings me back to reality. The poor man must be freezing. I flick the latch, and suddenly he's inside, shivering.

"Hello, Quilla."

How is it possible that the timbre of someone's voice can weaken your knees? I cannot speak. I can't believe how glad I am to see him. He seems taller, and the way his eyes light up when he looks at me makes me wish I had someone here with me to put distance between us.

Before I can think to return his hello, before I can close the second door, he's coaxing me gently toward him, giving me time to pull back, to resist, but I cannot. And then I am encircled by those long, strong arms and it feels so right.

I lay my cheek against his chest and feel my lashes connect with my eyelids.

Dear God, this is heaven!

Too soon I'm being pried free, and Edward's voice breaks into my stupor.

"Quilla, woman of my heart, I've missed you. Can I just stand here and hold you in my arms for a bit longer?"

Dear God in heaven! This man is a dream come true! Not even a minute in my house and he's calling me "woman of my heart."

My traitorous heart slams hard against my ribs.

Yes! Yes! Yes! It answers this question, and I move back into his embrace, only to ease away—slightly. What am I doing?

Father in heaven, You know I must not get close again to this man. I mean, I still have not worked through stuff with You. I must erase the feel of his chest against my cheek and how right it feels. Make it mean no more than just a greeting from friends long separated. No electricity, Lord. Please, erase the electricity.

But God, the inventor of currents and undercurrents, does nothing. My foyer is thick with it.

OK. OK. I can handle this. That . . . that momentary distraction was just a lapse. It will not happen again. I use talk, my best weapon, to chase the intimacy from the room. I become an overprotective, lint-removing fussbody.

"I didn't expect to see you till tomorrow. Look at you coming out in this weather with nothing on but this foolishness. What were you thinking? You should have called. I would have made dinner for you. Are you hungry? Take off your shoes. Come in. I was wrapping Christmas gifts and talking to God. I can make you some hot cocoa. Would you like some hot cocoa?"

Against part of my will I become a bleating, blathering idiot—speaking much and saying nothing. He reaches out a palm to brush my cheek ever so softly. I want to rest my cheek within his cupped fingers. Like a cat begging for a caress, I turn my head toward the warmth of his hand.

With his fingers still softly stroking my cheek I close my eyes, basking in it, forgetting my self-talk.

"Look at me, Quilla."

I don't want to, but I do.

"Maybe this was not such a good idea. Coming here tonight." His eyes and his voice tell a different story.

The undercurrent, which never quite left, is back. I cannot agree or disagree. I am adrift in a sea of mesmerizing need.

The caressing hand falls to my shoulder, then departs, returning me to the here and now.

Edward stares at the ceiling, takes in a deep, long breath, and blows out. When his eyes rest again on me, the pulsing current is veiled, and Edward, with "no strings attached," is back.

"Did I hear an offer of hot cocoa? I'm partial to it, you know, but only my mom and I make it just the way I like it."

I come back too, the practical, no-nonsense Quilla on the outside with fears and insecurities hidden on the inside. I can do this. Summoning a grin, I employ my gift of repartee. "Well, if you're going to doubt my hot cocoa before you've even tasted it, you can very well find your own pot. We'll have a hot cocoa tasting contest right here and now, mister."

Backing off his jacket and stepping out of his shoes, he pushes up the sleeves of his sweater. "Woman, you're on."

I allow my eyes to rest on this tall man as he strides into my kitchen, opening and closing cupboards in search of pots. When he finds one, he turns in triumph and catches me staring at him. He gives me the sexiest wink I've ever seen and turns back to fill his pot with water, softly whistling a tune I do not recognize.

Taking a deep breath, I select a smaller pot.

Four days.

It's only for four days.

I can do this.

It's Monday night. I'm so tired I cannot see straight, but having had no time to process anything since Edward's surprise visit Thursday night, I want to write down all that has happened. Starting with the hot cocoa face-off.

We each made our pots of brew, and Edward, quickly finding his way around my kitchen, selected the best of my china cups for his. Presentation, to him, was the key. Personally I think cocoa should be served in a thick, heavy mug—one that will help to retain its warmth.

While we bustled around the kitchen, he agreed that he could indeed use a snack since he'd literally dropped his bags at Gloria and Wendell's, grabbed a quick shower, and headed out to surprise me. We toasted bagels. He lathered them with butter, and we drank each other's hot cocoa. Surprisingly, his version was not too bad and tasted just right in the china cups.

Testing my proffered mug for weightiness, he took a healthy sip of my hot cocoa. A pleasant flicker of surprise crossed his face when the taste hit his tongue. I wished Susan had been there for a high-five moment!

"This is good," he said, taking another sip. "What did you put in it?"

I told him my secret ingredient—the unconquerable nutmeg—at which he raised his mug in a toast of concession.

"To the nutmeg, and to Quilla." China and ceramic clinked before we sipped again. "Now how am I going to break this news to my mother?"

He looked so forlorn that I wanted to rub his head in comfort. But I didn't. I changed the subject.

"So had you planned this surprise all along?"

"Nope. But as the days got closer to coming here I got more antsy to be on my way. So I finished my work a day earlier, and here I am, feeling as if I've come home after a long journey."

He started to say something else but checked himself. I think he was remembering his promise to come as a friend so we could get to know each other. (The weekend had many of those checked moments. I didn't ask about them even though I kept wondering what he would have said or done in each instant.)

He left my house Thursday night about 10:00. Expecting him to arrive Friday evening, I had arranged to leave work that afternoon at 2:00. Monday I'd booked off as well. After all, I had promised him some time.

He called Friday afternoon as soon as I got in the door. He'd be picking me up in an hour. I should dress warm. This time he had dressed for winter weather. Wendell and Gloria must have fixed him up. He drove us to Edward Gardens, telling me that any place named after him had to be worth visiting. With fluffy snowflakes dancing in the late-afternoon light, we had the perfect winter walking weather. As we strolled through the park, he talked about his childhood, his growing up years, the things that had left impressions on him. He told me of his work, what he'd still like to do with his life, and how his first stint as a Big Brother was challenging and satisfying. Some of these I'd heard before, but it was nice having the discussions in person.

Right before sunset he turned our steps back toward the car, where he surprised me with a picnic dinner. Scraping snow off a park bench, he unpacked a thermos of tea, Gloria's signature whole-wheat rolls, cheese, and fresh fruit. I couldn't believe he went through all that trouble just for me.

"What did Gloria and Wendell have to say about you running off and leaving them like this? After all, they want to see you too."

"They cannot say enough. Wendell literally chastised me for not picking you up from work—saving you from taking the bus."

"But how did he know I didn't drive today? Sometimes I do."

"I told him. How was I supposed to know it would become a bone of contention? They cannot say enough good things about you, Quilla. And the more I get to know you, the more I'm seeing for myself what they're talking about. You are one special woman."

Embarrassment made me protest. "Edward! How can you say that? You don't really know me. If you even knew the half of me you'd not say that. I'm just—"

"Don't!" he interrupted. "Gloria is your friend, but she's also my aunt. Not by blood, but by marriage. I know that woman loves me just as much as she loves her son Christopher, and I also know that not even for you would she compromise her principles. If she tells me that you're a good woman, that recommendation is worth its weight in gold. When she tells me how caring and kind you are to others, how you have a wonderful way of drawing people to you who just need an ear, someone to listen, I take all of what she has to say as gospel. So don't waste your breath trying to convince me otherwise."

I opened my mouth to continue my protest, but a look from him changed my words. "As long as you know I'm not perfect!" I mumbled.

He heard me.

"On that note, my friend, we are in complete agreement. I, too, belong to that club. Just know this. I like the woman you are, Quilla. I'm glad that the high regard I have for you is shared by people whose opinions I trust. I just wish you did not have such a low opinion of your own worth. You've lived too long in Susan's shadow."

"But Susan is . . ."

"Yes. Susan is beautiful to look at. So is that tree over there. So is this snowflake that has fallen on your hand. Indulge me for a minute. What parts of you don't you like?"

Why is it that in every conversation this man comes back around to the personal? Which parts of me I don't like? OK, he wants to see warts, I'll give him warts. Let's see how he handles truth.

"For starters, there's my mouth. I don't like my mouth. My lips are too thick, and my bottom lip slightly protrudes. Then there's my—"

"Shhh," he stopped me. "One imperfection at a time." He gave my mouth a visual inspection, making me wish I'd kept it shut. "Yes, I do see full-looking lips. You're right about that." He turned my face in profile. Sounding like a clinician, he reported, "And yes, the bottom lip does protrude slightly. I'd say about 1 millimeter." Turning my face back to him, he continued his assessment. "When I take into consideration the composite picture of your full mouth against the rest of your face, the whole effect is extremely pleasing. I like it." His voice dropped to a whisper. "Plus I'll let you in on a secret." He blessed me with a conspirator's look.

"What's that?" I heard a husky voice ask. Obviously being out in the cold was affecting my throat.

"You're a Black woman. African gold. You're supposed to have lips like that." As an afterthought he added nonchalantly, "I have been made to understand that lips like yours are the best kind for kissing."

Without giving me a chance to reply or react, he continued to tease. "Now, what about the other defects? Let's have them all. Come, come!"

"Why do you want to be with me, Edward? In all seriousness, why are you here spending your time with me, an ordinary-looking woman who does not even think that highly of herself and who is also nine years older than you?"

I wanted to get at the root of this ridiculous thing he had for me and nix it for good. I must not become attached to him. I must not love him. I must not.

His eyes did not leave mine, but when he spoke, the teasing was gone from his voice. "I don't know how I got here. However, here is where I am. I wasn't looking, not that my eyes were closed, but I wasn't actively looking to get into a relationship. Then four months ago, on a visit to Toronto, I discovered you at your own dining table, and from the time I returned later that evening for my Bible and took that quiet walk with you, I've been hooked. There's just something about you, Quilla, something about being with you that just feels right. And before you tell me that I'm looking for a mother figure, I have a perfectly wonderful mother whom I love very much. I don't need another woman in that role. I'm also not looking for a woman to take care of me. I've been doing that for myself for the past 10 years and can continue to do it for as long as I have health. I'm just drawn to you. That's all I'm going to say."

"Oh, Edward, what am I going to do with you?"

The teasing came back into his voice. "I promised you a weekend of friendship, no strings attached. Let's just get to know each other. Now do you want to hear about my warts?"

"Yeah, right! As if you have anything to be 'warty' about!"

"You think you're funny, don't you?" he said as I began to pack away the remains of our dinner. "What if I told you that I've never liked being this tall? I wanted to be six feet of raw, buffed muscle. As you can see, I'm way past six feet and lean and wiry. Not buffed."

"But—"

"Don't interrupt me, woman. I'm dredging up my insecurities here. What if I also told you I have never been good at sports? None of them. I can hit a ball, but I can't run very fast. Basketball, the Black American man's game, I am totally bad at! I'm good at Scrabble, chess, Balderdash, crosswords, Sudoku, stuff like that."

"Can you fix leaky sinks?"

"That I can do. No problem. My dad was able to teach me that much."

By then my toes were tingling, telling me I'd been out in the cold too long. On the short walk back to the car he carried the basket in one hand and held my mittened hand in his free gloved one. Still holding my hand, he stowed the basket in the back seat of the rental car and closed the door. Then drawing me to his side, we leaned against the car and watched the snow dancing in the light of the parking lot. In the distance Christmas lights glowed.

"I could get used to your white Christmas," he said. "It's pretty. On the other hand, the cold I could do without, so let me take you home, woman, before I freeze my buns off. Then what good would I be to you?"

"Hot and cross," I quipped.

That earned me a playful peck on the cheek.

I hugged him then. I don't know why. I just needed to. And then the long arms were around me, enfolding me, inviting me to my own homecoming.

No kissing. Just a hug that went on forever, ignoring our plans to keep things light. I wiggled to get some breathing space, and his arms loosened an inch or so. I looked up at him. "I don't want to love you, Edward."

But it was as if he did not hear me. He guided my cheek back against his chest and enfolded me again.

"*Shhh*," he comforted. "It's OK, sweetheart. I got you. I'm not going anywhere."

Never had I felt so vulnerable and woozy. Before I was ready to be exposed to the cold again, he opened the passenger door, waiting for me to fasten my seat belt before closing it. As soon as he started the car and I reoriented him in the direction toward home, he grasped my hand and held on till we got there.

He walked me to my door, opened it, crossed the threshold with me, and went no farther.

"I'd planned on having worship with you tonight, Quilla, but I don't think it's such a good idea now. Will you forgive me for leaving you? It's the only way I'll be able to keep my promise."

I didn't want him to go. I too had looked forward to worship. The books were already on the sofa waiting for our discussion.

"I don't want you to go."

"Quilla!" His whisper was hoarse.

"I know. You should go. But I'm just saying I don't want you to."

"Help me, sweetheart. Don't look at me like that. Help me keep my promise to you and honor God. I didn't expect this . . ."

Leaning against my front door, this man did something strange and sweet. He began to pray.

"Holy Father, thank You for bringing us safely home. Thank You for this unforgettable evening. My heart is too full even to put into words what I'm feeling, but I just want to say thank You for Quilla. Look into the vulnerable places of her heart and love her as only You can. As we go through this weekend, Father, help me to represent You in all that I do and to honor this woman You've brought into my life. She's come to mean so much to me, and already my mind wants to build castles in the sky. But not my will, Father. Only Yours. Amen."

At his amen I rose up on tiptoe and brought his forehead down to touch mine. "I didn't expect it either."

Then before I could no longer resist what I wanted to do, I stepped away from him.

The move brought some sanity into the room. He favored me with a lopsided smile. "I'm going to have to watch myself around you, woman. You're messing with my head."

I smiled, but said nothing.

He kissed me then. A quick brush of his lips against mine. And he was gone.

Later he called to say good night, insisting that he'd pick me up for church the next day.

Saturday morning he was at my door at 9:45. We sat together in church—Wendell, Gloria, Edward, I, and Susan—in that order. Even Lynn was at church with Katie. All during the service I was conscious of Edward's presence, his breathing, the rustling of the pages of his Bible, the same one he'd left at my house only four months ago.

We had lunch at Gloria and Wendell's. I can safely say that all during lunch my brain was in total befuddlement. Gloria and Wendell looked on us with benevolent understanding when, as soon as we'd all finished eating, Edward announced that he and I were headed out. He drove me back to my place, but did not come in. Before he allowed me out of the car, he gave me two options. Well, one really. He wanted us to take a drive to Niagara Falls. It was going to be a nice afternoon, sunny and cold, but no snow. My choice was whether or not I wanted the trip to include a stopover at my parents' house. I told him I'd think about it on the way.

I quickly changed my clothes, and in no time we were on the QEW zipping out of the city. Except for a slight slowdown in the Burlington area, we made good time, singing to some beautiful praise and worship music Edward had brought along.

As we passed through Stoney Creek he turned down the music and reached for my hand. "Are you having as wonderful a time as I am, Quilla?"

I decided to play. "Since I don't know how wonderful a time you're having, it's kinda hard to compare."

"Well, today I got to sit in church with three of my favorite people. Now I have the woman of my heart singing along with me on our drive to the honeymoon capital of the world. To top it all off, God loves me. What could be more wonderful than that?"

What's a girl supposed to say to a statement like that? Nothing prepares you for a declaration of that magnitude. This man was making my heart sing. I reached for my 'nine years older' reality checker but could not find it.

"Yes!" I agreed after a pause. "I'm having a really wonderful time."

He let go of my hand and pumped his toward heaven. "Did You hear that, God? She's having a 'really wonderful' time. Did You know this would happen?"

"You do that a lot, don't you?"

"What?" he asked, face bright with joy.

"Talk to God about everything."

"I try to. You don't?"

"I do. Most times. But on certain topics I pretty much tell Him what He should do as opposed to discussing things with Him and listening for His direction."

"Am I one of those topics?"

Honesty made me admit it. "Especially you. I was trying to work things out with Him the other night right before you rang my doorbell and surprised me."

He turned the music down. "You don't want to love me, do you?"

Joy drained out with the question.

"It's complicated, Edward. Mostly I don't want to be hurt. It wouldn't take much for me to love you. Already I think I'm . . ." I stopped, checking myself. "You just don't fit into any of the comfortable plans I had for my life. You live in another country. You're a much younger man than I feel comfortable being with. And here you are with your nice, caring self, treating me like a queen. I don't need this complication."

"I love you, Quilla. After one meeting and many telephone conversations I can say that with certainty. I have feelings for you that I've never had for any other woman. On top of that, the attraction between us could light up a small city. You feel it too, don't you?"

I could only nod.

"And don't ask me why you? I don't know. I just know this thing between us is good and it is right, and it would be a shame for a simple matter of age to ruin it. So unless you want to claim that you would have kidnapped me from my crib when you were 9 years old, then no one can accuse you of being a cradle robber. I also want you to know this. While I'm sure I love you, I'm not so foolish that I think we have no barriers to overcome. You've named a critical one. We live in two different countries. Second, while I would never willfully hurt you, I should let you know that if I'm not convinced that this relationship is sanctioned by God, much as it would hurt me to do so, I will not go against His will. He has to come first."

His admission sobered me. This man knew what he wanted but was prepared to give over to God's will—a lesson I still grappled with.

"I also want you to know that I've been talking to God about you from day one, asking Him what to do with you."

"And?"

"All indicators say proceed with caution and patience. So unless God tells me to step aside, I'm not going anywhere. I want you to know that I am single-mindedly committed to wooing you. How's that for an old-fashioned word? Get used to it, sweetheart."

"But I'm starting to get gray hairs," I wailed.

"And one more thing: I promise to do my very best to honor your virtue at all times. Now as for your gray hairs, not that I can see any, but if you have them, let them go gray. If the gray bothers you, color it. But don't color your hair to make yourself young for me. Do it if it makes you feel good."

"You're taking away all my excuses."

"Is it working?"

I turned up the music and ignored him. He laughed and took my hand again.

We drove along the Niagara Parkway, then spent a joyful hour walking by the falls. A brisk wind drove us back to the car, but we stayed around long enough to watch the lights come on. The Christmas season in Niagara Falls is very beautiful.

"So what will it be—dinner, or a visit with your folks?" Edward asked when my tummy rumbled.

I truly did not want to go home with Edward in tow. My folks were going to read way too much into it. But then again, I was certain to slip up in a later conversation with Mom and mention that I'd been to Niagara Falls. Then I'd get the lament of why I didn't come to visit.

"As long as you have a good excuse for a quick getaway, if needed," I finally said. "My mom can be overwhelming. She'll probably give you the third degree."

"My shoulders are broad."

"You've never met my mother."

Well, the long and short of it is that Dru Hazelwood greeted Edward and welcomed him into her home as if he were a long-lost son. Daddy, who we found napping in his wheelchair, woke up, and before I could properly introduce Edward to him, Mom did.

"Honey, this is the man who is going to help Tranquility get her 'groovy' back."

My dad, who is a bit hearing-impaired in one ear, thought she said gravy and wondered how I'd lost my gravy and what kind of gravy it was and would it still be good when I got it back. By the time we got the whole thing straightened out I was ready to high-tail it outta there, but Dru Hazelwood could be heard tinkering with saucers in the kitchen. Yep. We had to stay for tea.

Edward and Daddy then got into a heated discussion about servant leadership, and despite my hints, throat clearings, and other clues, Edward ignored me, looking as though he was having the time of his life.

Late that night, when he dropped me off at home, we both managed to keep the currents at bay. Edward saw me to the door, gave me a hug, and told me to get my beauty rest because we'd be having another late night on Sunday. He was joining his aunt and uncle for breakfast; then the rest of the day was ours.

Chapter 17

Did I get any beauty rest? That would be too much to ask. No sooner had the sun crept over the horizon on Sunday morning, than my phone began to ring. I exaggerate a bit, but any phone ringing before 9:00 on a Sunday morning, if not for an emergency, is pure punishment. Friends should know better than that. But Susan plays by her own rules.

My groggy hello was greeted with a squeal.

"Open the door, Quilla. I've brought breakfast!"

Groaning at my plight, I took my time in getting to the door, hoping the prolonged exposure in the cold would punish her.

In one hand she carried a bag from the doughnut shop and in the other two hot drinks. I let her in.

"Get back to bed. I'm coming up," she said, depositing her goodies on the floor. "You need to give me a key for the house, since you dislike me waking you up when I do my morning visits. I don't see why you keep taking the key back when you return from holidays. After all, if I can watch your house while you're away, why can't I keep the keys? I let you keep mine. You don't see me . . ."

I trudged back to my bed and pulled the blanket over my head, wishing on a star. My futile wishing produced the anticipated lack of result. She was coming up the stairs.

"Scoot over; I'm coming in."

I scooted while she placed her breakfast on my bedside table and stacked two pillows to support her back. She ripped open the bag from the doughnut shop to reveal two toasted buttered bagels with peanut butter and two apple fritters. Picking up the larger of the fritters, she bit into it with relish.

"Want yours now?" She didn't wait for my answer. "They're good. Yum, yum! Now tell me everything. Every single detail!"

"I don't want to love this guy, Susan. He's nine years younger than I am."

"Foolishness!" She licked bits of icing sugar off her fingertips. She was already halfway through the doughnut.

"Tell me, tell me, tell me!" She flapped her hands in anticipation, dropping crumbs and bits of icing on my bed. "Did he kiss you yet? I know he wanted to. That man is smitten with you, girl! He had eyes for no one else but you all day yesterday. Gloria told me that he even made you a picnic dinner on Friday. How romantic is that! So did he kiss you? How was it? Did he call you 'woman of his heart' again? Did he?"

I couldn't answer her. All the pent-up emotions from Thursday night onward came at me. I wanted to put a pillow over my head and give vent to the tears burning the back of my throat. Lying there on my back in my own bed, with my best friend eating sticky doughnuts beside me and a man a half hour's drive away who calls me 'woman of my heart,' I felt overwhelmed. A traitorous tear rolled out the corner of my eyes, and the eagle vision of Susan saw it.

She touched my shoulder in sympathy.

Wrong move!

The tears came then. Lots and lots of them. Susan slid down on her pillows and hugged me. "My poor best friend. You don't know how to deal with his tenderness, do you? You don't know why he loves you."

"He's nine years younger," I cried, attempting and failing to control my tears. "Why can't he see that? He'll want a younger woman one day. When the flesh of my arms start sagging like Mrs. Beatle—remember how the skin on her arms used to jiggle when she wrote on the blackboard? He's going to break my heart!"

A fresh bout of tears came on. Susan rubbed my arm and tried her best to calm me.

"Give your heart permission to accept love when it's offered, Quilla—love for a month or love for a lifetime. I know you might get hurt. There's always that possibility. But think of what you'll miss if you lock your heart away. You are one of the most beautiful souls I know on the face of the earth, and I am blessed to have you as my best friend. You've stuck with me through so many things. I know I've challenged your friendship more than I should, but still you love me because that's who you are. People can't help being drawn to you. And that's the beauty Edward sees and is drawn to. I'm sure that for him the years between you is just that—a nonissue. Now, my friend, why won't you accept for yourself some of the very love you so generously give to others?"

It wasn't really a question. At least I don't think she expected an answer, which was good, because I didn't have one.

"You talk to God all the time," she continued. "What does He have to say about Edward?"

"He wants me to give him a chance. Get to know him," I replied, drying my eyes on the two sheets of double-ply tissue Susan placed in my hand.

"There you go then. You have your marching orders. You're not marrying the man, not yet. Just getting to know him. So relax and enjoy the ride. What are you guys doing today?"

"I don't know. He told me to wear something nice and to plan for a late night."

"Romantic, to boot! I love it. Mystery and intrigue." She picked up the other apple fritter and bit into it. "I tell you, you'd better not keep dragging your heels with this guy. If I could sustain a relationship with him, I'd snatch him from right under your nose. Imagine a younger man (but not a baby) making goo-goo eyes at you, ignoring all the other swans in the room—young and old alike—calling you 'woman of his heart,' and you're here lying in bed crying on your best friend's shoulder. You should be running down the street yelling, 'Hey, people, I am loved!' "

I had to laugh. Maybe I was being a tad too cautious.

"OK. Fine. Tonight, at least, I will try to be happy and bask in the admiration of this younger man. Tomorrow he returns to his life, and me—I'll be back to reality. Today I will give myself permission to be loved. For me."

"Now, that's more like the Quilla I kno— Ow!" Susan stopped dead in her speech.

"What? Are you in pain?"

A look like surprise mingled with discomfort and joy crossed her face. She grabbed my hand and placed it on her tummy. I felt a flutter under my hand. We stared at each other. Susan was the first to speak.

"It's really happening, Quilla," she whispered. "I'm going to have a baby! A real live baby that's already kicking."

And then it was my turn to comfort her as her look of wonderment dissolved into tears of who knows what. What a pair we were!

Before Susan left that afternoon, she went through my closet with a clinical eye, then pulled out a black dress with a deceptively simple cut that had cost me a small fortune.

"Wear this tonight. You look like a million bucks in it." She then whisked the scarf off my head and fingered my extensions with disdain. "I don't know why you put these things in your beautiful hair. But at least the style of it suits you this time. Pin it up, then leave a few curls to dangle over your right eye."

She selected bag and shoes, gave me a quick hug for courage, and was gone, taking both bagels and one of the drinks with her. So much for my breakfast! Halfway home she called to apologize for eating my breakfast and to remind me to give myself permission to accept love. I promised her I'd try.

That night was the most unforgettable night of my entire life. It was so good that I asked God if He had plans to come right then, to please delay it till morning. I asked even when my mind reminded me that "eye has not seen nor ear heard" the things God has in store for us.

"Please, God," I prayed, "wait heaven for just one more night."

Any minute now he would be touching down at the Hartsfield International Airport in Atlanta. His flight had left Toronto at 3:45.

"Father, please keep him safe. Watch over him as he checks out, rides the shuttle to go to his car, and on the drive home."

To prevent myself from waiting by the phone and getting anxious to hear that he'd arrived home safely, I unfolded my ironing board and began to do this most hated of household tasks.

At 7:07 my phone rang.

"Hey." He sounded tired.

"Hey yourself." I sat down on the laundry hamper.

"Quilla, woman of my heart, I just got home, and already I miss you."

"I miss you too," I whispered.

"Good. I'm glad I'm not miserable all by myself."

"I'm ironing. It's a good distraction. I hate ironing."

"Another discovery! I'm going to enjoy getting to know you, Quilla."

My heart did again what I've started calling the Edward flip. I grabbed for a red herring. "You had a good flight?"

"Don't get me started on these flights. I want to know whom to write to so that they'll start serving real food on planes again. I bought this snack box for seven bucks. There was enough salt in the stuff to season a small island."

"That's what you get for rejecting my offer to make you a sandwich and salad."

174 The Waiting Heart

"Nag, nag, nag! Did I tell you how much I'm missing you?"

"Yes, you did. Why don't you get reoriented back to home, and I'll call you later. About 9:30. Then we can chat for a bit before going off to bed."

"How about I just take a shower, get to the airport, and fly back to Toronto?"

"You have work tomorrow, and so do I. Do I call you later, or do you prefer to call?"

"You call this time. I like it when you call me."

"Later then," I said and waited for him to hang up. He did the same for me.

I like this man. I really do. Even listening to his breathing gives me joy. When I finally broke the connection, I noticed tendrils of smoke coming from under my iron. Yikes! I'd left it facedown on one of my best pillowcases. When I lifted the iron, a brown imprint remained.

Focus, Quilla. Focus!

At 9:27, snuggled in my bed, I called him.

"You're two minutes early," he greeted me, a smile in his voice.

"Three."

"Still missing me?"

"Not as much now."

"Tranquility Victoria Hazelwood, what have you done to my heart? This weekend did not go anywhere close to my expectations."

"For me, either. I didn't expect the chemistry to be so strong. It's kinda scary!"

"Scary! It's a ticking time bomb! The weekend was for us to get to know each other more. That was the plan. We would talk, walk, pray, sing, have fun. No strings attached. That's what I promised you, Quill. But from the moment you opened the door Thursday night, something happened. Like a chemical shift. Then Friday night, after that wonderful evening of speaking from the heart with you, propped up against your front door, I had no desire left to keep my promise to keep things light—no strings attached. I had to pray, Quill. It was either that or run for my life. Thank you for your help."

"It's all your fault, you know."

"My fault! How do you figure that?"

"Well, if you'd come Friday night, like you were supposed to, I would have had my defenses firmly in place."

"I thought I had mine well in hand, enough for both of us," he replied. "How wrong I was!"

"What are we going to do?" I asked, but it was more a question for me. Friday night might have been his Waterloo, but Sunday, the day I listened to Susan's counsel to allow myself to receive love—Sunday was mine.

"Tell me you're falling in love with me. Even just a little bit. I know you don't want to, but tell me that God is working a miracle on your heart and softening it to love me."

"Oh, Edward! What am I going to do with you?"

"Is that a yes?" He checked himself. "No! Don't answer that. I'm doing it again. I can wait, sweetheart. When you say it, I want it to be of your own free will and not because I prompted you. Take your time. I'm not going anywhere. Not after this weekend. But hard as it will be, I'll keep my promise. We will defuse as much as we can our ticking chemical time bomb—buy ourselves time for reason to guide us. That and our heavenly Father."

I thought about our entire weekend. I thought about our Sunday evening date, and I wanted to tell him, "Yes. Yes. Already I'm loving you! Not just a little bit, but heaps." I wanted to tell him he's the most incredible man I've ever had the pleasure to know and that I admire and respect him so much. I could give him something to go on in spite of my fearful heart.

"Edward, I had the most fantastic time this weekend that I've ever had with anyone. I have never felt too treasured and cherished in my life. And even though I'm scared to death, I want to get to know you, too. Just give me time for my heart and my head to get synchronized, OK? After this weekend my heart is singing, but my head is freaking out."

"Is it OK to tell you that right now I wish I could kiss you?"

My heart did the Edward flip. This time with a double somersault.

"Promises! Promises!" I teased to lighten the loaded question. We managed to move the conversation to less-explosive topics, and after talking for a bit longer, we prayed and said good night.

Wednesday evening when I got home from work there were four messages on my home phone. One was from Mom, asking if Edward had gotten home safely and telling me to give him her love.

Her love? Can you explain that one?

The next message came from someone by the name of Justina. She'd heard of my project from Danesha and wanted to know if she could contribute her story. The next was Gloria, asking me to ring her when I had a free moment, and the final message was from a woman from church—Clare, the desperate. Yikes!

Is God creating a ministry from this project for single women who want marriage? As I said before, I'm not going to balk on this one. I will go where He leads.

After throwing a load of laundry in the machine and getting a bite to eat, I returned the calls from Justina and Clare, arranging to meet with one of them Monday evening and the other Thursday of next week. Anyone else would have to wait till the new year. I had a busy Christmas season ahead.

I'd arranged a special Christmas Eve feast for my friends. On Christmas morning Susan and I would drive to St. Catharines to spend Christmas and Boxing Day with our parents. Michael and his family were coming too, and as usual, Mom would have two or three other guests with her for the holidays. Bless her heart!

By the time I got around to calling Gloria, the first load of laundry was ready to go into the dryer and I'd tossed a second into the washer. Wendell answered the phone. When he discovered it was me on the line, he said in a deep bass voice, "Hello, Quilla, my soon-to-be niece."

"Wendell, don't you start teasing me, or I'll serve Susan's salad as the only dish next time you come to my house."

"Woman, you certainly know how to play hardball. I'll just hand the phone to Gloria before you threaten me with anything else."

I heard him calling to her, and then she was on the line.

"You can hang up now, Wendell."

"Outed!" he grumbled, hanging up.

"What's up, Glo? How are the holiday preparations going?"

"Almost done. Can you believe next week Thursday is Christmas Eve, and did I tell you Christopher will be home for the holidays?"

"Yes, you did. I can't wait to see him. As for the shopping, for a while there I thought I wouldn't be able to get it done on time, but I did it. Two more gifts to wrap, and it's a wrap!"

"That's such a puny pun! Anyway, the reason I called earlier is that I felt you might want to talk. After the weekend and everything. How did it go? I've never seen my nephew in such a mental state."

"Was he upset?" I asked in alarm.

"Not in the way you're worried about. You seem to have knocked him for a loop, Quill. He is completely smitten with and by you."

"But he said he would not go where God is not leading. What if God says no? He's going to get hurt, Gloria. That's the last thing I want to do. I didn't even ask to be in this relationship."

"Is it the age difference that's still tripping you up? You think the nine-year gap is too wide?"

Did I want to talk to Gloria about this? Or anyone else, for that matter?

Curious to hear what she thought, I decided to talk. "The age is a very big piece of it, but there's the matter of geographical distance, too."

"I hear you. I hear you. Now, indulge me for a minute. For argument's sake, let's pretend there was no nine-year age gap and that Edward lived in Markham. How would he fare in your estimation?"

"Did he ask you to talk to me about this?"

"Absolutely not! Actually, this conversation is coming out of my concern for you. Even though Edward is like a son to me, you're still my friend. I don't want you to be hurt either."

"Sorry, Gloria. I'm a bit sensitive these days. You're asking if there was no age or location barrier how would I feel about him. Honestly, I'd still be freaking out. I'm discovering that I don't have a very high opinion of myself when it comes to the opposite sex."

"You've lived too long in Susan's shadow."

"That's what Edward said too! I don't know if it's that or what, but I'm so afraid that once he discovers the real me, he'll run the other direction. But the age thing still bothers me too. And how are we going to sustain a relationship when there's more than two hours flying time between us?"

Gloria did not speak for a while, but I could hear her thinking.

"Based on what you've discovered about him, the kind of man he is, do you think he's worth investing your time and emotions in—just to see if things could work between you?"

"That's an easy answer. Of course he is. I really like and admire him. Every time we talk or meet, I find more to like. I have no doubt he'd be worth the investment. The problem is not if he's worth it—it's more if I'm worth it to him. I have so many strikes against me, and age is a big factor. Gloria, if this relationship progresses to marriage, I won't be able to give him children—at least I don't see myself risking it at my age. He's young enough to want kids. And don't tell me I'm being stupid for thinking about these things."

"That thought never crossed my mind, and you're simply voicing how you feel. There's nothing more legitimate than that."

"Now you sound like a therapist. Lynn must be rubbing off on you."

"Therapist-sounding or not, it doesn't make the statement any less true."

I sighed. "I know. Just being prickly again."

"I have one more question, and then we can change the subject if you've had enough.

"OK."

"What would Edward—or any man in his position, for that matter—have to do to convince you that you're the most precious person in his life? Is this a winnable scenario for the guy?"

My last deep conversation with God on this very topic came back to me. I'd have to accept God's love. All of it. Believe in my heart that Jesus would die for only me, if need be. Then knowing that I am loved by the God of the universe, that I am dear to His heart, then it might not be too difficult to allow someone else to love the beauty God sees in me. And even better, if that person, the human, should prove unfaithful, I'd know that God had my back and He would never leave me or forsake me. That's a confidence worth fighting for.

I said as much to Gloria.

"Then do it, Quilla. Allow God to love all of you, the beautiful, the ugly, and the unmentionable parts. Just so you know from where I sit watching you over the years, you are one of the most easy-to-love persons I've ever met. I want you to experience for yourself the joy you bring to others, and if I could be given the opportunity to select the man I believe most equal to the task and most deserving of you, I would have picked none other than my nephew Edward—nine years your junior. For whatever little my opinion counts, he's a man among men, Quilla. In this life when many men are becoming deadbeat duds, I have been blessed to be married to a diamond, given birth to one, and to be aunt to another. And I can take credit for influencing. Edward, on the other hand, is just who he is, along with some solid parenting from his mother and father."

Wow! Some commendation, eh!

What do you think? Should I take the risk and let God expose and love all the messed-up parts of me? I want to.

Then having done that, am I brave enough to defy societal expectations and allow myself to be cherished by a much younger man—one whose relationship with God is rock-solid, and who would help me grow in my own walk with God?

The distance issue is really a nonissue. With my nursing skills, it wouldn't be a problem to relocate to the U.S., if our relationship matures to that point.

Some time ago I came across a book that's stayed with me. It's called *Feel the Fear and Do It Anyway*. I don't recall who wrote it. I should look it up. But that's what I have to do. The fear won't necessarily go away, I see. I just have to walk in faith, living beside my fears, and trust that my Father in heaven will guide me in the way I should go.

"Thanks, Gloria. Thanks for asking some really good questions, and for being a friend who seeks me out."

"You're both in my prayers, you know. You and Edward. And remember, however things work out, I will always be here for you as your friend."

Immediately following that talk with Gloria I had it out with God. I'd done enough foot dragging. I opened up my heart and turned over everything to Him. Then I called Edward and told him of my decision. His elation brought tears to my eyes. Already God was showing me, through Edward, a picture of the joy in heaven over one soul who turns to God and says, "I'll do it."

The next day when I returned from lunch, one long-stemmed red rose nestled in a box of baby's breath and greenery was waiting on my desk. The card read simply, "You bring me joy. Edward."

Cherished? Am I feeling cherished? You bet your Christmas dinner I am!

Chapter 18

You're not going to believe this! Mara is engaged. This same Mara who just last week had all kinds of reasons for why a relationship with G. David would not work, remember? She liked her independence! She could not see herself being the wife of a pastor, too much water under the bridge, and all that jazz. That same person came to my door blinding me in one eye with the width of her killer smile and fully blinding me in the other with the glare of the rock on her finger.

I'm getting too old for these types of shocks.

Thursday is my last day at work prior to the Christmas holidays. (Isn't it nice getting off a week before Christmas? I love this job!) Anyway, as I was saying, on Thursday I got a text message from Mara telling me to please be home tonight by 7:00. She needed to see me. I cut short my grocery shopping and some other errands so I could be home. I'd braced myself for an evening of tears and angst, so when the doorbell rang I opened it wearing my best sympathetic face.

That's what I got. Exactly what I told you. Totally and completely blindsided!

My girl, this commonsense, no-nonsense woman, literally skipped into my house and gleefully informed me that she had gotten herself reattached to the man who had broken her heart many years ago. I couldn't get over it.

Noticing that I appeared incapable of speech, she led me to my own kitchen table and told me everything. How sweet he is. How he had met her at the airport with flowers and hadn't complained when she'd insisted on spending Friday night by herself in a hotel. How at church he had introduced her to the whole assembly as the woman whose heart he had broken years ago but who was giving him another chance. That he had hoped that one day soon she would do him the great honor and marry him.

She told me about some woman who had come up to her after the church service and hissed in her ear that in no uncertain terms would she, Mara, have G. David. He was *hers*, whether he knew it or not.

"Quilla girl, I felt my Jamaican roots rising up on me, you know? The nerve! I wanted to box her upside that curly weave she had on her head. But thankfully Garry came by then, and I remembered that I am a redeemed child of God. Man! Some of these women are brazen. Imagine, the guy makes a big announcement in church that I'm his supposed future wife, and then this little tough-calved heathen had the unmitigated gall to come give me a warn-off! She never see my wrong side, you know."

I'd revived enough by now to be able to calm her down. Needless to say, I'm really glad she's my friend, because the little glimpse she was revealing of her "wrong side" made me want to keep to the right of her.

She then went on to tell me how she and G. David had had a big argument over it that very afternoon at his mother's house, where they had gone for lunch. Thankfully it had been only the three of them. How his mother had wept when they met and kept hugging her and hugging her and calling David all kinds of idiot—"How could he have let me out of his sight for even a minute when he knew that those piranha women, those harbor shark women, were just waiting for an opportunity to run me out of town so he might finally pay attention to them?"

"It was all too much for him. He got up from the table and walked out on us. Left me hanging on to his mother, and she to me, with our righteous indignation and love for him. It was all nerves, you know. I was so nervous about going to see him and then when he made the announcement to the church, I wanted to scream, 'Why are you putting all this pressure on me? I just got here, and I can't promise you anything.' So when that woman spoke to me, it was like adding fuel to the fire. I had to yell at someone. I managed to hold it together till I got to his mom. When I saw her, I remembered how much I loved this woman and how angry I still was for what he had done to me."

"So what did you do?" I asked, blown away by this turn of events. "How did you get from there to being engaged?"

"I went after him. No way was he walking out on me this time. He'd done it before, and I would not have it. Not again! I'd come to have my pound of flesh—even though it sounds a bit cold-blooded. A part of me wanted to hurt him as much as he'd hurt me."

She shook her head at her own insanity and continued. "I found him walking down the street, still in his church clothes, looking as handsome as ever. Full of fury, I grabbed his arm and spun him around."

She stopped. Her eyes closed as if reliving the moment. I hate when people do that. Stop talking in the middle of a really good part of the story.

"What happened, Mara? What happened?"

"Huh?"

"What happened when you grabbed Garry's arm and spun him around?"

Chagrin replaced her bemused look. "There were tears running down his face. Not only that—he looked defeated. That's what I'd reduced him to. Something melted in my heart then. All the anger I had, all the bottled-up resentment, just went up like a puff of smoke. I realized something. I still loved the man. I could not bear to see him so . . . vulnerable. I wanted that strong, happy, capable, warm man back."

"So then?"

"I threw my arms around him. Right there on the street, I kissed his tears and told him how very sorry I was. I told him how much I loved him, that I'd never stopped loving him, and if he ever broke my heart again, I would sit for days at the doors of his church and pray his soul into hell."

"You didn't say that!"

Mara's right eyebrow arched in a question mark.

"OK, tell me that even if you did, you didn't mean it!"

"I did mean it. Who knows what I meant? But Quilla, listen to this! Taking my hands in his, the man knelt down on that dusty road, still wearing his beautifully tailored suit, and begged me to marry him. He told me how much he loves me. How he'd never found anyone like me and how sorry he was for hurting me. He asked me to forgive him for not giving me the time he'd promised to redevelop my trust in him, but he didn't know how he'd manage if he ever lost me again."

" 'Marry me, Mara,' he begged. 'Please don't go back to Toronto without giving me some hope that I will one day be your husband.' "

"I had to ask him, Quill. I asked him, 'What about God? I thought you desired to do God's will above everything else. That's what you said to me back in Toronto. How do you know that reuniting is God's will for us?' "

This woman is tough. Would I even think to do that in the middle of such a scene? Would you?

"What did he say?"

Mara's voice dropped to a whisper. "When I asked him about God's will, it was as if time stopped. I felt a physical reaction go through him. Right in front of my very eyes I saw a war taking place, the war of a heart wanting something so badly, struggling to let it go and give it to God instead. How long he remained quiet I have no idea. It felt like forever. He finally gave a huge sigh, and then his whole body shuddered and became still. I could feel it since he, still on his knees, was holding on to my hand. After what seemed like forever he stood up looking spent but resolute.

"'Then I would have to let you go,' he said. 'I'd have to keep to my commitment to put God first.'

"I knew then that I had nothing to fear. Knowing that someone is prepared to give you up for the love of God should have made me upset. Instead it's like I got smothered in peace. Like this man whom I knew but didn't fully understand had matured into someone worth risking my heart for again. He had integrity. This time he might just keep his promise."

"Mara!" I gasped. "This is . . . I don't know what to say. It's incredible."

Her killer smile flashed. "I know. So to make a long story short, I told him that we would seek God's direction together, and that I would be his girl until or unless God told us otherwise. When I said that, he turned me around and put his arm around my shoulder. Then he took my inner arm and brought it around his waist. Holding it in place, he walked us slowly back to his mother's house, pausing every now and then to look at me as if to make sure all this was for real."

"Wow!" I said. "Wow!"

"The rest of the week was a bit mundane after that. But that's just what I needed. I wanted to be with him—normal like, you know. Every day while I was there, he'd come by his mom's house and sit with us or take me out on one of his home visits, or just go do grocery shopping. It allowed me to get a feel for his life and what day-to-day with him might be like."

I sighed. I love a good romantic tale. "So how come you're just now calling me? You've been back since Sunday night!"

"Actually, I just got back last night." Her eyes danced with mischief at my confused look. "Knowing my boss goes to the office early, I made plans to call him on Monday morning and ask for a few extra days. He's usually pretty accommodating. So Sunday evening when Garry came by to take me to the airport, I played it up. I got in the car with my bags and said goodbye to his mom and everything. We started down the road. Poor Garry looked so sad. Then I asked him if staying a few extra days would get rid of that sad face. 'Yeah, right,' he said.

"I told him to turn the car around and take me to dinner."

"You have a mean streak, Mara, playing the man of God like that. There's probably a special category in the books of heaven for mischief made against men or women of the cloth. I'd watch it if I were you."

Mara continued as if I'd not spoken. Actually, she waited for me to finish and then continued as if I had not spoken.

"It took him a while to take me seriously. 'You mean this for real?' he asked. I assured him it was. Then the man of God did a U-turn in the middle of a no-U-turn zone and whisked me to a cozy restaurant where he dined me in style. The next day he took off work early—he has office hours on Tuesdays—and when he came to pick me up, he took me to the beach. There he gave me this ring and his promise to love me and cherish me all the days of my life, unless God said no. Would I marry him?"

"H'mmm! I wonder what answer you gave him!"

Mara grinned. She is so beautiful, and this happiness makes her simply gorgeous. She looked at her finger.

"There wasn't an ounce of no left in me."

Let me skip over a few things and get to the next story. I know you want to hear all about what happened the Sunday night Edward took me out. I'm no fool. But I'm not ready to share that yet. I want to keep it just between us for now. Not even to Susan have I disclosed what happened that awesome night.

May I also remind you what this documentation is about? It's about the stories, the conversations, I have with unmarried and wannabe married women about why they're not yet married. This is not really about me. Their stories are supposed to help me make sense of my own situation. So if I choose not to discuss some personal aspect of my life, it really is my prerogative. Just thought I'd mention that . . . for the record.

Justina

On the Monday before Christmas Justina Calderone and I met at the Starbucks near her office. Not the place I'd have picked given how emotional some of these women's stories become, but I did not know her, so she got to choose the venue. (As a reminder, Justina is one of the women who'd called me the day I had that conversation with Gloria.)

A petite woman with a slightly protruding abdomen, she looked the quiet introverted type. I'd told her that I'd be wearing a red jacket (my favorite Christmas one), and that my hair was in extensions. She identified me immediately as I walked in the door.

"You're Quilla, aren't you?"

"Justina?"

She nodded, guiding me to a table at the back of the café. At least here we had a bit of privacy. Speaking as if she'd rehearsed her introduction, she told me how Danesha had kept on and on about the discussions we've had, to the point where they'd begun to debate the issue themselves. That was when Danesha told her to talk with me. Apparently she and Danesha were gym buddies.

"So here's my story," she began. "I'm 38 years old with one child and another on the way, and I've never been married. When I found out I was pregnant with this one, I came this close (a breath of space separated her fingers) to aborting it, but I just didn't have the nerve."

I touched her hand, inviting her to pause. "Justina, before you go any further I think I should tell you that almost all the women I've spoken with on this topic experienced a lot of emotion during their talk. It's been the same for me. Even though I will not be discussing your story, the personal pieces, with anyone, you don't know me and have no reason to trust me. So with that in mind, are you sure you still want to talk?"

I had to give her an out. Make sure we were doing the informed consent thing, you know. Too many times I find myself the unasked-for confidant to people's stories. I must have sympathetic eyes or something. Then, when in a moment of weakness they bare their souls to you, things can become awkward thereafter every time you meet. With friends it's not an issue, but with strangers I make myself stop them—give them a moment to back out. It's just the right thing to do.

"Thanks for letting me know, but I still want to talk. Danesha told me I could trust you, and I trust her judgment of people. She can be pretty hard on the human race."

"Tell me about it!"

I meant to agree with her assessment of Danesha, but she took it to mean I wanted her to continue with her story. I didn't bother to explain.

"My firstborn is 6 years old. A boy. He has a learning disability, and even though managing his care is difficult some days, I love that little guy with all my heart."

I wished I'd thought to bring some tissue. I'm never prepared for when the emotions are going to kick in, and any minute now Justina's would. I sensed her telling would be draining for us both.

She had been promised by the father of her firstborn that he'd marry her. Actually he'd given her a ring, not an engagement ring but a promise ring—whatever that means.

"Call me old-fashioned, but even though I'm not a religious person I wanted our first sexual experience to wait till we got married, you know. I loved him, but I wanted it to be special, something to look forward to."

She picked at her short, nicely manicured fingernails.

Well, the guy had been understanding at first, actually told her he respected her stand and loved her for it. Soon after the promise ring, however, the pressure for sex increased. If she loved him, why withhold the very thing he needed to feel even closer to her? She didn't really love him. Now that they were almost as good as engaged, what difference did it make if they celebrated their love for each other now or six months from now?

"I reassured him how much I loved him. I told him how special our wedding night would be—to have this new thing to look forward to—but he would not be convinced. Why didn't I want him as much as he wanted me? Was I frigid? Did I even like sex? Did I understand how hard it is for a man to have someone he loves in his life and not be able to be intimate with her?

"He wore me down," she said, "Maybe he's right, I reasoned. If we love each other and are planning to get married, what difference did waiting really make as long as the first time was very special? And because I hadn't planned to have sex before I got married, I wasn't on any birth control. One night, after flowers, champagne, and dinner to celebrate our 'soon to be nuptials,' we slept together. After that, there was no turning back. I went on the pill, but two weeks later something didn't feel right in my body. I was pregnant."

She stopped, working to control her emotions. "You hear these stories all the time. The girl thinks the guy loves her, gives in to the pressure for sex; then he disappears. I thought I knew better than that. After all, I was 32 years old! I had dated a lot prior to this guy. I thought I knew my way around men, but this one played me for a fool. As soon as we started to have regular sex, he started to be regularly absent. He had to work late, he wasn't feeling well, all kinds of excuses. When guys do stuff like that, it messes up a woman's head. Was I that awful a sex partner? Did I not satisfy him?

"When I told him I was pregnant, the distance between us just grew. The more he wanted to be gone, the more I clung to him to the point that I didn't even like myself. Quilla, for someone who had kept her virginity till she was 32, waiting for marriage to have sex, I could not bear the thought of being an unwed mother. But that's what happened. I couldn't hold on to him, so I had the child alone, with my family and friends to support me. I love my son, but I wanted marriage. I wanted the white wedding dress and the whole shebang—my chance at happily ever after."

I wondered then at the losses women experience. Justina had lost her dream of being a virgin bride. She then lost the man responsible for the loss of her virginity, and now she's feeling the loss of a white wedding gown. I mean, some things in life, once you lose them, you never get them back. One has to learn to live with what remains, even when our hearts experience wistful longings for what might have been. Sad. So sad.

"What happened next?" I asked.

"Well, I counted my losses, got my body back into shape, and made myself available for a second chance. Even though being a single mom decreased my prospects for finding someone, I still wanted my dream. Fool! That's what I am. A @%&# stupid fool!"

She used an expletive that didn't sound right coming out of her mouth. I must have winced, because she quickly apologized.

"Forgive my 'French,'"

There's a point in listening to these women's stories where I have to really control my need to interrupt and ask all the questions that pop into my mind. It's like my presence has punched a tiny airhole into a bulging sac of pain. So I sit and let them talk, allowing my hand to jot questions and my mind to record their stories through active listening. Their need to talk, to hear their own stories in the presence of another, takes precedence over my need to discover why *I'm* not married by now. I guess that I also have to be prepared for the occasional 'French' and, as in this case, school my features to display no censure.

I let Justina talk. Who knows what the outcome of this aired laundry will be?

As her story unfolded, she speculated that her dream must have blinded her to the kinds of men she dated. An attractive, petite brunet, she looked the type to attract men who needed a small woman by their side to make them feel strong. However, all the men she dated eventually disappeared.

"So how come I'm sitting here, three and a half months pregnant, eh, Quilla? I'll tell you. I don't learn from my own mistakes. The sad reality is that once you've had a child, men assume you're an easy lay. I never hid the fact that I had a son. It was important to me that the men I dated knew

188 The Waiting Heart

that up front. So imagine their response when I told them I wanted to wait until marriage to have sex with them! One guy laughed right in my face. He found the whole idea so funny that he announced it to the whole bar where we were having drinks that night. I know he was a bit drunk at the time, but can you imagine my mortification? That was only our second date!"

I made a note on my pad about the current pregnancy. Obviously possessing the ability to read upside down, she replied to it.

"Yes, I'm beating around the bush. You see, the father of this baby is the sweetest guy I've ever been with. He's kind, giving, and protective, *and* he loves me. Problem is, he'd been married once. Got burned really badly and has no desire to do a repeat. I love him, Quilla, but he can't bring himself, even though he loves me, to risk marriage. Not again."

The hard café chair forced me to shift position. I decided to ask another question.

"So getting pregnant this time was deliberate?"

The only tears she would shed for the evening spilled out of her eyes when she acknowledged my question.

"I was so sure," she eventually replied. "How could such a kind loving man not respond to being a father of his own child?"

"Maybe he felt you'd forced his hand?"

Fully in control of her emotions again, she continued. "Who knows? When I told him, he got very quiet. Went to some place deep inside himself. Then he got up from the couch, kissed me on the forehead, and left. He didn't say goodbye or anything else. He just left. I knew then that I'd gambled and lost. When I got home from work the next day, I found an envelope containing a check for $10,000 under my door. There was also a square sheet from a yellow Post-it saying in his bad handwriting that he was sorry and to 'please use the money to help with the child' and that he'd try to send more when he could. He must have emptied his savings.

"So what do you say about this second bomb of my life? What do you say to women who want marriage so badly, yet every year they watch another birthday pass and the dream get more and more impossible? What do I do with my need for companionship, for someone to walk through life with, have babies with, grow old with? someone to hold my hand in sickness or death?"

Her questions tugged at my heartstrings. When dreams die, when the expected does not come to fruition, I guess, as I've said before, you just have to deal with it and eke out the most you can of what remains.

Her questions and my thoughts brought me back to that first meeting with Natasha. She talked about the letting go of a dream being like a death, except there's no one to grieve with you.

Who grieves with those of us who must let go of cherished dreams? Shouldn't there be a ritual in society in which these dearly loved and departed dreams can be acknowledged and laid to rest among the dust and ashes of life? What hope is there for us?

What am I thinking? Of course there's hope. Not all of us get to do the things we dream for our lives. Not all the things we dream and desire are even good for us. But for those who believe in God and the promises of heaven, there is hope. While we may experience disappointments here, earth is just a temporary home. We believe that God is preparing more bountiful rewards for us, more fulfilling than anything we could ever imagine.

And that, I think, is my assignment. As I listen to these stories of dead or dying dreams I must remind myself and others that we have a God who sees and hears and who has gone to prepare a place for us.

Oh, yes, I hear what some of you are thinking. More religious pie-in-the-sky mumbo jumbo to sugarcoat the real pain of people's lives.

But that's not it at all. Life is full of disappointments. The fact of the matter is that we will not, in this life, get all the things we dream of. Some people don't even get the things they *need*—food, clothing, shelter. Against the backdrop of their raw basic needs, my desire for a husband and marriage pales. However, for me, for Justina, Martha, Natasha, and all the others I've spoken with so far, this pain from our lack of fulfillment that we live with day in and day out is not to be dismissed. It hurts. The only way that I personally can survive the loss without falling apart is by the grace of God.

What then do I do (other than listen and nod) for unbelievers such as Justina? What answer do I give this woman who so desperately needs to have hope in something above her situation? What will happen to her and to her children? Already she worries me even as her words drip with such pain.

Trusting my gut, I did for her the same thing I did for Mara and Lynn. I prayed for her. I took her small hands in mine, her short nails shining with vivid red polish, and without asking permission, in her hearing I talked to God about her questions. Softly I did this—with eyes wide open, I asked God to look at her sad, disappointed heart. I asked the Great Physician, the Balm in Gilead, to heal and soothe her. I appealed to the Creator of the universe, the Maker of heaven and earth, to help her discover the ultimate purpose for which she was born and to give her hope, joy, peace, and love. To get her through life—not just survival. To give her a sense of redirected passion. Then I asked God, if it was His will, and if it would be for her best, to still find a way to let her have her dream.

I didn't end my talk to God with 'amen.' I just said, 'Thank You for listening,' squeezed Justina's hands, and let go.

"You just prayed for me—why?" she asked.

"Because when circumstances in life challenge me, I need to remind myself that God is in control of the circumstances."

"Even for people who don't believe?"

"Yes. God knew you before you were formed in your mother's belly. I believe He knew the path your life would take up to and including this moment when I would take your hands in this coffee shop and pray for you. I also believe that when we tune in to God on the spiritual channel He put within each one of us, He will help us fulfill the purpose for which He created us, and help us find the path that leads to full joy. This joy allows us to rise above our seemingly desperate situations and leaves onlookers astonished at our peace in the middle of life's nastiness."

Justina eyed me somewhat sceptically. "A spiritual channel? You're saying each person has one?"

I nodded. "I don't know if I've ever really verbalized it like that before, but yes. We all have a spiritual imprint in our souls, whether we use it or not."

"I see now why Danesha has nothing but good to say about you, Quilla. You have the kindest of hearts. Thanks for letting me tell my story. I think I got more from talking to you than I expected."

"One day I hope to pull all the stories together and see the common theme, if there is one," I told her. "When that's done, I'd like to have a gathering of all the women who contributed. Do you want me to include you as well?"

Justina reached for her handbag and produced a business card. "Justina Calderone," it read. "Chartered Accountant," followed by the name of an accounting firm that even I had heard of. This little woman—a CA? What do we know about people—the successful and the accomplished, the poor and the middle class? No one is immune to pain and to having dreams money can't buy. I wondered how those senior partners would deal with this second single-mom pregnancy.

Justina stood, and I stood with her.

I gave her a hug. "Merry Christmas."

She hugged me back, a hard short hug. "Merry Christmas to you, too."

I watched her walk away. Then before I could second-guess myself I called her back and gave her an invitation card to my Christmas Eve soiree. "The only condition is that you must bring along a food item that you love and a nonperishable something for the Grant a Wish Foundation. You don't even need to tell me in advance if you're coming. Just come. Bring your son. I'd love to have you both."

She fingered the invitation, nodded, and left.

Chapter 19

Obviously my brain was addled when I made the decision to meet with this other woman from church—Clare—the day before my Christmas Eve party. I still had a few things to prepare, and the house needed a thorough cleaning. Not that it's really dirty, but it could do with a little sprucing up. There were Christmas candles to set up, music to select, and plates of goodies to arrange. This year I also planned to begin the evening with the reading of the Bible's Christmas story. Too bad Edward wouldn't be here. He has the right voice and method of delivery for it. Ah, well. I'm sure I'll be getting grief over the fact that we again had fun without him.

Before heading out for my lunch date with Clare, I called Natasha to remind her I'd pick her up at 2:00 tomorrow. Jason had put in a special order for pierogies, and Nat wanted to make them fresh for him. Personally speaking, it's not a food I associate with Christmas, but "to each his own."

I wish I'd asked Martha for her phone number. I'd love to invite her, too. "Dear Father, please don't let her be lonely for the holidays. And if she is, please remind her to call me. You know I'll welcome her to this expanding circle of friends."

I left the matter in God's hands and switched to fretting over the things I still had to do.

My list of invitees include Gloria and Wendell, Christopher (home for the holidays), Susan (of course), Natasha, Jason, Mara, Stelle and a date, and two of the three musketeers. (Mia's family is going to be celebrating, so given the time she has off work, she's not able to do both events.) I'm hoping that Justina will come and that Martha will call. Lynn and Katie might . . .

Wait a minute!

Lynn!

I've not updated you on Lynn.

I tell you, between Edward messing up my head, Susan with her ongoing antics, and Mara's reconciliation, I completely forgot to provide a Lynn update. So where did we leave off? Oh, yes! She had decided to write a letter to Katie's father and wanted me to give it a once-over before she sent it. So of course I did. I mean I gave her letter the once-over. I figured it'd be a shocker to the poor guy, but it was well written.

Seems he didn't respond quite the way she'd anticipated. Out of the blue, two or three weeks ago, and a week after she'd mailed the letter, he just showed up. As I understand it, late one afternoon he called her at her office and said he had to see her that very day.

I can't believe I let this slip. I'm supposed to be recording these important happenings. Yes, I know it has nothing to do with my "Why am I not married?" question, but these are outcomes to the conversations.

Just so you know, I found out about this stuff *after* the big showdown. But guess what? There was no big showdown. It seems the letter had done its work, so that by the time Katie's father came he'd wrapped his head around the facts and wanted more than anything to see his kid. That's all I know right now.

I'm desperate to know what happened, but I will not call to find out. It feels intrusive somehow, so I'm waiting and hoping that Lynn will call me again or that Gloria will tell me something. Anything! The suspense is killing me.

Clare's Story

I know Clare, at least I think I know her. But I don't really. I know of her. I know what people say about her behind her back. Everyone at church talks about Clare. She's desperate to be married. I mean, really desperate. When the guys see Clare coming, they run in the other direction. They tell me they can spot these desperate women a mile away.

You see, Clare is at the stage (seems she's been at this stage for years!) when her chief concern is her biological clock and her disappearing eggs. And she's not quiet about it. She has no time to waste getting to know a man who has no intention of entering a serious relationship with her. From what I hear, by date number two she produces a list of questions: Does he have a job? How long has he been working at the company or for himself? Any children? Ever married? What does he look for in a woman? Does he want to have children someday? Etc.

I wish someone would tell her to ease up on the intensity. Her anxiety is so palpable that she can't relax long enough to get to know a guy. If publicity and word-of-mouth marketing could have produced the results she wanted, she'd be long married by now, with a bunch of kids. But like me, she's not married, and worse, the few guys who are around make it a duty to warn all newcomers about her.

OK, let me confess here and now that I don't like Clare very much. I don't like what she stands for and how she parades herself. Her whole personality and attitude put my teeth on edge. Twice on my way to this meeting I asked God to help me be nonjudgmental and kind. Many times we Christians are not kind. We try to be good, but boy, oh boy, sometimes we are not nice at all. We love to slay the other saints with our tongues or condemn them with our prejudgments when we know nothing about the state of their hearts. I don't want to be that way—regardless of how I feel about her.

Clare is a teacher and had asked me to meet her at her office (technically her classroom). She'd told me she had some end-of-term grades to enter in the computer system at work, then she'd be officially on holiday. When I got there, she had pizza, Christmas cookies, and a couple bottles of water waiting on her clean desktop.

Clare, typically, is dressed to the nines, including stiletto heels that make my back hurt just looking at her, and today was no exception. Knee boots with impossibly high heels (those expensive soft leather ones that fold over at the top) hugged her slender jean-clad legs. Tall and slim, not slightly rounded like me, her whole presentation ensured she got attention. It's hard to ignore Clare when she walks into a room. Actually, she never just walks into a room. She makes an entrance! She likes clothes that hug and highlight. As far as her body is concerned, she's in the advertising business.

And true to form, before I'd even said a proper hello and fitted myself into the small child's desk closest to her, Clare pounced.

"So what's this I hear that you're interviewing unmarried women—asking them why they're not married? What kind of stupid question is that? You don't think unmarried women have enough to contend with without someone blaming them for the fact that they have no husband?" She took a slice of pizza, snapped her teeth into it as if it had offended her, then inched the box in my direction. "Help yourself."

I counted to five, then five more. Not working!

Imagine, this woman called my house and left a message that she wanted to be interviewed for this project. I did not seek her out. Even when I returned her call and we set up the time and date, she gave no hint that she considered the whole thing a waste of her time. She wanted to talk with *me!*

Fighting for control, I took a slice of pizza even though I wasn't hungry—anything to prevent my saying the first, second, or third thing that came to my mind.

God, help me to be kind.

Knowing that fear or pain sometimes masquerades as aggression, I willed my mind to take the high road.

"Actually," I replied with a commendable degree of calm, "the first time I heard the question I got a bit hot under the collar myself. That's what started me on this project of interviewing other unmarried women."

"Well, I'm not hot under the collar. I just think it's a stupid question and a complete waste of time."

My high road choice came to an abrupt end. I dropped the pizza back in the box. "Why did you want to talk to me, Clare? Did you ask me to come see you just so you could tell me how stupid my project is?"

"Now look who is getting high and mighty! Sheath your fangs, girl."

Sheath *my* fangs? Sheath *my* fangs? I extricated myself from that desk with the agility of a viper provoked, but because the angel of the Lord whispered in my ear I heard a calmer voice than I thought myself capable of saying, "Let me not waste any more of your or my time. I'm outta here."

Clare swung her lithe body into a standing position. "Cool your jets, Quilla. I guess I came on a bit strong. Sit."

She motioned me back into the seat. When my reluctance manifested itself, she raised her hands pleadingly. "I'm sorry. I'm sorry. Please, Quilla. Sit down."

I perched on the desktop and dropped my handbag on the chair. Clare opened her mouth as if to say something else but closed it when she saw what must have been the no-more-putting-up-with-nonsense look in my eyes. Folding my arms across my chest, I just sat there looking at her. The silence became longer and larger, but she was going to have to be the one to break it. And if she didn't break it soon, I'd be gone.

After what seemed forever, she stepped to her desk, reached into her handbag, and pulled out an envelope. Then she removed a square of paper from the envelope and handed it to me. It was a faded photo, one taken long ago with those ancient Polaroid Instamatic cameras. A tall young girl whom God had not blessed with an ounce of good looks stared sullenly at the picture-taker.

"Meet Clare Williams, 15 years old."

"Is this a relative of yours?"

"Nope. That's me in the flesh—BS."

My jaw dropped. I couldn't help myself. "This is . . . you? No way!"

She produced a wry smile. "Shame on you, Christian girl. Don't you believe that with God all things are possible?"

"But . . . I mean, this looks nothing like you. And what does the BS mean?"

"Yeah. *That* does look nothing like me. Not anymore. Thank God for plastic surgery. That's what BS stands for—before surgery. I got the nose redone, had them shape up the lips, enlarge the eyes just a tad, and rebuild the jawbone. That was the hardest one. My jaw hurt for months. To this day when the weather is too damp it still sends me reminders." She massaged her chin as if today was one of those days.

"I don't know what to say," I replied eventually. And I didn't. What does one say to a confession like that?

"Not a lot of people know. I did the surgeries slowly, bit by bit, so it was almost like someone gradually losing weight and then all of a sudden people notice the person is slim. That's how I went about redoing my face. With the jaw job I had to take a couple months off work, of course. But anything was worth the sacrifice of not having to look at that ugly mug in the mirror every morning."

I took my bag off the chair and sat down heavily. Clare walked over to the edge of the wall-to-wall chalkboard that sported "Merry Christmas and a Happy New Year" in flourishing penmanship. Leaning a shoulder against it, she turned to me.

"It's a curse to be ugly. A curse. For most of my life I've been cursed with ugliness. Through no fault of mine I was a freak genetic joke. My parents are ordinary-looking people. No one has to avert their eyes to avoid gawking at them. Maybe that's why I'm an only child. In their quiet moments they probably wondered how they managed to produce such an ogre and dared not risk a repeat."

While my brain digested the disclosure that had me rooted to my chair, I couldn't help noticing the inspirational sayings above Clare's head, the kind that you see plastered on the walls of classrooms where dedicated teachers work diligently to help build a child's self-esteem. One read "You are unique and precious." Another said "You can be anything you want to be!" Still another read "Discover the beauty that lies within." All around the room words and sayings provided soul restoratives.

I looked at the face of this woman whom I seriously did not like, and wondered why she'd chosen me to unburden to. Her story continued to pour out.

"When I was a child, my mother would tell me that while man looks on the outward appearance, God looks at our hearts." Clare's shaking head and slight sneer communicated what she'd say next. "But then I'd look at my face, the outward me, and know that compared to all the other faces I knew, mine had been cursed.

"As soon as I learned to read, books became a way to enter other worlds. I read everything. As my body matured, I wanted to learn about boys and love. Girly stuff, and I discovered the Harlequin romances. Wow, did I get hooked on them. I loved the love stories. Couldn't get enough of them. But even then I knew I was more of a voyeur. I knew that I could view romantic love on the pages of a book and even in real life, but I'd never experience it myself. Not with this face. My heart cried out for a chance to show a young man how much I could love him back, but nowhere in the stories were there women I could relate to—not outwardly. They were all beautiful. And me, I was cursed. I longed to be desired like those women in the books, but throughout all of high school and then college, not one single, solitary guy ever asked me out. Not one. A woman's need to be loved shouldn't be determined by her features. But mine was!"

Clare shifted positions, resting her back against the board. I remained glued to my seat.

"The times that people were cruel to me weren't that many. Kids can be, you know. Cruel to each other. I see it all the time in my classroom, and trust me, I have no tolerance for it. My parents did an excellent job of loving me, and I've been blessed with kindness from many people. But sometimes kindness is really pity in disguise. I know the difference.

"One night—it was near the time of my high school prom—I heard my parents talking. They were hoping that someone, anyone, would ask me to go with them. 'Honey,' I heard Mom say to my dad, 'we can love her as much as we want, but we can't make other people love her, so how do we help her?' Not having an answer, he suggested they do the only thing they knew how. They prayed for me, not asking God to make me beautiful on the outside, but prayed that God would help me navigate through life and if it was in His will, to one day find someone to love me and to share my life with."

I have allowed the stories in these interviews to pull at my compassion but not to overwhelm me. But this one . . . this story from this aggressive, irritating woman whom I didn't even like very much . . . made me lock my jaw and swallow repeatedly against the urge to cry for the child, the teen, and the young woman in the photo whose heart dreamed of love, but who might never get it because of her face. Nothing—from my moments of wishing for some of Susan's beauty, of thinking myself undesirable—compares to the agony Clare must have lived through. Again I looked at the photo, then at Clare. Unbelievable!

Here I am again, being forced to face things I've never thought about. You think your life is the pits until you hear about someone else's pain. "Growing up ugly" could be a whole other project. Dear God in heaven, it's a wonder some people keep going at all. We seem to be all riddled with crippling baggage of one sort or another.

Clare unscrewed the cap from one of the bottles of water and took a long swig as if the liquid could serve another purpose than that of hydration.

"I'm not married, Quilla, because up until my thirty-fourth year there was no man in the world who wanted to be seen with me. But long before that, I'd made a plan. It was way back when I heard my parents pray for someone to love me. I decided that I would work hard and save every penny I earned, and then I would rid myself of my cursed face. So in addition to getting a formal education, I studied fashion. I watched women and how they dressed, how they carried themselves—beautiful women, sexy women, confident women. In the privacy of my house I practiced to be like them, to walk like them, talk like them. When the final piece of surgery was complete, I was ready. I'd planned it for years. I would move to a different city and there I would be the new and improved Clare Williams—not a cover girl, but someone just shy of drop-dead gorgeous."

I felt a question coming, but Clare must have read my face.

"You're probably wondering why, when I look like this, when I've gone through all this trouble with my face, I'm still single? Why have I become so desperate that I drive away the very men I want to attract?"

She saw my look of surprise.

"Yes, I know that's how I'm described, and I deserve it."

She stood in front of me now, looking down from her great stiletto height, a lean and well-proportioned beauty. It seemed that whatever quirk of nature had maligned her face had repented of the evil and blessed her with a body other women dream of.

Taking the seat beside mine, she explained. "As I said before, when my makeover was complete, I was 34 years old. My parents hadn't had the financial means to help me, so I had to do it alone. It wasn't cheap, these surgeries. I worked and saved, determined not to go into debt, but it took that long to do it all, and by then my childbearing clock was ticking way too fast. The surgery did what I hoped it would. Immediately I put all my in-room practice in motion, and it paid dividends. I started to attract guys. But . . . how could I attract the right one, the one who would love me back, the one who didn't need all the time in the world to know that I was the love of his life and that he couldn't live another day without me? With each day that passes, the very thing I sacrificed my youth and young adulthood to secure—a husband and family—becomes more and more an unreachable goal. You see my dilemma, don't you?"

I nodded. I did see it. I also understood the desperation.

"The right man, Quilla. That's what we all want. Mr. Right. I wanted to find a nice Christian guy who loved me, but there is no such guy in any of the churches in Toronto, and trust me, I've attended them all. No, I lie. Let me modify my statement. There are still a few decent, unmarried men around, but my reputation has preceded me. All the others—the not-so-decent ones—are interested only in sex."

"Speak the truth, girl," I added. "Some of these men make you wonder what Christianity really means to them."

"We serve a cruel God, Quilla. He must be. How could a God of love read my heart, see what I need, and not look with compassion on my situation? June coming I will be 50 years old. Fifty years old, and still alone! Made beautiful on the outside by surgery, but alone. Does God not understand how that loneliness eats away at a woman's self-confidence? Doesn't He care that I go to bed hugging my pillow—a pillow that can't hug me back—when I long for a warm body beside me? Cruel, I say! He's gotta be. Why would He punish us like this when He is the one who created within us this desire for companionship and without which many of us will never feel complete?"

What a provocative question! I mulled it over and started to reply, but Clare had more to say.

"I'm spitting mad. So mad that it spills into every part of my life, even when I don't mean for it to. I'm mad because I've been gypped again." She took another long swig of her water, washing down her ire.

"Three years ago when it started to dawn on me that I might not get my dream, the anger came. The thought popped into my head as clear as day—what was the point of 'saving myself' till marriage? There might be no husband. Not ever. What was I saving my precious virginity for? So I gave it up. Any guy I dated who wanted sex, I gave it up, for free. And God could put that in His heavenly pipe and smoke it!"

My body cringed at the blasphemy. But I had no answer. Sometimes, meeting up against the rawness of someone else's pain, there is no appropriate scripture to quote. Sometimes the best scripture is allowing the person's pain to be howled to the universe while we accommodate it in the silence. So I waited.

"Have I shocked you, Quilla?"

"Well, no one can accuse you of not speaking your mind," I half-joked.

She gave a fleeting smile, and gradually the pulsing anger left her voice. "Do you think God looks out for us even when we're spitting in His face and openly defying Him? Even though I have been, and still am, mad at Him, lately I've been feeling the loss of the connection we used to have. Fifty is staring me in the face, and I need to let go of some of my stuff, give it over to someone more capable. Why not God, I think. But every time I try to talk to Him about coming back—not to church, but to Him—I feel the anger. I can't even pray. How do I go back to the God who's let me down? If He's got the whole world in His hands and can do all things, certainly He must have the power to grant me my desire. If anyone should be held accountable for what's happened to me, He should! He knows how I've suffered. So tell me, how do I forgive God for what He's done to me?"

It's been more than four hours since I met with Clare. I'm now at home recording our conversation as closely as I can recapture it. Forgiving God? Isn't that a twist on things? There are those of us who not only need for God to forgive us, but we need to forgive Him too? Clare raised a good point. How do you forgive and move on when the person responsible, the one to be held accountable, is unidentifiable? Isn't it logical, then, to conclude that since God is ultimately responsible for all things, He should take the blame?

I wish I could tell you that I prayed with Clare before we parted company. I didn't. We parted more amicably than I'd expected, but I did not pray with her. I prayed for her as I drove home. I promised her that I'd pray for her. I even opened my mouth to invite her to my Christmas Eve gathering, but changed my mind. Her interview had done something to me that none of the others had. It left me rattled and uncertain of my ground.

That night when Edward called, I told him everything. I know I'd promised the women to keep their stories confidential, but I needed to talk about this one in particular. And he doesn't know her. When I'd come to the end of my tale, Edward put a name to it.

"The problem of pain. That's what it is. It's the Christian's Achilles' heel."

"Why is that?"

"Think about it. How can we say there's a God who loves us when He allows the innocent to go through unspeakable pain?"

I sighed. "You might be right. That's how I felt as I listened to Clare. Normally I can think of a passage of Scripture or share a personal experience to help encourage or comfort the women I speak with. But today I felt completely bereft of speech. Her pain was so great and her anger so justified that I knew nothing I said could touch it. I had no defense for God, Edward. What kind of Christian am I if I can't respond to charges like that about God?"

"Don't be so hard on yourself. Listen, God did not leave us without some tools to help defend His character. But one of the critical lessons we all need to remember is that we cannot always explain why God allows things to happen. How can you ask an ant to explain the universe? The ant can tell you only about its experience of the universe. We are kinda like the ant. We know only what we've read or have been told (and neither may be true), or what we've personally experienced. That's what we're asked to share with others—what God has done for us."

But I had nothing to share. Nothing that came even close to what this woman has lived through. My little problems seemed nothing compared to hers.

Edward continued. "Sometimes the things that happen to us are part of a larger drama that's unfolding. When you get a chance, read the book of Job again. Pay special attention to the opening chapters. Then, assuming you're familiar with the debates taking place within the middle chapters, skip to the end and see what God does when Job demands an audience with Him. See what God says when Job demands that He answer the question of why people suffer."

I knew the answer, at least to the last part. "God didn't answer Job's question. Instead He asked him a few of His own. And when Job heard all God's questions, he repented in dust and ashes."

"Trust God to defend Himself for Himself, Quilla," Edward advised. "God also understands that beneath our anger there's a whole lot of pain. He can relate to pain. He suffered and was tempted in all the ways we were, not necessarily with the mediums we have today, but the same root temptations. The temptation to cheat, steal, lie, deny God, covet, lust, etc. Yet He didn't sin. Quilla, you must have had moments you were mad at God. You can share that experience with Clare and tell her how you worked through it. Tell her why you still believe despite the struggles. That's your testimony. Leave God to be God of the bigger issues."

I felt some of the stress I'd been carrying since my talk with Clare ease. Here, with Edward, is a true illustration of Christian camaraderie. We can help to prop each other up and provide answers and perspectives through the unique lens God has given to each of us.

"Thanks, Edward. You've given me a lot to think about."

"Are all your interviews this intense?"

I chuckled. "Prying, are we?"

His tone was all innocence. "Who, me? Of course not. Just curious."

Sobering, I said, "I'd say that to different degrees, all are intense. But this is the first one that left me so rattled."

"Better you than me, then. I like the coolness of logic, and wouldn't know the first thing to do with all that emotional intensity."

"Yeah, right! What did you call that big debate with Susan—that was highly intense."

"But she didn't start crying on me or telling me about some childhood abuse. That's intense and emotional."

"The man with an answer for everything."

"I wish!" There was just the slightest pause before he spoke again. "Then I'd know if God will grant me the desire of my heart . . . for you to be my wife."

"Edward!"

"Everything tells me this is right, Quilla. I know we haven't known each other for a long time, but this is right. Maybe not for right now, but our being together feels right. I'm not saying this to pressure you. I'm just reminding you that I'm not going anywhere or looking for anyone else. Being with you feels like home, and I going to keep praying that God will reveal that to you too—or convince me that I'm wrong."

Like parched earth, my heart longs for the companionship Edward offers. I'd given him my word to give the relationship a fighting chance, but fear continues to stalk my decision.

"Oh, Edward, what will I do with you?"

"Just let your heart love me. That's all. And if you don't cooperate with me, I might be forced to return for another unannounced visit and ignite that chemistry all over again."

A tingle of anticipation raced up my spine, and a voice I hardly recognized purred, "You drive a hard bargain, Mr. Grainge. OK, I'll cooperate as much as I can, but you never know when a girl might get lonely and decide to be a bit uncooperative, especially around New Year's Eve, or the first full moon, the last quarter, Valentine's Day, times like those to name a few."

"Would you happen to be flirting with me, Ms. Hazelwood? You wouldn't be one of those who's all talk and no action, would you?"

"Trust me, Mr. Grainge. I'm very good at acting on what I say."

Edward crowed with delight. "In that case, if I were you, from now on I'd sleep with one eye open."

I smiled to myself, feeling strong. "Promises, promises."

Silence greeted my comment.

"Edward?"

"You're messing with my sanity, woman! Give me one good reason I shouldn't get on the next plane and come teach you a thing or two about playing with fire."

"You promised your mom you'd be home for Christmas."

"I did, didn't I?"

"That's what you told me."

"All right. When is your next school break?"

"In March. Why?"

"I want you to come to Atlanta. See where I live, and meet my folks."

My flirtation deserted me. "What?"

"You're going to love them, Quilla. They're the best. I've been telling them all about you and they can't wait to meet you."

What could I say? Heart hammering with fear and trembling, I managed a small "OK."

I heard his whispered cry of happiness through the line. "Yes!" Out loud he said, "I love you, woman of my heart. God knows why He picked a woman so far from home for me, but I do love you. Hold on to that when you question the rightness of our being together."

Words of reciprocity rushed to my mouth, but I swallowed them. "OK. I will."

When we prayed together, Edward prayed also for Clare and all the women I'd interviewed. Then before we said our goodbyes, he said, "Quill, have you ever considered that this project of yours is beyond the marriage question? People have chosen to tell you some pretty personal and painful stuff. Stuff that they've kept inside for a long time. Think what you're going to do about it. I'll be praying for God to show you His will as well."

My stress barometer rose, but he was just verbalizing something I'd known for a while. This ministry in the making—because that's what I think it is—what does God want me do with it? I have no idea.

Chapter 20

Happy New Year! Whew! What a busy Christmas season! Since Christmas Eve I've hardly had a moment to myself. However, today, being January 1, I am making a few resolutions. I don't normally do resolutions, but this year I'm determined.

I will spend at least 30 minutes of each day nurturing myself spiritually.

I will bring my "Why am I not married by now?" project to a close no later than April 30.

I will continue to be there for Susan.

Despite my fears, I will give this relationship with Edward a fighting chance.

That's it. I should probably include such things as exercising more frequently and giving up chocolate, but who am I kidding?

I've been back in the city since last week, but between one event and another it's been crazy. Just to get you caught up, my Christmas Eve party turned out very nice. I didn't hear from Martha, but to my surprise Justina and her son showed up. Jason, bless his heart, took the boy under his wing, and he had the time of his life. Natasha, Wendell, and Gloria performed a lovely rendition of "We Three Kings," and the food was to die for.

And Christopher! He's as handsome as anything. The two years away from home has really matured him. He carries himself with such a lazy confidence it has to be something in the European air. I saw him talking to Danesha for quite a while—I'm not saying anything's brewing, just writing down what I saw.

Mom and Dad are doing fine. Their celebration was just as much fun, but in a different, more understated way. And I went to Susan's parents' for brunch the Sunday after Christmas. The atmosphere was strained, everyone trying too hard to pretend that everything was all right. For the first time since she became pregnant, even Susan looked tired. There was no denying her growing belly, which she made no pretense at hiding. In fact, her bright-colored fitted top left no one wondering "Is she, or isn't she?"

She's a bit of a rebel, my friend Susan. Why would she come home and be so brazen with her belly? Her parents are one of the most conservative couples I've ever met, and Susan knows how uncomfortable she's making them. But like a child who continues to push at the edges of her boundaries, it's almost an act of open defiance—daring them to still love her no matter what.

What is it about the human psyche that makes some people able to surmount the circumstances of their birth, parentage, and environment and emerge as fairly whole persons, while others can't quite swing it? Let me take that back—at least partially. Some people *look* as if they've surmounted their circumstances, but my interviews have demonstrated that nothing is as it appears. No one is as they seem. All of us carry stuff left over from our past, or we're blown away by fears of the future. It's just that some of us are better at living with our stuff and striving anyway than others.

On a parallel note I think things are going to start brewing at church where Susan is concerned. I felt eyes boring into our backs as we walked into church this morning. Susan is showing, and the saints are curious.

For the record, the church we attend could be described as somewhat liberal. Clare's a member, and a few other edgy types are too. Most people know stuff goes on in the lives of the laity that flies in the face of our standards, but most church members at least make some attempt to cover up their dirty laundry.

However, a pregnant unmarried woman still gets the looks. How could she not? If nothing else, people would be curious. Of course, her "sin" is very obvious. And our Susan, since she fully believes herself free of blame in this matter, holds her head high and walks proud, rubbing the itchiness from her stretching belly as often as needed. Any day now someone will phone me to get my opinion. It never seems to enter their heads to phone Susan directly.

Then last week, before Gloria left my party, she said she wanted to talk with me. That was her second meeting with some of the women I've interviewed, and already her brain is working. I can tell. With Christopher gone I can expect to hear from her soon.

I picked up the phone and punched in Edward's number. Placing the phone to my ear, I heard a woman's voice.

"Quilla?"

I looked at the phone, wondering who I'd called by mistake.

"Hello?"

"Quilla, it's Gloria. I didn't hear your phone ring."

"But I just dialed Edward's number. How come you're there?"

"I'm not there, silly. I'm here, at my house. How could I be in Atlanta when you just saw me at church a few hours ago?"

Forcing my heart to calm down, I pieced together what must have happened. Gloria's and my call must have overlapped, ergo the missed connection. But you know where my mind went, don't you? I thought Edward had a woman at his house. I was ready to assume the worst. Imagine! Within those few seconds I had judged him guilty of two-timing me. Even if a woman was there, it could have been his mother, his sister, or a friend. What does that say about me?

"Quilla, have you been struck dumb?"

I collected myself. "No, Gloria. Just a bit disorientated. I'm OK now."

"Listen, Quill, we need to talk."

She is so predictable. I thought of her, and here she is on the phone.

"What ideas do you have for me?"

"Ideas? I'm hoping you'll help *me*. People are beginning to talk."

"About me? What about this project can people be gossiping about?"

"Quilla, stay with me, please. I'm not talking about your project. I'm talking about Susan. People are starting to gossip."

Didn't I call this one? Even in the most liberal of circles, an unwed mother will still raise at least one set of eyebrows. "What is there to do, Gloria? Susan is pregnant. People assume she's gotten this baby by the usual method. How are they supposed to know this situation is different?"

"Now I'm lost. What *are* you talking about?"

Yikes! Gloria doesn't know. I thought for sure Susan had told them. I could have sworn that they'd called the night she told me, and she had told them then. How am I going to dig myself out of this hole?

I racked my brain in search of a way to retract my last statement, to not betray the confidence of my best friend. Come to think of it, I'm sure Susan told Edward. So how come Gloria doesn't know?

"Quilla?"

Gloria sounded like she meant business.

"Yes." My tone is indifferent, I'm sure.

"Susan didn't do that thing she's been talking about, did she?"

Maybe I could try stalling. "What thing, Glo?" *Dear Father, help me not to lie and not to betray Susan.*

"The sperm bank thing she went on and on about last time. Tell me she didn't."

Caught! I am so fried!

Dear God, give me words.

"I'm not at liberty to say one way or the other. You'll have to ask Susan."

"Then I'm right! Silly, silly, child! What could she have been thinking? Doesn't she know how difficult it is to be a single parent? How is she planning to raise this child alone? No, don't tell me. She's roped you in, hasn't she? You're going to be the partner."

"Gloria," I implored, "please talk to Susan. I can't tell you what you want to know."

Gloria backed down—a little. "OK, I'll talk to her. But humor me for a minute."

Here it comes. The fictitious situation and what my opinion is.

"Let's say someone you know, a fellow Christian, became pregnant this way—through a sperm donor. Do you think it's wrong?"

"Gloria, if you'd asked me that question four or five months ago I would've said yes, it's wrong. But now I don't know. During these past few months I've listened to all these women who are desperate to be parents. None of them can find a Christian husband, Gloria, and they're not getting any younger. Now, I was never big on kids to begin with. It would have been nice to have one, but I'm not bent out of shape because it's not going to happen. For other women, however, being a mother is a crying need. But here's the catch. They want to be obedient to God and not have sex outside of marriage, and they don't want to have sex just to get a kid. Is it my job to tell them that this option—that they see as not breaking any of the rules—is out of the question?"

"But—"

"Listen to me, Glo. Think of how much you love Christopher. What if you hadn't met Wendell and together had a son? I know you wanted more children and couldn't. Think about how you feel even now, missing the ones you never had. Then think about these women who are getting old with no Wendell in sight. Can you, in all honesty, say that if you were in their shoes you would not even once entertain the thought of pursuing this option?"

I surprised myself. Given my earlier unvoiced arguments to Susan, who would have thought that I'd be here defending this very issue?

Gloria heaved a sigh of frustration. "Your questions are good ones, and when I think of things from the mother's perspective I find myself in total sympathy. But when I think about the child! Oh, Quill, even though I know Wendell loves me and I have a son who adores me, there are still days I wonder who I came from—where my parents are. I can live without knowing, but the wonder is there, every so often tripping up my complacency. I had loving adoptive parents. They secured my world, and I am forever grateful to them. But as I said, the wondering still lives in me to this day.

"So what about the children, Quilla? When these boys and girls ask about their daddies, what will we tell them? That they came out of a petri dish and were bought for a price? Look ahead 20 or 30 years. What kind of people will these children become? Will they be a different kind of 'damaged' child that requires a whole new specialization of psychotherapy to make them whole persons? The issue isn't just about the mothers and what they need, Quill. Somebody has to think about the impact and how we as a church and a society will support these kids."

"You won't get any arguments from me. But once the deed is done, just as if a daughter comes home and tells you she's pregnant 'the old-fashioned way,' the path I must take as a Christian, despite all my arguments and feelings about the 'rightness or wrongness' of the situation, is to love the mother and the soon-coming child."

"Rubber-meets-the-road religion, eh?"

"Something like that."

"Good thing this discussion is about a hypothetical situation, isn't it?"

"Call Susan, Gloria. I'm not saying anything more on the subject."

"Fair enough. I will."

And she will. I have no doubt.

I was more than ready to talk to Edward, so I told her goodbye.

"Not so fast, young lady!"

I stifled a groan.

"Just now, as you were talking, you reminded me about an idea I had for your unmarried women's group."

"What women's group?"

"Those women you've been interviewing! You need to do something about it. Have you thought about forming a single women's support group? Lynn can't say enough about how you've been there for her. Women trust you, Quill. You have a way of getting to the heart of things with them. I don't know how you do it or what you do, but Wendell says you have a listening presence. Whatever it is, I think this is your purpose, your calling."

"I don't know, Glo. I'm the least like a 'support group leader' type. I'm not—"

"Shut up and listen. I'm not kidding about this. You are kind, understanding, loyal, trustworthy, patient (most of the time), tolerant, compassionate, approachable, and all those other nice people qualities. You're a natural, so think about it. Something to focus on in this new year."

"OK . . . I'll think about it."

"Now go call my nephew before he starts wondering if you still love him."

"Gloria!"

"Oops! Did I say that out loud? 'Bye!"

She hung up before I could give her a good tongue-lashing. That woman! Good thing I love her dearly.

After talking to Edward, I went to the kitchen in search of a snack. I would not eat any chocolate. That's just the wrong thing to do on New Year's Day, even if the day is almost over.

Wait a minute. Now that I think of it, I didn't see Clare in church today. I must call her before too much time goes by and I lose my courage. I'm not afraid of her, but I don't want to have to deal with her unpredictable aggression. It puts my back up.

Searching through the fridge for something to whet my palate, I spy a container of mango juice way behind the milk and water containers. That's right. Mara had brought it by on Christmas Eve.

Thus inspired, I decided to make myself Mara's tropical nectar with ginger ale. I had no ginger beer. I sipped at the cool concoction. H'mm! Not half bad. The ginger beer would have given it a bit more of a kick, but it wasn't bad at all. As I turned to go back upstairs, the doorbell rang. I looked at my watch: 8:42. Probably one or all of the three musketeers. They'd told me they might drop by, but I'd had my doubts, and it was getting late.

I opened the door. It was Lynn.

"Tell me to go away if you have plans for the evening. I dropped by on the off chance you might be home. Actually I was taking a drive, trying to clear my head, but the car headed in this direction. Can you talk?"

Of course I invited her inside. *Brr!* It was spicy outside. "Come in! I have no plans for the evening. After the hectic last few days I'm taking a reprieve, and you can clear your head in my presence any time you want to."

Lynn removed her shoes and I took her coat. "What's that you're drinking?"

"A Caribbean dream catcher. Mara introduced me to it, and at the first sip I saw the man of my dreams walking down the beach toward me with a come-hither smile on his face."

"Can you make me one? I could use one of those. Imaginary or otherwise."

"At your service. One CDC coming right up!"

Lynn looked at me suspiciously. "What's in that drink, Quill? You sound way too chipper."

"Just having difficulty holding my ginger ale. The bubbles, you know. Goes right to my nose and tickles."

Lynn chuckled, seating herself at the kitchen table while I took out the mango juice and ginger ale.

"So how are things with Katie's dad?" I asked.

"OK, I guess."

I gave her the drink. She took a tentative sip, then a long swallow. "This is actually quite good."

"Are you seeing any dream guys yet?"

"Not unless you count the one who just reentered my life. He's a bit angry with me."

"Because you didn't tell him about Katie?"

"That and maybe because I didn't tell him a lot of things before he left town that last time years ago."

Joining her at the table, I waited for the story to unfold. Even though curiosity urged me to pump her for information, I made myself do the right thing and let her disclose what she felt comfortable with. She was halfway through the Caribbean dream catcher before she rested the tumbler on the table and began to talk.

"I had to cancel my last two appointments when he summoned me for the inevitable meeting. Not because of him, but because I knew I wouldn't be any good to my clients that afternoon. Even though I knew this first meeting was going to be difficult, I wasn't prepared for how nervous I'd be.

"I'd been racking my brains trying to come up with a place for us to meet. Someplace with privacy, but definitely not my house. In the end we met at my office. Gloria kept Katie for me. Needless to say, I didn't mention anything to either one about it.

"I had so psyched myself out that when David actually showed up in person I was able to greet him with a degree of courteous emotional distance. I thought I was doing quite well, but when I extended my hand to shake his, he just stared at it.

" 'Is that what we've come to, then?' he asked in disbelief. 'Even with a child between us?' All my nervousness returned. I didn't know what to say or do with myself. He looked almost the same. He's gotten a little gray at the temples but is still a very handsome man. He never did shake my hand, but he took time to look around my office.

"'So you finally did it.' I knew he was talking about my opening my own business. 'Good for you.'

"Then his eyes fell on the photos of Katie I have on the credenza, and he stepped closer to study them. Quilla, you could have cut the air in that office with a knife. 'Is this her?' he asked. I nodded. He just stared at the pictures, moving from one photo to the next. Then he dropped heavily in the same chair you sat on when you were last there and gave a huge sigh. 'My daughter. I have a kid,' he said as if trying the words on for size. I felt so bad. Not only had I not told him about her, but I didn't even think to send a photo of her with the letter!"

Then Lynn told me how they finally got through that first difficult meeting and made arrangements for David to meet his daughter the next day. That would give Lynn a little time to prepare her.

"So how did Katie react to him?" I asked. "How did she react to the news that she suddenly had a daddy who wanted to meet her?"

"Better than I expected. I told her the truth, Quill. I told her as simply as I could that it was my decision not to tell him about her, that I thought it was the right decision at the time but then realized that it was not fair to her or to him to keep them apart.

"What I hadn't counted on, or even realized, was how much Katie wanted a daddy of her own. So even though she was a bit shy with him at first, he eventually got her to open up. When he asked her if it was OK for him to give her a small hug, she threw her arms around his neck, nearly knocking him over. I knew then I'd done the right thing."

A bittersweet smile lingered on the corner of Lynn's mouth.

"That's good," I said. "The worst is over, and it looks like things augur well for the future—whatever that will be. So what has you roaming the street this Saturday night?"

"He's in a relationship."

"Married?"

"No."

"Living together?"

"I don't think so. But he mentioned that he's seeing someone and wanted to know if I was too."

"That's not unreasonable, of course. That he'd be in a relationship. How long has it been since you've seen him? Five years?"

"More like six."

"Do you think you still have feelings for him?"

"That's the trouble. I will always have feelings for him. For years he was my best friend. Then we became lovers. Now we have a child together. I don't think all that can be erased, but I guess you're asking if I still love him, aren't you?"

"Something like that."

Lynn took another sip. "I told myself that six years is a long time. Too long to expect anything, to hope . . . but it wasn't until he told me that he was seeing someone and I felt such a let-down sensation that I knew I'd been hoping that we could get another try. Stupid, eh?"

"The heart wants what it wants," I said. "Sometimes our mind has to remind the heart that it can't always get what it wants."

Lynn studied the last bit of her drink as if trying to read her future. "He's just as handsome. He's just as kind and just as nice as I remember him. Katie can't stop talking about him. It's been little more than a week since she saw him, but all I hear is when can she see him again? He calls her every night at 8:00 to ask about her day and to say good night. Thursday night when he called I told him we were reading the *Junie B.* books together. When he called the next night, he told me that he'd bought the whole set and wanted to know if he could join us for our nightly readings. How sweet is that?"

The tears were there, in her voice and behind her words, but none spilled. I wish I could assure her that David would come to his senses, realize that she was the woman for him, and come back to her. I wish life worked like that. In the movies it does, the sappy movies in which I can take leave of life and live for a couple hours in dreamland. But in real life the guy moves on, and the girl is left with the kid and a heart full of unrequited, unexpressed love.

"Can you pray with me again, Quilla, the way you did that first time we talked? And tell me I did the right thing. After all, my daughter is happy. That's what a mother is supposed to do, right? Put the needs of her child above her own?"

Taking the glass, liquid now warmed, from her hands, I grasped her fingers and prayed for God's sustaining power to be with her and with Katie and with Katie's dad. I asked God to prop Lynn up, guide her, and comfort her as only He can do. Then I asked God to reveal Himself to her, to show her His glory, not just through me, but that she can experience it for herself.

That's how my New Year's Day ended. Not even Edward's call later that night cheered me. For how could I be happy that I had a man, even a younger one at that, when so many of my sisters were grieving with loneliness?

Chapter 21

How many more of these interviews should I do? Since the year started I've had five more, and the stories are as different as the women who tell them. Those whom I've talked about in these pages continue to call me, to touch base. I feel as though I've grown an extended family, and somehow I've been appointed big sister, counselor, advisor, and confidant.

With each story there's been an opportunity to either introduce Jesus as the greatest comforter or to interject a word, pointing my sisters to a power bigger than their situations. Sometimes I've taken advantage of the opportunity, and at other times I haven't. I've learned that Jesus need not be sold or promoted in every conversation, because He has many different ways of speaking to people—friendship, a listening ear, a pot of soup, and a kind word are some of the other ways. I try to use the one that feels right at the time.

I need to wrap up things, though, or at least change focus. Already it's late February, and Edward has begun his countdown to my March visit. Thinking about it makes me nervous. How does an older woman meet the parents of the younger guy who considers her the woman of his heart? How will they deal with the fact that this older woman will not be bearing their son any children and that they will not be grandparents through his particular bloodline? How . . .

Let me give you an update on Susan. Don't say anything! Just work with me here. I know I just abruptly changed subjects, but I have to. OK?

Susan is in her twenty-third week of pregnancy and glowing. Even with her growing belly men still try to pick her up. She's taken to wearing a wedding band on her ring finger—she says to cut down on the approaches. I think it's also her way of pretending she's "legal." In three weeks we start her birthing classes, and I've already met her midwife. Susan wants her parents to be in on the birthing process too. That's good. She plans to work right up to the date of her delivery. Lucky her! Had I been in her situation I'd probably be confined to bed with some strange ailment that affects only one in one million pregnant women.

I'm not sure how I feel about being part of this birthing process. It's not as if I've never seen a birth. After all, I'm a nurse, and I spent three years of my career on the maternity ward. But to watch a friend giving birth, to see a child come into the world that you have been anticipating since her mother told you about her conception—that's got to be different. Something Edward will never experience if he wants me in his life.

I know. I know. I'm back here again with my new harangue. What if his mother hates me? What if his siblings completely dismiss me when I visit? And his dad. I've seen pictures of him. He looks kind, but what's behind the kind eyes?

*"Trust in the Lord with all your heart and lean not on your own understanding; in all your ways submit to him, and he will make your paths straight."** Lord, help me to trust and not doubt. Most likely things will be nothing close to what I'm imagining. Calm my heart, Holy Spirit, and take away the fear and anxiety.*

I speak my prayer out loud even as I write it, and once again the fear retreats but does not go away. I must think of something else.

Some time ago I started looking at my questions—the original list I jotted down at the outset of this project. Remember? I recall answering three or four of the 10 questions. Hang on. Let me check the list again. Here it is.

1. Was there something or a set of somethings I *did* to end up still single?
2. Was there something or a set of somethings I *didn't* do to end up single?
3. Is there something I *can* do about my single state, and if so, how badly do I want to get married?
4. Can I live with being a never-married woman?
5. Where does God fit into my current unwed state, and if my being married would have been good for me, wouldn't He have sent someone my way by now?
6. How do I deal with the pain of loneliness and lack of sexual fulfillment?
7. Is there a defect in me that turns men off?
8. Are my expectations about the qualities I want in a husband too high, not grounded in reality? And if so, how do I know that for sure?
9. What am I prepared to do about my single status?
10. Am I marriage material?

I dealt with questions 1, 2, and 7. Let me back up and look at question 3: What am I prepared to do about my single state (in other words, how badly do I want to get married)?

Don't even say what you're thinking. I know. I have a man who loves me. The age factor gives me a good reason for putting up roadblocks, and even though I say I'm giving the relationship a try—and I am, really I am—I'm just so afraid that I won't be good enough for him. How am I going to be able to love this man when I have difficulty loving me?

Maybe it's number 10 that I should be dealing with. Maybe I'm just not marriage material. If that's the case, then the rest of the questions become irrelevant. It's obvious I'm not prepared to do anything about my single status. All these years I blamed the world, blamed Susan's beauty, blamed the church, blamed society, but it's been me all along. Me not wanting to take a risk. Me who doesn't have the chutzpah to fling myself into the maelstrom of life and trust the tide and God to carry me to a destination I did not prebook.

And because of that fear I condemn myself to loneliness, lack of companionship, and lack of sexual fulfillment. Obviously I'm not prepared to do anything—anything too risky, that is—about my single status.

You think I'm nuts, don't you? How many times have I been down this road? Every time I go there God brings me back, assures me how much He loves me, and asks me to trust Him. Yet here I am again. Edward loves me. I don't know why, but he does. Do I love him enough to risk my half-a-loaf life for whole loaf with him—no guarantees?

On Valentine's Day I got the shock of my life. The man flew to Toronto for the *day* just to have lunch with me. With me! It must have cost him a fortune. How he found me at the particular school where I was working, I'll never be quite sure. But Susan looked a little too smug when she dropped by that night to find out how my day went.

He had the restaurant booked, bribed my colleague with expensive chocolate to cover for me since I'd be gone an extra hour, then spent the next two hours reminding me how much I mean to him and watching me hyperventilate my way through the ricocheting effects of his surprise. When he dropped me back to work he didn't even kiss me goodbye. He just grazed my cheek with his thumb and left me speechless in the parking lot, holding a bunch of blood-red roses in my arms.

Later when I removed the cellophane wrapping so I could put the flowers in water, I found his card. It read, "Red roses, for the passion you inspire in me and the hope of one day experiencing fully." Imagine! Me! A forty-something not-so-young chicken inspiring words like that! The man must be crazy. What happens when the scales fall from his eyes and he sees the real me?

That's it. I'm done writing for the evening. When Edward calls later, none of this self-doubt must be present. I don't think he has the patience for it. But . . .

Never mind. I've said enough.

Martha finally called me. *Thank You, Jesus!* I didn't actually talk to her, but she left a message on my phone telling me she'd been thinking of me and wanted to see how I was doing. Who cares about how I am? I want to know how she's doing. Needless to say, I called her back right away and guess what? She agreed to join me for lunch on Saturday. I'll pick her up after her church service is over. I don't know why, but I'm so excited she's coming.

I know what I'll do! I'll invite Natasha to lunch as well. Susan, as you know, is a Saturday lunch staple, so it will be us four—two older and two "getting older" women.

While I'm at it, I better figure out what I'm going to pack for my visit to Atlanta. I'm not going to ask Susan's opinion on my wardrobe, because the last time she picked out an outfit for me. . . .

I guess I never did get around to telling you what happened on that Sunday night date with Edward, did I? The night I decided in my heart, even though I didn't say it out loud, that I would give this relationship a fighting chance. How could I not after what happened! I have never in my life been the recipient of such an unfettered demonstration of being treasured. I should have known he'd be the kind of guy to do what he did. But I'm a hard learner.

When I opened the door that Sunday and let him in, his jaw literally dropped. I kid you not! He stood there staring at me.

"Wow! Quilla, woman of my heart, you look absolutely . . . wow!"

And I did look "wow!" Susan had returned that afternoon and made sure I was "drop-dead gorgeous"—to borrow a phrase from Clare. I felt like a million bucks and had decided that at last I was going to let myself experience love.

Reveling in the heady power of my discovered femininity, I did a slow pirouette for Edward. "You like?" I asked flirtatiously.

Imagine me, flirting with a guy!

As for him, he looked so handsome in his fancy black suit, tailored to show off his broad shoulders and his lean form. (This man needs to get into the habit of wearing a coat designed for Canadian weather!) Anyway, mesmerized myself, I felt like Cinderella heading out to the ball. The chemistry came back, but it was the teasing kind, not the kind that blindsides you. Tingles of awareness danced up and down my skin and I let myself, my controling self, my fearful self, take a holiday.

I had my coat draped over a chair in the foyer, and when I reached for it Edward took it from my hands and opened it. I slipped my arms into the sleeves, and then he turned me around to face him and proceeded to button up my coat from bottom to top. When he'd secured the last button he blessed me with a slow, lazy smile that communicated all kinds of things, then he tapped me on the tip of my nose.

"Come along," he whispered, tucking my arm in the crook of his. "Let's get this evening started."

We went to a lovely Italian restaurant downtown, close to the Skydome. From the time we were shown to our seats the ambience revved up. A musician playing the violin and who obviously had an eye for romance soon came to our table, and not only did he play us a beautiful tune, but when he finished, in true Italian style he broke into song. I have no clue what the words said, but I could tell from the expressiveness of his singing that the woman he loved did not love him back, but he would continue to woo her because he loved her so much.

All the while he sang, Edward held on to my hands and looked at me with the same wistful longing that the singer sang about. When the song ended and the musician had bowed his goodbye, Edward took a piece of the warm bread that had been delivered to our table, dipped a corner of it into the olive oil, and offered me a bite. I bit down daintily, and then he took the same bread and had a piece for himself, still holding my hand and treasuring me with his eyes.

How does a guy treasure a woman with his eyes? I don't know if I'm actually naming it right, but that's how I felt. Treasured. That whole evening. I can hardly remember the food. I know I ate, of course. I recall being really hungry, too, but my overall feeling was of being treasured. When I got up to go to the washroom, Edward stood. When I returned, he stood again and waited until I was seated. Before he took a drink, he offered me one. Before he served himself, he served me, and before he took a bite, he saw to it that I was eating.

Have you ever had something like that happen to you?

I never had.

Later, when the meal had been cleared away, the musician returned, this time playing a beautiful love song. I knew the melody but not the words. To my surprise, Edward got up from the table and held out his hand to me.

"Come, woman of my heart."

My panicked look must have communicated itself to him, but still he held out his hand, telling me with his eyes that it was OK. Tentatively, gingerly, attracting the attention of the other diners by then, I eased out of my seat. Edward drew me close enough to him so that he could watch my face and then guided me gracefully within the small square space next to our table. I gave over to the joy bubbling in my heart and let my fears go. The musician, probably seeing magic in the making, cocooned us with his song in a blanket of rapture.

When the song ended, Edward gave me that same slow, lazy smile again, the one that said so much. I felt my walls of common sense crumbling. Why would I not give this a try? I had no more reason left.

That God-blessed man, probably knowing by now how much I wanted him to kiss me, kept his word. I knew he struggled. I'd see his eyes close at times, and I guess he was praying, but when the eyes would land on me, these windows to his soul could not fully mask his desire.

We left the restaurant amid the indulgent smiles of those who remembered this kind of loving magic, our "personal" musician trailing behind us, underscoring our heart's longing with his instrument. Snow had started to fall, that thick, sticky kind. Looking down at my sandaled feet, Edward left me in care of the musician to go get the car. He, taking his job seriously, continued to serenade me until Edward returned. When Edward offered him a tip, he brushed it away.

"No tips for love," he said in his rich Italian accent. "For bella, for her beautiful eyes."

Seated in the car with the engine running, Edward did not immediately drive off. Instead, he turned to me, and this is what he said.

"You ever wonder about heaven, Quilla, and about God? As I walked to get the car all I could do was praise God for His wondrous works. A man meets a woman and somehow God created within us the possibility for this chemistry to happen, this effervescent joy. I felt like shouting to the buildings that I was indeed the happiest man on the face of the earth.

What has God done? While I knew that I loved and admired the woman that you are, I didn't anticipate this magic. I have no other word for it. That God created this too makes me wonder about Him. I never equated God with joy, but I do now."

So he felt it too. That made me glad. I was not risking without reason. We drove by the waterfront and parked. There we talked and talked, intermittently running the engine to ward off the cold. At one point Edward abruptly stopped talking.

"I take it back," he said.

"Take what back?"

His head tipped back against the driver seat headrest, and he looked off into the night. "The untested person sometimes speaks in ignorance and condemns when he has never gone through a real situation. I take back what I said to Susan that August day at your house. I can understand now how couples run into matrimony without taking time to really know each other. Right now I feel like doing the same with you."

I nodded in understanding.

"I love you, you know," he said, turning to me. "I'll keep telling you until you believe it. I will wait till you and God give me the complete all clear, but I want you to have no doubt or wonderment. Edward Anderson Grainge loves you."

My eyes are tearing now, just remembering. I have mentally gone over every moment of that evening time and time again. I have and analyzed and savored. Those few hours were the closest to paradise this girl has ever been in her life.

---

* Prov. 3:5, 6, NIV.

Chapter 22

Natasha and Martha, extroverted artist and introverted analyst, kicked me and Susan out of the kitchen after our Saturday lunch and insisted on cleaning up. My job was to go take care of Susan, who was experiencing swollen ankles. So that's what I did. I made Susan and her tummy sit down, and I propped her feet up with cushions.

The chickpea salad she'd made for lunch did not seem a favorite of the baby, so I gave Susan a couple of Tums for her heartburn. As the music played softly she fell asleep. I could hear Martha and Nat in the kitchen talking as they washed and dried the dishes. Pretty soon I found myself drifting off to sleep too.

I woke up about 30 minutes later to a quiet house. A note on the kitchen counter informed me that "M & N have gone for a short walk and will be right back," and that Edward had called. How did I miss the ringing phone?

Feeling the need for something sweet (since we hadn't gotten around to dessert), I peeked into the oven and found the apple pie was still there, warming. I took it to the dining table along with a carton of French vanilla ice cream and four plates.

Susan woke up when the others opened the front door. I brought in a kettle of boiling water and a variety of tea bags, and soon we were all enjoying our second repast.

"Guess what?" Natasha asked.

Without giving us a moment to answer, she announced, "I'm going to church with Martha next week. She and I have decided that we're already good friends, so I'm going to go see this church of hers. Maybe we'll find two old widow preachers to marry."

"Don't hold your breath," Martha deadpanned. "We'll hope for the start of a beautiful friendship instead."

"Here! Here!" toasted Natasha.

We all drank to that.

Martha shyly asked Susan. "When is your little one due? I bet you can't wait for the great expectation to happen."

"June. But 'the great expectation' is starting to take up too much space in my body. It's getting really uncomfortable to sleep."

"A June baby. That's good. I think summer is the best time to give birth," Nat said. "I'd hate to have to stay indoors in winter with a baby."

"I don't think anything's wrong with having the baby exposed to a bit of winter air," Martha countered. "You just need to bundle up. I love taking walks in the winter. It's so peaceful."

Throughout the conversation my mind drifted back to my ever-present anxiety about going to Atlanta. I wish I'd not promised Edward that I'd come.

"What's the matter, Quilla?" It was the perceptive Martha. "You OK?"

"Probably just stressing over the fact that she's going to Atlanta to meet the parents of her beau," Susan said with that mischievous look she has.

"Tell us about him," Martha urged in her quiet manner.

"Who? Edward?"

"Is that the name of your young man?" she asked.

"Yup!" replied Susan, all mischief now. "That's her 'young man,' all right!"

"Is he kind? Does he love you, love the Lord? Is he handsome?"

"All of the above," Susan spoke for me. "He calls Quilla 'woman of his heart.'"

"Susan! I think I can speak for myself."

"Then do so, my friend. Tell the good ladies here what has you so tied up in knots. No, I'll tell them. Quilla doesn't think she's good enough for someone to love. This really sweet guy loves her. He really and truly does. But he's nine years younger, and Quilla, so far, has not been able to convince him that he's way too young for her. Personally, I don't see a problem. He is an adult male capable of knowing his own mind and what he wants in a woman, and our Quilla here is his choice. She, however, cannot handle it along with the thought of meeting his parents."

"Keep this up, Susan, and you'll be birthing this child all by yourself," I warned darkly.

"You love him?" Natasha asked.

"Nine years is a lot of years, Nat. I'll never be able to give him children."

How many times do I need to say that? I know Edward loves me, but there is still that nine years between us.

"Do you love this Edward?" Natasha's accent became more pronounced.

224 The Waiting Heart

"When you look into your heart, does it respond for this man? Does it tell you that this is the real thing?"

Three pairs of eyes looked at me, each registering keen interest in my answer. I felt cornered. Did I love Edward? If I told these women that I did, it would mean that I had to follow through and tell him, too. But how could I be sure? I love talking to him. I love the fact that he loves me and frequently tells me so. But every time I think of saying those words back to him I pull back. Saying them will change my life.

"How about I tell you if I love him *after* I return from this visit, assuming I survive it?"

"Chicken!" Susan whispered loud enough for all to hear.

I made a face at her and got up from the table, effectively putting an end to that part of the conversation.

"Quilla, come back here." It was Natasha.

"I don't want to talk about Edward, Nat."

"Fine. You don't want to talk about him, we won't. I do want to talk about an idea I have for your unmarried women."

I edged back to the table. "That I have no problem talking about. What do you have in mind?"

"I think you need to have a memorial service to wrap up your interview project. Martha and I were comparing notes about you, how we met, and how we've shared things with you that we don't normally talk about to people we don't know well and even some of the ones we do. We both think that you have a way about you that is just your way—a kind heart that accepts people for who they are. So since all these women you've interviewed are concerned that their dreams for husband or child might never or won't ever happen, I think you should bring everybody together and share your findings."

"OK," I said hesitantly, "but where does the memorial service come in?"

"It would give people some kind of finish, a closure, you know—a way of acknowledging that their dream has died," Martha explained. "Dead dreams deserve to be mourned. A service would help people move on . . . I think."

"What a crazy idea!" declared Susan. "Now, why didn't I think of it myself?"

"Are you serious about this?" I asked. "You don't think that's bordering on the macabre?"

"What's this 'macabre'?" asked Natasha

"It means ghoulish, gruesome, morbid," Susan, the encyclopedia, supplied.

"No, I don't think it is what you say," replied Natasha seriously. "I think it is necessary."

Susan nodded. "I agree."

"Me too," added the quiet Martha.

I tried to wrap my mind around the logistics. "So . . . how would this work? Would people talk about their dream in the way we pay tribute to someone who has died, and what the loss means to them?"

Martha spoke up. "I don't think everyone would feel comfortable discussing their cherished dream in the presence of strangers. I know I wouldn't. But you are the glue that will have brought everyone together, Quilla, so you will probably have to take a more active role. In your speech you should touch upon some of the issues people have discussed with you—without revealing names, of course."

"But," said Susan, thinking hard, "you could provide paper for people to write their dreams on, or to record the loss, and then we could have a cremation."

"That's maudlin!" I cried. "That's awful."

"Work with us here, Quill," said Susan. "All of this is symbolic. And burning the paper with the dream will be like letting go of the pain and the mental baggage. It's a symbolic purification. The end of something, and the beginning of something else. I know what I'd write. And maybe it's time for me to let that go, with the baby coming and all."

"It will work, Quilla," Natasha urged. "Remember how I told you I burned the picture of the man I should have married but foolishly didn't? Doing just that helped me move on. We don't always get what we want from life, but when we want it so badly that we spend our lives trying to get this thing, thinking it will be ours, and it doesn't happen, it's like—like someone died. We need to mourn for these losses. I am sure there are psychologists who write books about this, and think it's good idea."

"Who am I, then, to argue with the wisdom of my three friends and their psychological compatriots?" I said.

"So you will do it, yes?" Natasha asked.

"I'll think it through. When I come back from Atlanta, if I survive in one piece, I'll try to put some more clothes on this idea of yours. It still looks pretty naked to me."

Susan uttered a long-suffering sigh. "She makes statements like these all the time. Just get used to it, ladies. I have."

⁂

Dear Father in heaven, help me not to embarrass myself or You during this visit.

I repeated the prayer I've been praying since I left Toronto. The Air Canada Jazz flight now circled over Atlanta. Looking out the window, I noted the absence of snow and what looked like clay soil spotting the ground between the trees. I repeated my favorite text, the one that had helped me weather so many storms past: "Thou wilt keep him in perfect peace, whose mind is stayed on thee: because he trusteth in thee."[1] I know it's old-school King James, but that's the Bible version Dru Hazelwood taught me from.

Peace, Father. Keep me in perfect peace.

Touchdown!

My heart did another flip-flop.

Why, oh, why hadn't I done the smart thing and booked a couple nights for myself at a nearby hotel? But no, Edward has me staying with his mom and dad, and now I am stuck.

Please, Father in heaven. Help me not to embarrass myself.

Like a lamb to the slaughter I hauled my one piece of luggage up the ramp and through long corridors, following the crowd of fellow passengers who seemed to know where they were headed. At last we went down to the tunnel where I boarded a train—as Edward had instructed—and counted the stops till it got to the terminal and baggage claim area.

My heart started to do the funny flip-flop thing, but this time I didn't know if it was the excitement of seeing Edward or trepidation at meeting his parents. Five days at their house! How will I bear it? They're going to hate me.

"Breathe, Quilla," I reminded myself. "Breathe."

My lips felt dry. I should have gone to the restroom to freshen up. Foolish, foolish woman. I probably look a sight. Why hadn't I found a restroom and gone in to freshen up?

"Peace I leave with you, My peace I give to you; not as the world gives do I give to you. Let not your heart be troubled, neither let it be afraid."[2] Trust in Me, My child. All will be well.

Oh, dear God, why am I such a wreck?

Don't worry about that. Trust in Me and lean not on your own understanding. I've got you, Quilla. Now, breathe and put on a smile for the man who calls you "woman of my heart."

I felt a measure of peace then, truly a gift from God.

Thank You, Father. I really appreciate that.

And before the panic could return, there he was, his long arms outstretched, and I was running to that blessed homecoming, face all smiles and heart glad. Dropping my luggage, I held on to Edward for dear life and loving the sound of his heartbeat against my cheek.

There on that Friday afternoon, in the middle of one of America's busiest airports, we became an island, forcing the crowd to shift and separate around what must look like two lovers who were finally reunited. The beep of an airport trolley brought us back to the here and now, but even then Edward did not let me go.

"I missed you, too, woman of my heart. I missed you too." He kissed my forehead and picked up my suitcase. "Let's go home."

So maybe I overdid the panic thing a wee bit. What's a girl supposed to do when she has to meet the parents of the man who loves her! True to Edward's word, his folks were rare gems. Especially his dad. His mom was a bit reserved, but she was very nice and went out of her way to welcome home in style "the very first woman Edward has brought home to meet the family." Her voice had a slight Southern drawl, which I loved instantly.

Edward was commissioned to show me to my room. The lovely rambling old house with an actual veranda that overlooked a large yard welcomed me too. The room, which I understand used to be his sister's, had a double bed covered with a beautiful quilt of blue, green, white, and purple.

"I'll leave you to unpack, then I can take you on the grand tour. Can you find your way back downstairs?"

I nodded.

"Are you OK, Quill? You're a little quiet."

I smiled at him, reassuring him that I was indeed OK. But I did feel like crying, and I didn't know why. Relief from anxiety, I guess.

He looked at me long, and I held his gaze. "See you in a few minutes, then."

I shook out the dress I'd brought for church and hung it in the closet, then quickly packed away my other clothes and toiletries. Then before going downstairs, I checked to make sure my face and the rest of me were presentable.

"Mr. and Mrs. Grainge, I am in envy of your beautiful home," I told them following the 'grand tour.' You have added so many nice touches to make it worth taking a second and third look. And your garden! You already have flowers blooming. Back in Toronto even our tulips are afraid of showing their heads. It's been a cold March."

"Thank you, Quilla," Mrs. Grainge said. "Claude and I put in a lot of hours on the house and yard, but we knew from the day we bought it what we wanted to do with it." With a smile toward her husband, she changed the subject. "I'm not sure how much Ed has told you, but we don't stand on a lot of ceremony here. However, on Friday nights we set the table in style. We light candles and dress for dinner. It's our way of welcoming the Sabbath. You OK with that?"

Thankful that I'd added an extra dress just in case, I said, "I think that's a really nice tradition. What time is dinner?"

"Sunset's in about an hour and a quarter. Ed, why don't you take your young lady out for a drive? Show her the neighborhood. Just get back in time for dinner. You know I hate to have to keep a meal warming past its eating time."

"Yes ma'am, your majesty. As you will."

"Now don't get cheeky with me, young man, just because Quilla's here. Go on you two. Have a good time."

We ended up driving to Edward's house about a half hour away. I wanted to see where he lived so I could picture where he calls me from when we correspond by telephone. We didn't stay there long.

Next we drove past the church where we'd be tomorrow. It looked smaller than my home church back in Toronto, but I couldn't wait to meet Edward's friends.

Dinner was simple—a hearty vegetarian stew and freshly baked bread, followed by homemade apple-rhubarb pie and the infamous hot chocolate—a drink his dad loved. We read, sang, and prayed together, then just sat and chatted. That was one of the most relaxing Friday evenings I've spent in a long time. I think that's the way the Sabbath should be welcomed.

After worship Mr. Grainge asked me if I sang. I told him that I did a little, but I surely wasn't a solid soloist. "Well, Evelyn and I are going up to do our own special Sabbath ritual, but get Edward to play something for you. He's not half bad on the piano. It's time to start making your own

Sabbath rituals, you know. Good night, Quilla, and welcome again to our home and into our boy's heart."

I stood up to say good night, thanking them for making me feel so welcome, then watched them climb the stairs. I noticed how much care Claude took with his dear Evelyn.

Curiosity made me whisper to Edward. "What's their Sabbath ritual?"

He sat down at the piano. "That, my dear, is a trusted family secret. If I tell you and you're not family, I'm going to have to kill you. So you might as well decide to marry me if you really want to know."

"OK, then, maybe I should hear you play first. All these factors must be taken into consideration before one makes such a momentous decision, don't you think?"

And that's when he played the most beautiful rendition of "It Is Well With My Soul" that I've ever heard. I mean it was beautiful, on par with Richard Smallwood, who is my standard for gospel music excellence.

"Edward Grainge! What else don't I know about you? That was awesome! You are good, very good. That just took me right to heaven's gate and reminded me that no matter what happens, God is in control. I love the interpretation you gave it. Thank you!"

My effusive praise embarrassed him, but I couldn't help it. It was truly remarkable.

"Play something else," I begged.

He did. I sat there in awe watching this man who says he loves me create this new, to me, magic. After he finished playing the second piece he motioned for me to sit beside him, and we sang together. Now, as I told Mr. Grainge, I'm no soloist, but that night with Edward accompanying me on both piano and vocals, I sounded ready to release my debut album. And to think I was afraid of coming here.

The clock tolled 10:00 just as I stifled a yawn. Edward's eagle eyes saw it, and he walked me up to my room, reminding me again how glad he was that I had come.

"Drive home safely," I cautioned.

"I'm not going home tonight. Actually, for this whole weekend I am as close to you as three doors down this very hallway. I want to spend as much time with you as I can, so get used to it."

"Well, then, have a safe walk to your room. Thanks for . . . thanks for being you. You are a very nice man, Edward Grainge."

Whatever he was going to say he checked himself.

"Good night, Quilla. Dream of me. I plan to do the same."

"'Night, Edward."

He closed my door, and it was a few moments before I heard his steps going down the hall.

The church service next morning was lively and meaningful. It seemed everyone, from the children to the adults, could sing or play an instrument. Riding back to his parents' house with Edward, I learned that while this was the church he grew up in, his membership was at another congregation on the north side of the city. His brother and sister and their families were joining us for lunch. My mind reminded me that I ought to be nervous, but I was in too mellow a mood to worry.

And what a boisterous crowd they were! There was his brother Mark and his wife. Mark is the oldest, and their teenage kids were away at school. Edward's sister, Esther, was expecting her second child, and her 4-year-old daughter, Amanda, plopped herself on my lap, telling me I was going to be her new best friend.

Have you ever been in a room where everyone is talking and then suddenly the room hushes and one voice can be heard saying something typically embarrassing to someone else? Well, that's what happened to me. Little Mandy had been grilling me. Was I really going to be her new auntie? Would I be marrying Uncle Edward? Were we going to have one or two babies?

I managed to adroitly field her questions, and felt a little proud of myself. Next she reminded me she was 4 years old, and asked how old I was. Now, telling my age is something I've never shied away from, so I told her I was 44. Holding up four fingers on each hand, I said, "I'm 44. Four and four."

Into the conversational lull her voice carried clearly to those in our immediate vicinity.

"You have two fours in your age, Miss Quilla. I have one. Mommy," she called, "Miss Quilla has two fours in her age."

You could have heard a pin drop in the room.

Before she could check herself, Mandy's mother, Esther, said, "Oh, so you're a bit older than Edward. There goes getting more grandchildren, Mom." She rubbed her extended belly. "This one is the end of the line."

"You didn't mention that Quilla was older, Edward," accused his mother in her quiet voice.

Whether or not Edward heard her, I do not know. All I recall is that I died. Right there among all those nice people my heart gave out. God bless the innocent sweetheart of a child, but I couldn't play with her anymore.

"What's come over this family!" chided Mr. Grainge. "Have we forgotten our manners?"

All the fears that I had imagined came rushing back. I had to get out of there. I knew it! I knew it! Rejected. They believed all the fears I'd expressed to Edward. A nine-year gap was way too wide, and now, now . . . I had to get out before I made a complete fool of myself.

Blindly I deposited Mandy on the floor, and like one condemned, not knowing where to look but knowing I could not meet their accusing or pitiful eyes, I walked out of the room with as much dignity as I could muster.

Edward, who had been chatting with his brother on the other side of the room, must have caught on that something had happened. He ran after me. "Quilla, wait!"

But I was beyond waiting. Out the front door and down the steps of the veranda I flew, wanting to put as much distance as possible between me and his awful family. He caught up with me at the bottom of the steps, grabbing hold of my arm to slow my momentum.

"Where are you going? What happened? Tell me what happened!"

"Let me go! If you want to know what happened, go back in there and ask. Just leave me alone!"

With a move I'd learned in a self-defense class, I wrenched my arm from his grip. He started to follow, but I took off down the drive and out onto the street. Then I heard his footsteps taking the stairs in leaps, going back to the bosom of his family. Good! They deserve each other!

I could have kicked myself. How could I have allowed this to happen? Why had I let myself be beguiled by this young man? And here was his family throwing my age in my face!

"Stupid! Stupid! That's what you are," I berated myself as I tried to add distance from the house of condemnation. "Stupid and foolish and . . ."

"Oh, dear God . . . help me!"

The tears came. I couldn't stop them. I felt them racing down my face and had not a single tissue to use to dry them. Thankfully, it was a quiet neighborhood, but even had there been a lot of people on the street I was beyond caring. How would I get past this? I must go home. At home I could lick my wounds and kick myself in private. But how would I manage? I was the "woman of his heart," and now? Now I'm just—

What am *I now?*

I didn't know.

I railed at God. It was His entire fault. *"Why did You tell me to come here only to get a broken heart? I tried doing Your will. I listened to Your voice even when I didn't want to be here, but You welcomed me into Your heart just as Edward did. But it's all a lie. I—"*

With the suddenness that accompanies some divine interventions, something or someone turned me around right there in the midst of my godly lament. Just like Balaam's donkey! I don't know how it happened or how to explain it. One minute I couldn't get far enough away from Edward and his mean old family, and the next my feet were propelling me with purpose and determination back to confront them.

How dare they? What kind of Christians were they to treat me like this? Didn't I ask my Father in heaven to direct my steps? Then why should I let them get away with this, and run away like a shamed dog with its tail between its legs? No! My bare feet pounded out my purpose. No way was I going to take this!

The closer I got to the house, the angrier I became, and by the time I reached the veranda I possessed a cold and righteous indignation. Who were they to judge me? Why should my age dictate whom I marry? It's not as if the man in question is a child. How dare they dismiss me like that? Discuss me as if I wasn't even in the room!

Wrenching open the front door, I marched into that living room and laid into them. Edward reached for me, a look of relief on his face, but I pulled back with a glare. *Oooh,* I was peeved! Voice clipped and quietly emphatic, remembering just in time that I too needed to model God in my anger, I said my piece.

"A long time ago I gave my heart to God. However, it's been during these past few years that I'm discovering what discipleship truly means. I've chosen to put my life and plans in God's hands and allow Him to guide me, sometimes in ways I don't want to go but trusting it's for my best. Now! I did *not* ask for this relationship with your son and your brother. I had 50 million reasons we should *not* get involved. But every time I said no, God brought me back, reminding me to trust Him. And let me tell you something: If there was any doubt in my mind before today, there is no doubt now. None at all! I love this man. Do you hear me? I love him. Yes, he's nine years younger than I am, a far cry from the same-age or older man of my dreams. But that's the only thing that's different. He fits all my other criteria to a T. He loves the Lord with all his heart. He loves me as no other man has loved me, and he is, I believe, God's plan for my life."

I came up for a quick breath of air and with it a defined confidence in what I had to say. "Now I came here to meet you because you are important to Edward, but I will not be made to feel inferior or apologetic about my age. I am what I am, and if he will have me, I would be honored to be his wife. I just pray to God that you will get over yourselves and support us. Do we understand each other?"

I continued glaring from one to the other, to ensure my message came through loud and clear. Too bad if they didn't like it. I would take nothing back. The nerve!

Then from the back of the room I heard hands clapping. It was Edward's dad's. Then all the others, including an excited Mandy, joined in.

"She's got spunk, Edward," declared his dad. "You've got to marry her so she's on our side and not an enemy."

Esther rushed to me. "I'm so sorry, Quilla. I didn't mean to hurt your feelings. Mitchell is always telling me that I think too much with my mouth. I didn't mean that you were too old for Edward. What I was trying to say was that I was not having any more children after this, and when Mandy mentioned your age I just assumed that it might not happen with you and . . ."

Her voice petered off as she realized what she was saying. "Oh, Quilla. I am an unthinking fool today, and I offer my sincere apology and beg your forgiveness. I'll do all I can to make it up to you." Her face became bright with inspiration. "I got it! I'll name this baby, if it's a girl, after you. That will serve as a reminder, every time I call her name, of you and how much you mean to my brother."

"And maybe the importance of thinking before talking," added her husband, Mitchell, coming up to put an arm around her.

Esther nodded. "I'm really sorry. Say you'll forgive me, please." She lifted her clasped hands as if in supplication. "I feel so awful about all this."

Evelyn Grainge made her slow way to join her daughter by my side. "I, too, was not dismissing you when I said what I said to Edward. Had he told me you were older, I would have anticipated that you might be sensitive about the subject of age. I'm glad you came back, however, and put us all in our place. And I'm glad, as Claude said, that my boy is marrying a woman who can speak up for herself when she needs to. Welcome to our family. But most important, I'm glad to hear that you love my boy just as much as he loves you. He's done his best to be patient, but waiting for your love has tried him more than you will ever know." Her eyes met mine as a smile lit her face. "God's blessing to you both."

One by one, they all came and hugged me, greeted me, dried my tears, and embraced me into their family. Little Mandy begged to be let in. I picked her up, tears of relief and gratitude and who knows what still running down my cheeks.

"Am I an unstinking fool, too, Quilla? Like Mommy?" Her serious eyes looked at mine in concern.

Thus the little angel who inadvertently started all this became the means to break the tension. I swallowed the urge to laugh as I corrected her. "The word is 'unthinking,' honey, not 'unstinking.' It's means that sometimes we don't think before we act."

She hugged me long and hard. "I'm glad you love Uncle Edward. He gives the best hugs, and he needs someone other than me to hug."

Edward put a stop to it. "Mandy, I need to have some time with Miss Quilla now. OK?"

Mandy obediently released me, and I put her down.

"When will you make her my auntie?" she asked.

"As soon as I can!"

Then he took my hand and led me upstairs. "Grab your jacket and put on some shoes. We're going for a drive."

My heart did the Edward flip then. A seriousness in his tone and an indefinable look in his eyes made me edgy. We drove the half-hour distance to his house in just under 20 minutes. He held on to my hand the entire time, but didn't say a single word. Once we got inside the door, he closed it behind him and turned the lock.

Then easing me around to face him, about 12 inches separating us, he said, "Tell me again what you told my family, Quill."

I knew what he wanted, what he needed, to hear. Looking him full in the eyes, with no hesitation, I told him.

"I love you, Edward Grainge, with my whole heart. And I would be honored to be your wife."

The muscles in his jaws clenched and unclenched.

"Can I get you to say that one more time?" he asked, his voice a tight whisper of control.

I reached for him then and drew him to me. Pulling his head down close to my face, I whispered in his ear. "I do love you, Edward. I do. I have loved you for a long time but wouldn't allow myself to say it till now. I love you with my whole, entire, fear-filled insecure heart."

No kiss greeted my declaration. He just held me, squeezing the daylight into my life and reminding me again, "I'm not going anywhere. I got you."

He seemed content to hold me like that forever, but I really wanted a kiss to seal the moment.

"Edward, I need for you to kiss me right now."

I felt his body grow still. That's all I remember for the next long minute as my guy gladly offered what I asked. The chemistry thing kicked in with a vengeance, weakening my knees and leaving us breathless. Edward surfaced first, taking in calming breaths, and I joined him as we waited for the planet to stop its mad spin.

With my head against his chest and his arms surrounding me, he did his signature thing. He talked to God. "Father God, Quilla, the woman of my heart, loves me back. I don't know how to thank You for this precious gift. My heart is so full right now that . . ."

His voice broke. I squeezed him tighter, my own eyes brimming, and continued his prayer. "Lead us, please, Father, the way You have led us to date. Continue to guide and direct our paths. Help me to be deserving of the love of this wonderful man and to do all within my power to treasure him all the days of my life. Amen."

"Amen," Edward echoed, looking at me with wonder in his eyes and allowing me to see the mist of tears glistening there. "I love you, Quilla. I'll spend the rest of my life showing you how much."

With that he kissed me on the forehead and ushered us out of his house. We hadn't moved a step beyond the foyer, but I knew why we had to go. It wouldn't take much to set off that ticking time bomb. Like Joseph, we ran from the temptation, willing ourselves to wait for the right time.

---

[1] Isa. 26:3, KJV.

[2] John 14:27, NKJV.

Chapter 23

My flight back to Toronto was delayed for an hour. To pass the time, I pulled out my project book to record all that had taken place during my visit to Atlanta. Anything to distract me from the loneliness. I missed Edward. Going home felt wrong. I wanted to remain where I was, or have him come with me. It's like once my mind and heart became synchronized in jointly loving him, he became necessary to my sense of completeness.

We'd clung to each other at the airport. He came with me as far as security would allow, and even there we'd hugged and kissed again, wishing that circumstances and distance stood not between us. I thought of calling his cell phone to alert him that the flight had been delayed, but I stopped myself. What was the point? He'd feel bad, and I'd feel worse. Too close, and yet too far. I decided to wait until I was on the plane to tell him that I'd arrive home later than we expected.

Recording the weekend brought it all back. I can't believe that I actually said all that to his family, but in hindsight I wouldn't change a thing. Nothing I said was inappropriate, disrespectful, or rude. Yes, I might have prejudged the meaning of what Esther and Mrs. Grainge said, based on my own sensitivity over the age issue, but it did force me to own up to my love for Edward.

Following our flight from temptation, we'd returned to his parents' house only to find most of the family were already gone. Mandy had left me a note, written by her mom and signed by her in large letters, to ask if I could come and visit her the next day, that Mommy was making breakfast. I showed the note to Edward, who chuckled.

"I guess you've made a hit with my niece." Looking at me through narrowed eyes, he'd asked, "What is it about you that draws people to you?"

I had no answer. Until I started my project I had no idea I had the ability to "draw" people. It seems that God can use anything to help us grow into the persons He designed us to be. I have to talk to Him more about what His plans are for my life with this supposed "new gift."

Mr. Grainge happened to come into the kitchen just as Edward asked that, and he answered it. "Don't look a gift horse in the mouth, son. God has sent you a virtuous woman whose price is beyond rubies. Just remember to treasure her every day of your life."

Then taking me by the hand, he told Edward to go visit with his mother or find something else to do, because he wanted to have a talk with his prospective daughter-in-law. I kid you not. That's exactly what he said.

Taking me to the back of the house where he had his study, he closed the door and sat me in one of the two chairs in the room. Reassuring me that I was not in for an inquisition, he again apologized on behalf of his family for any discomfort I'd felt earlier. Then he asked me something that I should have expected but had not anticipated.

"Quilla, do you love my son?" he began.

"Yes, sir."

"Do you know why you love him? Why this man?"

Nervousness made me almost joke that he was my last possible train to Zion, but I restrained myself. Why do I love Edward? Is he just an escape from my loneliness? Is it because I'm so physically drawn to him? Why this man indeed? Is it because he's the first man to make me feel treasured, loved, special?

Trying my best to put into words what Edward means to me, I said, "I wish I could tell you that it was this thing Edward did, or this particular trait that he has. But I don't know why, why Edward. I know that he makes me feel treasured as a person. Love should do that. I know that seeking God's will for his life is more important to him than having me. I love that about him, because if God is first in his affections, I'm going to be OK. I like the chemistry between us, the humor, the mental stimulation that we have in our talks, the prayers we can share, and that he never seems to compete with me but rather he is helping me grow into the person God wants me to be."

Now, before you say anything, I realize that what I'm documenting is not the typical kind of conversation a woman has with the father of the man she plans to marry, and before I continued, I told Mr. Grainge as much.

"Sir," I said, "I want to tell you something that's very personal. Earlier I mentioned the chemistry between Edward and me. Edward has promised himself and God that he will protect my honor, and by that he means that he will not have us get into sexually compromising situations. However, neither one of us anticipated that the chemistry between us would be so potent, if I can use that word. There are times it flares up so suddenly, and is so palpable, that it is very easy to forget our good intentions. But you know what? Your son talks to God in my presence about it and asks for strength to honor me. That is the nicest tribute any man has ever paid me. Making me feel I'm worth waiting for."

Mr. Grainge nodded and smiled approvingly, but I actually had more to say. That surprised even me. I couldn't believe the things I was talking about to this quiet man. Rarely do I let anyone I don't know extremely well into the inner sanctum of my heart, yet there I was, telling this man some really personal stuff.

I told Mr. Grainge about my incident at the convention center, and how it led to my project of interviewing single women. I told him about my own self-evaluation and the lessons I had learned along the way, lessons about leaning on God, trusting Him, dealing with fear, and facing my own insecurities.

"I wanted a husband, or I thought I did. But when Edward showed up with his nine-year age gap and expressed his interest, I completely dismissed him. And even when I started to develop feelings for your son, I could not, I would not, allow him or God to convince me to move in that direction."

"'Trust in the Lord with all thine heart; and lean—'" Mr. Grainge began quoting.

"Mr. Grainge!" I interrupted. "How did you know? That's exactly the text God kept bringing me back to. That I must not lean on my own understanding. But God had to be wrong, I argued. I wanted Him to admit that my being with Edward made no sense. I listed all the reasons for Him: I was too old to give Edward children, the divide was too wide, I'd be in retirement years before he was, and so on and so on. Had Esther not said what she did, it's likely that I would have gone back to Toronto and somehow come up with all kinds of reasons to say no to the love your son offered me, denying what I already knew in my heart—that I loved him too."

Throughout my long speech this wonderful man just listened, nodded encouragingly, and allowed me to verbalize in his presence. When I'd wound down, he told me something I did not know.

"Back in October Edward asked me if I thought it was possible to love someone you've met only once. Having never been through that, and thinking that love needed time to grow, I didn't have an answer. That's when he told me about you and how he felt God leading him to seek you out. Now, of my two boys, Edward tends to be pickier when it comes to women, and of my three children, Edward is the one whose spirituality is the most mature. Therefore, when he put the matter to me, I knew it had to be serious. So I told him to do the one thing that never leads us astray. I told him to pray about the matter. I advised him to seek God's will above his own."

"I didn't know," I said with wonder.

"There's more. My son told me your name—Quilla, short for Tranquility—and asked me to also pray that if indeed your life was meant to be joined with his that God would reveal it to you, too. So, my child, I have prayed for you ever since. And now that I've met you, I see why my son loves you. Your age isn't a problem for us, Quilla. What I prayed for from the time I first held my children in my arms is that they learn to love the Lord with all their hearts, and that when they grow up, should they choose to join their lives with another in marriage, that the person who would share their lives would also be a seeker after God's heart."

"I'm not a saint, Mr. Grainge. I don't always even want to do God's will. Being a Christian is not the easiest path one could choose. I don't know why people keep spouting that silliness about religion being an opiate. Try submitting your will to God's will day in and day out—it's not easy."

"No, it's not! Some people come to God hoping He'll clean up the one or two things about them that are bothersome. What they don't know is that once we let God in, He's not about patching us up here and there. He wants to make us into new creatures. To do that, He has to get rid of the old nature—all of it."

"C. S. Lewis talks about that in *Mere Christianity*," I said.

"Ah, so you're a fan of Lewis?"

"I like his reasoning. It's interesting to see Christianity from the perspective of someone who was once a nonbeliever."

"So you are the questioning heart, then?"

"Not always. But sometimes I do have more questions than answers. I suppose one has to live with a bit of doubt in order for faith to be exercised."

Mr. Grainge's eyes shone with pleasure. "Marry my boy, Quilla. I'm going to love having you around. We will have the best discussions!"

Just then there was a sharp rap on the door and a voice said, "Dad, can I have my girl back?"

Mr. Grainge stood up and let him in. "You can have her back only if you promise to marry her soon. I love this woman's brain. Just think! When your mother gets tired of my constant discussions, Quilla will be able to provide another brain to bounce ideas off. You're not planning to move to Canada, are you?"

Edward's face took on a resigned expression. "There falls another victim to the Quilla effect." His sigh was exaggerated. "And Dad, please! Allow me to get used to the idea that this woman loves me before you start making plans for her life! You have your girl; now leave me with mine." He pulled me to my feet and placed a possessive arm around my waist.

Mr. Grainge held up his hands in surrender. "Yes, sir!"

Sunday, Monday, and Tuesday flew by in a flurry of activities. Including brunch with Esther and her family, I saw where Edward worked, took long walks, went downtown to visit the sights, including the Underground, did a bit of shopping, and even took in a gospel concert at one of the local universities. Edward and I talked and planned and basked in mutual adoration of each other. It was heady and a soothing balm for my too-many-years-lonely heart.

Mrs. Grainge and I had a bit of a heart-to-heart as well. She asked only that I love her son and that together we would trust God to lead our lives. Mandy made me promise to come back in the summer to visit her, and could we have a whole day just by ourselves. At that, Edward shook his head in despair, wondering if he would ever get any time with me. I reassured him with a kiss to seal my words that no one else would ever take the special place reserved in my heart for only him. He shut up when he saw how serious I was.

Wednesday night, when I finally got home and let myself into the house, it felt uncomfortably empty. Turning on the lights, I gave my head a chance to readjust, but it was only when I called Edward to report in that I realized what was missing. It was Edward. By choosing to love this man, I'd created a self-extension as necessary to my life as breathing.

My voicemail, which I'd ignored during my absence, showed 14 messages. I just couldn't face them at the moment. I called Edward again.

"OK," I said when he answered, "I don't know how to do this."

"Do what?" he asked, concern leeching through his voice.

Plopping down on the floor by my bed, I rested my head against the mattress. "I don't know how to return to normal or whatever normal is. I miss you, and it feels awful being here without you. This love thing's the pits!"

"I miss you too," he commiserated. "I found the card you left under my pillow. When did you sneak upstairs, by the way? Oh, never mind. Your card made me appreciate your thoughtfulness even more. I wish I'd thought to do something just as special for you, but writing isn't my favorite means of communication."

I wanted to reassure him that it was OK, but this new loneliness overwhelmed my ability to talk. I just couldn't find the strength to say anything. Is this what it means to open your heart in love to another—that you feel weak? Is this what G. David felt with Mara? Heaven help me! What if Edward changed his mind and decided he didn't want me anymore? What if his family actually didn't like me and convinced him to bow out? Now that I had accepted that I loved him and actually said it out loud to most of his family, it would be devastating if he had second thoughts. Where would I be then? I'd feel just like I felt now—a stranger in my own house, missing a critical part of me that could never be restored.

He must have read my mind, or maybe God gave him words to say. "Quilla, woman of my heart, please remember that I love you. Don't consider for a moment that I would ever change my mind about you. Your coming here convinced me even more that God is in this, and my love for you is as true as steel. But I know how you feel. When I came back from visiting you in November I felt the same way—worse, because even though I knew you were developing feelings for me, I wasn't sure of your love. Now I am, and it makes a big difference. I can't wait to see you again but until we do, I can start planning for our lives together. It will make missing you a bit easier to deal with. Are you hearing me?"

I nodded, suddenly realizing that he wasn't right there standing in front of me. We had just a phone connection. "Yes, Edward," I said aloud. "Thanks for reminding me of your love. I guess I'm feeling really vulnerable right now."

This was exactly what I needed to hear. To be reminded that I remained the woman of his heart and that he'd treasured the time we'd had together just as much as I did.

"You know you can call me anytime you need me, don't you? No matter what hour of the day or night. Trust me when I say I'm not going anywhere. I got you, Quilla. In you I've found the woman of my heart."

That brought a smile to my face. I love this man. Yes indeed I do. Every word he said restored my confidence, and I told him as much. "If you can express your feelings so eloquently, Mr. Grainge," I teased, "why can't you put the very same thoughts in writing? I *love* hearing how much you love me."

"You do, do you?"

"Yes, I do."

"So when will you marry me?"

"When do you want me to?"

"Now!"

"Really Edward, when?"

"Now!"

"Edward, we're not going to get married now."

"You mean you want me to be realistic? Why didn't you say that before?"

"Edward!"

"OK, let me think. If I say summer, you're going to tell me that's too close and that it's going to compete with the birth of Susan's baby. Next you'll tell me that Susan has to be your matron of honor, and knowing Susan, she'll insist on getting her body back in shape before that."

He had that right . . .

"So, let's see, a realistic date would be in November or December. H'mm, I wouldn't mind experiencing one of your Canadian white Christmases, and it would make things easier for your parents. Plus the winter cold will give me lots of excuses to snuggle up to you. How's that?"

Tears filled my eyes. He'd thought of everything and left me with no words other than "Let's do it!"

I was so ready.

What?

You thought I'd bargain for next June? Listen, when you're 44 going on 45, and love comes knocking, you don't ask it to come back later or wait for a more convenient season. I've done enough foot-dragging. I want this man in my life for better or for worse. I just pray that the better will far exceed the worse.

With my blues a thing of the past, after we prayed together I blew my honey a kiss, then got out my book to record this last bit. Then I called Susan, told her the news, and hung up before I was deafened by her continuous screech of excitement. That night I sang in the shower. There was indeed much to thank God for.

Imagine! Me! Quilla Hazelwood! About to make wedding plans.

Pinch me.

The sun had barely broken the eastern horizon on Thursday morning when the ringing of the phone dragged me out of a really nice dream.

"Quilla," cried Gloria before I could even say hello, "I'm volunteering to be your wedding organizer. This is so exciting! Edward called last night to tell us the good news, but he made us promise not to call you till today. I've hardly slept, and have been wide awake since 5:00 trying not to call you too early. When can I come over to begin our consultation? You don't go back to work till next week, do you?"

I heard a rustling across the phone line, then Wendell's voice.

"Hey, Quilla, we're going to be family! Fantastic! You couldn't have picked a nicer guy, except me, of course, but you'd have to knock off Gloria to do that. Can I be your giveaway uncle?"

The phone changed hands again.

"Never mind him, Quilla. He at least slept, but as soon as he woke up he wanted me to call you. So tell me everything. Did he take you out someplace romantic and it was there you told him you loved him?"

Wendell came back on the phone. "Edward said something about you telling his family where to get off. What happened? No, let me guess—did Esther say something stupid again?"

I heard more scuffling in the background, and finally Gloria was back. "I shooed Wendell away on the pretense that I could do with a cup of tea. Talk quickly before he comes back."

I gave her a short version of everything—after telling her that her crack-of-dawn call nearly sent my blood pressure sky-high. By the time I'd finished the retelling I was as excited as she was. Talking about happiness is contagious. In the middle of our talk I heard footsteps thudding up my stairs. That could only be Susan—taking advantage of the fact that I'd left her a key so that she could collect my mail and water my plants. What is wrong with these people!

A large bouquet of flowers preceded her into my bedroom. Puffing hard, she dumped the flowers over the foot of my bed and as usual, pushed me aside, snagging three of my four pillows for herself. Then she opened three different bride magazines to several dog-eared pages and handed them to me.

"Gloria, Susan, the Goodyear blimp, has taken up residence in my bed. Talk to her for a minute. I have to go to the bathroom, something I plan to do unaccompanied."

Not waiting for an answer, I tossed the phone into what remained of Susan's lap and backed off the bedcovers, spilling the flowers across the floor.

It was 8:30 before I got rid of Gloria. Susan, having the day off, I had to put up with for a lot longer. Thanks to her advanced pregnancy she fell asleep by 9:00 a.m. That gave me time to talk to my Father in heaven, to thank Him for friends, even though they were irritating at times, and for this love that leaves me breathless.

Chapter 24

It's time to put this project to bed. A recent conversation with Clare decided that for me. I'd also done a few more interviews, and while each woman's story had its own unique set of circumstances that needed to be documented, if only for the record, my interest had begun to lag. I suppose that's partly because of having Edward in my life and being so busy helping Susan get ready for motherhood. But there's another reason. I'm becoming drained. I can't, without compromising my health, continue to sustain or support the growing number of relationships that follow my interviews.

What does all this have to do with my conversation with Clare? I'm glad you asked. We were talking after church, and she asked what I'd learned from my interviews and if someday I'd share what I'd learned.

"Maybe we can all learn something that will help us come to terms with things," she said without her usual fierceness. "I can't go on the way I have been, Quilla. At this point I'm open to hearing anything that can help me deal with my own situation."

That's what made me revisit Natasha's crazy idea. Since, as I said before, I can't continue to maintain the relationships developed with my interviewees, a memorial service might provide closure for me and everyone else. It could be a point of looking back and moving forward. First, though, I need to think things through.

In reviewing my notes, I found the following statement written way back at the beginning of the project: *Maybe in their stories* (that of other women) *I will find a way of reconciling myself to my single state of affairs and make contentment my new partner.*

Interesting how life has a way of messing up our assumptions along with our best-laid plans! It looks as though I was ready, back then, to throw in the towel, doesn't it? Reconcile myself to singleness. And look at my life now. What do we know about the future and the plans God has for our lives? Nothing at all!

What about you? As you took this journey with me and these women, did anything stand out for you?

While you ponder this, let me talk about what I have learned during the past 10 months and from these 21 interviews. More accurately, what I have learned in response to my original question, "Why am I not married by now?" and to the broader question of why these other women who desire marriage are not married.

First let me acknowledge right up front that there is an appalling paucity of men in our churches, let alone eligible ones. There is no getting around that fact. I don't know what our churches are doing, or not doing, that keeps away the male species, but it's a growing concern to me. It should be to our church leadership, too, who, to state the obvious, are mostly men.

Why is it that as soon as our boys get to a certain age, somewhere between age 16 and 20, they start withdrawing from the fellowship of believers? Why is that?

I have two theories. You want to hear them? Of course you do.

My first is this. The type of passive Christianity that we now practice—the sit and listen, the emotional testimony times, the vegetarian cooking classes, the income tax clinics, the opening-of-the-heart men's ministries—none of these kinds of activities appeal to our men. So where do we find the few young men in our churches actively engaged? It's not as elders, deacons, or pastors—at least not where I go to church. I see them clustered around the musical instruments and I see them hanging out in the hall during services chatting with friends. Not all of them, but too many. So I can't help concluding that the way we practice our religion nowadays has a greater attraction to women than to men.

My second theory is this. Something about the submission of ourselves, which is required to become children of God, flies in the face of men's need to exercise control over their lives. Asking of God, yielding to God, prostrating the self—these are not qualities we teach our boys to exemplify. How, then, when they are desperate to prove their mettle as "real men," do they reconcile societal expectations against what faith demands?

The result? They leave the church.

Now see what happens. The young women, peers in age, who choose to stay in church, have fewer choices from which to select potential marriage partners. It's not that I'm saying young women don't also leave the church. They do, but not in the same high percentages as their male counterparts.

We now have a situation on our hands. With each passing year there are fewer and fewer eligible men in the church, and every woman is looking *and* waiting or looking *and* fighting for the few "slim pickings" that remain.

Imagine the pressure, the crying need of these women who by the grace of God are trying to do the right thing, save sex and sanity until marriage. Yeah, right! No wonder Mara just lost it when she came across the text about waiting on the Lord.

So before I go any further I want to give out a big high-five to my sisters who've hung in there and kept the faith. I know your pain, and God knows it too, even though sometimes His silence makes you wonder.

Plain and simple, men who are practicing believers are scarce to nonexistent. And truth be told, a few of the ones who are available should be left alone. They have too much baggage to deal with. My advice, if you're open to it, is that unless you're sure you can manage your baggage as well as these men's, stay single, my sisters. These guys are not for you to marry! You've seen it happen. The marriage that shouldn't be, but the woman wants it. She knows the guy is bad news. She knows he's got a dozen issues that only God can understand yet alone fix, yet she thinks *she* can change him, reform him.

That's not our job. Reformation belongs to God and God alone! Don't ever let your mind convince you that these gents with severe issues are OK just because they could provide a little sexual gratification or whatever else you're hoping for in marriage. Maybe they will and maybe they won't. And if they can't, then where will you be? Stuck in a relationship you entered for the wrong reason, that's where. I know that I have enough trouble managing my own stuff without adding some bad-news-guy's complications on top of mine.

So what do we do while we wait for the dream guy that might never show up?

I have to believe deep in my heart that God knows my situation and will not deny me the things necessary for my soul's salvation. I then have to remind myself that God's primary concern is not my earthly happiness. What I know in my moments of strong faith, and based on the assurance of His Word, is that God is most concerned with transforming my character so that heaven will be a haven for me. I know that once I give control of my life to God, He is going to take every opportunity, use every circumstance, every hard thing, every trial, even every pain to help me grow or to bring Him glory. Everything!

Is singleness God's desire for your life? I don't know. Is marriage in your future? I wish I could say yes, but I don't think marriage, even for those of us who want it so badly we ache with the longing, is for everyone. I'm old enough, and I've seen enough, to know that many of those who married and subsequently divorced, or those who are living miserable married lives, should not have married in the first place. I think that an even graver tragedy of married life is the husband or wife realizing that now they're married, they're lonelier than they ever were as a single person. How awful must that be!

While I've recorded here a few of my interviews with single women who want to be married, two of my recent interviews were with married women who wish they were single. They wanted me to know that marriage is not always the bed of roses we think it's going to be. That our stuff— the insecurities, selfishness, the character flaws—will all come back to haunt us in marriage unless we take time to face up to and deal with these things *before* marriage. One of them told me point-blank, "I should not have married him in the first place. All the danger signs were there. He was easily angered. He was cheap, inconsiderate, and selfish. But you know what? I thought that with gentleness and good loving I could change him to be more like the guy of my dreams. What a wake-up call!" she concluded dejectedly. "What a wake-up call."

These two women are just a small sample of those who are unhappily married.

And lest it be thought that this is all a railing against men, it's not. Listen, sisters, some of us have got to get real. (I know! I know! I'm starting to climb on my soapbox, but this is important.)

Seriously, what do you and I expect from the men we hope to marry? Have we examined our expectations? Do we want him to treat us the way our father did—the good or bad daddy? What if he doesn't? For those who experienced childhood abuse—physical, psychological, sexual, or verbal— at the hands of the dominant male figure in our lives, we must give serious thought to the impact those early perceptions of men will have on our marriage relationships. In essence we need to consider if we're emotionally healthy enough to enter into and maintain a marriage relationship. More important, if we ever find ourselves in an abusive situation, do we have the wisdom to know when to leave—if it comes to that?

And while I'm still on my soapbox, answer this. Do we truly understand the meaning of love? Are we aware of how love forces us to confront our selfishness while valuing our personhood—the type of love that does not need to put our partner down so that we can lift ourselves up?

These are questions I've been asking of one Quilla Hazelwood. And I must confess that when I honestly examine my heart, I find myself seriously lacking in some of these areas. I mean, I need a major intervention!

I'm not implying that we need to be perfect people before we can enter marriage. That's not what I'm saying at all. I'd hate to be married to any pariah of perfection. But years ago I heard something at a seminar that has stayed with me ever since: *awareness is the key to change.* That statement takes us to the crux of the matter: self-examination, another of my takeaways from this project.

From all these women's stories, amid the pain, anger, loneliness, heartbreak, and honest disclosures, in between the lines there lurks a crying need to come to terms with stuff. This coming to terms, I think, can be done only through honest, painful, anxiety-ridden but ultimately liberating self-examination.

For those of us who are wondering why we're not yet married, this is the part of the equation over which we have a degree of control. We don't have much control over the woefully few men in the church to choose from, but we do have full control over our mental attitude. Because if today, tomorrow, next week, or within the next three years the opportunity for marriage presents itself to me or to you, are we equipped to carry our share of the partnership? Here I am, about to join my life to this man, Edward Grainge. But I really don't know him. I don't know the day-to-day reality of life with him, not the good *and* bad in him I am yet to discover. I don't know the things about him that he doesn't even know himself, but which will shape his decisions and his behavior toward me throughout our life together.

I know that I love him based on what I see, hear, feel, and assume about him. But soon will come the day-to-day-living kind of adjustment. There will be times, probably lots of times, that either he or I will have to take the high road so peace can reign in our home. That was a question Dru Hazelwood asked during one of our recent conversations. Am I ready for that kind of give-and-take? It's enough to make the devil I know in the form of loneliness (and what Crystal calls "the freedom to consider only my needs" when it comes to taking a certain course of action) seem like the more attractive partner.

Bear with me. I'll soon step down from my soapbox, but honestly and truly, do you disagree with anything I've said? Feel free to disagree. However, I stand unmovable by my point about the importance of self-examination on this issue of marriage readiness.

In revising my original list of questions, in listening to the stories of these wonderful women who've been so kind to share with me such personal information, and in looking within the dark and not-so-dark places within myself, here's what self-examination has revealed to me about my stuff.

Quilla's conclusions about herself and the question "Why am I not married by now?"

1. I am deathly afraid of heartbreak.
2. I do not think I'm lovely or lovable where men are concerned.
3. I lack confidence in my own attractiveness and femininity.
4. My assumptions about the qualities I wanted in a life partner revealed some uncomfortable biases, especially concerning age, race, and ethnicity.
5. My passivity and lack of initiative in seeking out avenues to meet Christian men limited my options.
6. When it comes to my deep-seated fears, I am not as open as I thought I would be to letting God into that part of me.
7. With patience, perseverance, and trust, I can learn new ways of behaving and thinking.
8. God sometimes allows us to experience the unthinkable.

What does your list look like? H'mm? If you haven't made a list, please do it soon.

I wish I could wrap things up by assuring you that you'll get all the desires of your heart. But I can honestly say that I'm glad I don't always get what I desire, because sometimes what I want isn't what's best for me. I have to trust God, and not just for the fringe benefits, such as peace of mind, a shoulder to lean on, someone powerful who's got my back, but for who He is, and that He wants me in heaven with Him.

When I examine how God kept begging the children of Israel to return to Him, not to go after other gods; when I see the illustrations of Jesus showing us through stories such as the lost coin, the lost sheep, and the prodigal son how relentless is God's pursuit of us—how eagerly He desires us to love Him in return—I cannot help concluding that God is madly in love with the human race, and with you and me in particular. I think it was the apostle Paul who said that no eye has seen or ear heard or mind imagined the things that God has prepared for us in heaven.* Just as Edward, while preparing for me to join my life with his, takes pleasure in our daily conversations and loves to hear me tell him how much I love him—in just the same way, God wants that fellowship with us. Whether or not there is a husband in our lives, He still wants it.

I have denied Him that. Too many times. Even though God's love overrides any earthly love I can have. That may feel like cold consolation when our hearts are burdened with loneliness, but it is a consolation nevertheless. God's love and the hope of experiencing the abundant bounties He's preparing for us, bounties that, in comparison, make our loneliness here a trifling thing, are what will allow us to traverse this journey here on earth without slitting our wrists in despair. God promises us peace of mind.

Can you fathom feeling at peace about not having a husband? For those of us who want a man in our lives so badly, but with every passing day our hope grows dimmer and dimmer, God promises to be with us and never leave or forsake us.

Will Edward and I live happily ever after? Who can say? What I do know, however, is that I must never let him come between me and my relationship with God. When imperfect humans fail us, and they can and will, God provides a rock-solid constancy that will sustain us through thick or thin, better or worse, beginning and end.

So my final takeaway is this: I must make God first in my life. I recommend you do the same. You won't always understand His ways, so my best advice is that you start a list of all the things you would like for Him to make plain to you when you get to heaven. I have my list, and I will add new items as I face situations here on earth that challenge my faith. I look forward to discussing these with Him in heaven under a section of the tree of life where mangoes grow in abundance. There, sipping that heavenly ambrosia untainted by earthly imperfections, we will confer, my God and I. And I'm certain that it is I who will, like Job, be left without words.

Again, accept my apologies if my "preaching" offends you. At least, see these words as a sincere expression of how passionately I feel about this subject. And in the final analysis, please hear this: God is God. I am but a mere creation who is trying to understand the Omnipotent. But when I cannot fathom His ways and His leading, the thing that anchors me and keeps me holding on is how much He desires a relationship with me. I continue to be inexpressibly awed by that inescapable fact.

---

* See 1 Cor. 2:9.

Chapter 25

I regard the women in front of me, each face with a different story. In the background soft music plays, the kind that makes you want to speak in whispers.

They are all here.

I cannot believe that these women have come on this Sunday morning in response to my invitation to participate in this weird ceremony. I kid you not. They are all here, all 21 of them, including Susan, Mara, Clare, Justina, Stelle, Crystal, Danesha, Mia, Martha, Natasha, Lynn, and me.

Today we face the issue head-on: saying goodbye to cherished dreams.

If you are thinking that this is a premature action, a lack-of-faith ritual, I wondered the very thing myself. After all, we don't control the future. If we'd done this ceremony one year ago, if I had closed the chapter of my life that still hoped to someday marry, would I be here right now planning an upcoming wedding, once this is over?

This ceremony, to which I'm about to say words of welcome and share my findings, is more than just saying goodbye to cherished dreams. It's also about coming to terms with the unmet expectations in our lives and choosing to refocus our attention on other things.

It was the "out-of-the-box-thinking" Stelle who directed me to this venue. I cringed when she first suggested the idea. *No way*, I thought. But Mara, who was there while we discussed the matter, kept silent as I protested the inappropriateness of the suggestion.

"Stelle's got a good point," she finally said to me. "It's a bit off the wall, but it will make this real for people." Shrugging her shoulder, she added, "Plus those who find it uncomfortable can choose not to participate. You can send them your notes by mail or e-mail."

So it was decided. Stelle knew someone who knew someone, which helps to explain why I'm standing right now in the chapel of a funeral home, 21 women in front of me, to have a service—or whatever it should be named.

Don't these women have anything better to do? I don't know that I'd have come if I was in their place. Would you?

Trust me when I say I prayed about it and waited for God to tell me it was a stupid idea.

Nothing!

All I got were increasing responses to my invitation, responses delivered by phone, e-mail, and even a couple handwritten ones. Up until Saturday afternoon I had 16. Saturday night the list climbed to 17. This morning before I left home I received two more confirmations, and now there in front of me, seated at the back and looking apprehensive, are the last two holdouts. I provided no reminder follow-up to the invitation. I told the women what I was planning to do and where it would be held, and gave them an opportunity if they so desired to participate.

They're all here.

What does that tell me? I don't know yet, but obviously this is more important to them than I thought. What I do know is that I need to get started. Let's see how this thing will play itself out.

I've arranged the chairs in a loose semicircle so the women won't be sitting in rows, as if they were in church or a courtroom. It felt friendlier somehow. "Wow," I begin, meeting the eyes of each woman in the room, "I can't believe you're all here with me at this strange ceremony. What does that say about us?"

"That we're all as nuts as you," Susan deadpans.

This breaks the ice. A few smiles and chuckles greets her comment. *Thank you, Susan!* I silently bless her.

"I have written some notes so I won't leave out anything I want to share with you this morning. And by the way, later this afternoon there will be a little get-together at my place. Good food for the calorie-conscious and decadent delights for those of us who need it." I raise my hand to indicate I belonged to the latter group.

I quickly glance over my notes, curious about my lingering reluctance to dive right into the talk.

God, I pray silently, *is there something else I need to do?*

Speak from your heart, Quilla. Don't be afraid to be real. That's what these women appreciate most about you.

OK, God.

I begin at the beginning and tell how I got started doing the interviews, beginning with my personal list. I'd received permission from Nat to share her illustration about unmet expectations and how they affect our lives. I tell how each woman's story forced me to face things about myself that I didn't want to deal with, and I share with them my conclusions and what I've personally taken away from the project—information similar to what I last wrote about.

I don't know if you, dear reader, often have the opportunity to do public speaking. I've done a bit in my time at church or work-related conferences. There are times in the middle of your talk that it dawns on you that every single mind is on the same channel as yours, tuned in to every nuance or expression of your presentation. I feel the same now. These women are with me in body, mind, and spirit.

"What I did not plan for," I tell them, "was how much your stories would affect me. By just sharing a piece of your life for that hour or two of our meeting, you forced me to examine my faith, my prejudices, and my tolerance of ambiguity, to name a few. What can I, a fellow seeker with you, tell you about how to deal with this thing we all have or are experiencing—our unmet expectations? I feel inadequate in your presence. I don't have answers to give."

Natasha raises her hand, indicating she wants to say something.

"Everyone," I nodded toward Nat, "Natasha would like to say something."

Nat walks to the front of the room with the poise of a diva about to deliver her signature number.

"I don't know about you, but meeting Quilla has been one of the best things that has happened to me in a long time. When she told me about her project I suspected where it might take her and take us. But as I talked with her and shared my own story, she provided a safe place to talk. Quilla has very good way at listening with her heart. I don't know how she does it, but you feel comfortable sharing things with her."

Her English becomes less certain as she continues. "I just want to thank you, Quilla, for embracing, no . . . that is not word I want . . . for, how you say, ack . . . ack . . . acknowledge me [she taps her heart and her head] and for inviting me into your warm circle. It was not something I expected when I met you that day at park, so maybe miracles happen still, yes?"

The whole group of women stand to their feet and give me an ovation. Susan is sitting, but her arms are raised high above her head, clapping as enthusiastically as the rest.

Where did this come from? I must not cry!

Blinking back the threatening tears, I shoo Nat back to her seat, scolding her with my eyes for what she did.

"Thank you, everyone, but this is not about me. Everything today is about us—who we are and what we will choose to do with the rest of our lives, whether or not it includes a husband or some of our other cherished hopes and aspirations. Today, in this setting, we have an opportunity to bury some things, to pay tribute to some others, or sing a eulogy to our souls. We can do it privately or publicly, but let today be the start of something new."

Oh, boy, talk about introducing tension into a room. I can feel the looking outward turn inward—not a bad thing, actually a necessary part of the ceremony, but the struggle is there in the room in every woman's downcast, upturned, spaced-out expression.

I press on. "The small notepads I placed on your chairs are for you to record the thing you will let go today. The thing that has influenced your life or dominated your aspirations— whatever it is—simply write it down in your pad.

"Now, I know that not all of us here are believers in God, but I am. I believe in a God who is interested in a personal relationship with me, and it is to Him I will give this thing that I need to let go of. Please indulge me as I take a minute to publicly ask Him to watch over our proceedings and guide our decisions."

Most of the heads in the room bow.

"Father in heaven," I pray, "before we speak You are already listening. Today we come to mourn for lost dreams. We grieve for the things we have so strongly desired that we now must find a way to come to terms with, living without them. God, You know the loneliness that haunts our waking moments, the arms in this room that are achingly empty of that dream of a child to hug, to love, the child we wanted to help fill the maternal heart You put within us. We hold out our empty arms to You, Father. Look at them— some Black, White, Brown, all the colors You made us, some wrinkled, some smooth—but most empty. Father God, I know You know all things, but we don't know what You know, so I ask You to bless the empty arms, and if it is for the good of us, please fill them one day with young ones to embrace.

"Then, Lord . . . , turn Your eyes of compassion on the hearts that are aching for a special man to love. Not just any man, Lord, but a man who will treasure us, honor us, support us, cherish us, and to whom we are precious in his eyes. God, You know how this loneliness eats away at the core of our confidence. Fill that empty void, please. If not with a man, then with something else so that we can be at peace and feel ourselves to be whole, fulfilled women who can walk proudly with no apologies because all is well with our souls.

"If there is anything else we need to bury today, Lord, anything else we need to let go, reveal it to us so that today can be the beginning of our healing. Your Word tells us that not a single sparrow falls that You do not see, so please, Father in heaven, see the tears that fall from our eyes today. Let them not fall in vain, but in Your time and plan, warm our hearts with joy in exchange for this blanket of grief.

"I want to ask that every woman in Your presence here will have the desires of her heart fulfilled. You know that's what I want. But I won't ask for that, Father, because I know that what we want is not always what is best for us. So instead I pray for Your will—a will that is passionate about doing what's ultimately best for us—that Your will be done. And months or years from now, when we see the things that are happening in our lives, we can look back on this day of mourning as the turning point of our souls. I pray this prayer in faith and leave all things in Your hands. Amen."

Not wishing to break the solemnity of the moment, I softly ask everyone to begin writing and when finished to form a circle around the special container prepared for us by the funeral director. Yes, as macabre as it is, there will be a cremation component to the ceremony after each woman, who desires to, gets a chance to say what she wishes before committing to the fire what she has written.

The heaviness of the moment weighs on me. I too have a few things to let go, but I had already done my homework, recording my own stuff in advance.

One by one, all the chairs empty of their occupants, and the circle expands to admit each newcomer.

Red eyes, pink eyes, somber eyes, and empty eyes focus on the simple brass basin sitting on a table in the middle of the room. This is it. My own jaw is hurting from holding in my emotions, but I keep control as I ask the women to step forward, one by one, acknowledging their pain. I remind those who desire to say a few words that they can before placing their folded papers in the basin.

This is really, really hard and I am not so strong.

I wait along with the others in the circle.

No one is moving.

Oh, dear God, this is difficult.

Sill we wait. The music, which was soft before, sounds loud in our silence.

Somewhere to my right I can hear crying, but my own eyes are full, and looking to see who it is will set me off.

Clare's grip on my hand tightens. I feel a shudder run through her body. I grip her back. Then she detaches herself and walks toward the basin. There she stands, arms raised to drop her notes in the bin.

"Today I choose to say goodbye to the ugliness inside and outside me. For a long time I've been preoccupied with attaining beauty, but today I let it all go and choose, instead, to become beautiful within, so help me God."

She lets the folded papers fall. They ping softly against the metal, and then she's beside me holding on to my hand, tall and resolute.

The next three women do not say anything, but they too, like Clare, stand in front of the basin, pausing to silently acknowledge the thing being offered up before opening their fingers and releasing their small square sheets of paper.

Two women down from me, to the left, is Susan. Like a baby learning to balance, she takes a wobbly step forward. This is costing her big, I know. As she lifts her foot to take the next step she breaks down. I freeze, resisting the urge to run to her, knowing how important it is for her to do this alone. She turns panicked eyes in my direction, and her cry breaks my heart.

"I might never meet them, Quill. How can I bury them when I never even met them? I kept hoping and hoping that one day I'd hear the doorbell ring, and there he or she would stand, glad to have finally found me. How can I bury them, Quill?"

I cannot bear her pain, so I do what I've been doing for years. I release the hands now gripping mine and go embrace my friend, rocking her in silence and wishing for a balm to ease her sorrow. After a while she pulls herself together. Mumbling under her breath about letting bygones by bygones, she waddles with steadier steps to the basin.

"For you, baby girl," she whispers as she defiantly releases her crumpled wad of paper.

With equal measure of solemnity or drama each woman commits her stuff to the basin of grief, saying goodbye to not having children, or grandchildren, or a dream of a life partner. Saying goodbye to controlling temperament, selfishness, a white wedding gown, romantic moonlight cruises, and the daughter who will not be there to help during the passage into old age—surprisingly mentioning many things that have little to do with not having a husband.

The process is long and heartwrenching, but finally it is done. Thank

God! Going through this has been harder than I ever imagined. In the end there is no one left to say the hateful words but me. So I say them. They must be spoken aloud for this to be real.

"Dust to dust, ashes to ashes," I say, turning my back and hiding my tears as the director enters to remove the basin.

We walk behind him in silent procession, me lagging behind with heavy feet, to the place where he will put fire to our stuff. New tears flow at this last piece of what feels very much like an actual funeral. Hugging and supporting each other for as long as we can hold on to the moment, we eventually part company. I remind them of the later repast at my house for those who wish to come.

Fourteen come. The mere two hours of separation have given us back our appetites and allow us to start practicing our new walk toward only God knows where. As for me, I will trust Him to make something beautiful from the ashes of our dreams.

Epilogue

January 1

Happy New Year! I am awake early on this January morning. Before my brain starts cluttering up with the many things I have to do or should be thinking about, I am taking a quick minute to have a silent conversation with God.

"*What's the rush, Quilla?*" He chides me gently. "*Be still.*"*

And know . . . My mind completes the next phrase of the verse.

So I do what I should do. I obey.

I'm learning to obey more immediately instead of questioning everything. That's what happens when you've proven a relationship and know the person is in your corner.

I still my mind. I hear the blood pulsing in the side of my neck. I feel a pain in my left shoulder from sleeping in an awkward position. I feel my breath entering and leaving my nostrils and with each one, the rise and fall of my chest. My tummy rumbles.

Next God reminds me that not only did He design my body with all its complicated parts—He also keeps them in motion every day, every minute, whether I'm aware of it or not. He tells me that today, whenever I feel the wind on my face, to remember that He controls the wind and He will also take care of me. I wait a minute longer in the stillness and acknowledge my Creator.

Taking care not to wake Edward, I tiptoe downstairs with my journal. Snuggling up in the corner of the living room couch, I tuck my feet under me so I can bring you up to speed with my life.

Yes, I still write to you, even though my project is over. I've decided that ours is one of the relationships I want to maintain. I've come to rely on seeing things through what I imagine your perspective to be. And even though I've yelled and berated you with more questions than any relationship should have to put up with, keeping you in mind also helps to keep me accountable.

So what's up with you?

Me?

259

Quilla Hazelwood-Grainge is OK. Edward and I married in November on the Sunday of the U.S. Thanksgiving weekend. Gloria and a much slimmer Susan, along with most of my project friends and well-wishers, ensured I didn't have a care in the world on my wedding day.

Daddy gave us a scare in late October. We almost lost him. Thankfully, he rallied and, driven by Dru Hazelwood, was able to wheel by my side down the aisle and present me to my husband. Old-fashioned, I know, but doing that small thing was important to him.

Edward. What can I tell you about him? Well, he has habits that I need to get used to. For example, he snores. Not the rumbling train down the track kind of snore, but a quieter version. It's annoying at times, but what's a girl to do when this is part of what comes with the man she loves. And I love him even more than I did before. Let me tell you what this man did, why I am still living in my Toronto house and not in Atlanta with him.

On Labor Day weekend he came up for a visit. In one of our many planning conversations I'd been worrying about how I would get my house sold before I had to move to Atlanta, what with planning the wedding and reception, etc. This man, wise beyond his years, knew at once how wrenching it was becoming for me to leave my home, my church, my family, and friends so that I could be with him in Atlanta. So you know what he did? He asked for and received permission from his company to work out of Toronto for a minimum of six months. He has to fly back to Atlanta about once, sometimes twice a month, but immediately after we returned from our honeymoon Edward took up residence in my house. *Yaaaay!* He did that just for me. Imagine that!

He loves me. I can't get over it. I am indeed the woman of his heart.

And the honeymoon?

Glory hallelujah! Friend, that honeymoon blew to bits all my preconceptions of what rapture is. Don't ask me where we went! OK, fine! We went to someplace warm. In the Caribbean. But that's not what I want to talk about. Work with me here!

Listen, I knew Edward was a bit of a romantic. I knew of the self-control he prayed for every time we so much as hugged or kissed. I knew that he loved me, desired me, even liked me, but I knew nothing about sexual joy. Nothing! The chemistry equation that has always been there between us, when it combined with the oxygen in our lungs, the love in our hearts, and something special placed in the tingling pores of our bodies by our

Creator, during our honeymoon it set off the ticking time bomb that would not be diffused, and we were blown away on that island paradise.

Waiting till marriage for that experience was worth every single frustrating minute. And I kid you not! The time bomb keeps resetting itself, surprising us at the most unusual times with its power.

This girl, Quilla, is being supremely blessed by God in the middle part of her life. Every day I wake up wanting to pinch myself to make sure I'm not dreaming. I can't help praising the Lord at all times and agree with whoever said that we are fearfully and wonderfully made! There's no other way to say it. I pray to God that I will continue to love and treasure that honey of a man lying upstairs in my . . . (oops!) our bed every day of my life just as much as he treasures me.

Now on to other business.

Susan gave birth to a boy on June 12, one week prior to her due date. A boy! Why did I not anticipate this? It's Susan we're dealing with! She talked about having a girl. I assumed she would have a girl. What do I know about how these sperm donor things work? I thought they could predetermine the child's gender, so it didn't dawn on me to question Susan when she talked endlessly about having a daughter. I guess she had her heart set on a girl even though she later told me that she'd asked them not to tell her which it was, a boy or a girl.

I had to return all the girly stuff I'd bought. Good thing I had the receipts. A week after Susan got home from the hospital we threw her a huge baby shower. All the regular members of the sisterhood—Mara, Danesha, Mia (Crystal had left two weeks earlier for her mission trip to Africa), Natasha, Gloria—plus a few of the others who are fast becoming regulars—Clare, Lynn, and Martha—showed up. It was the silliest baby shower I've ever attended, but it was such fun. Later that evening Jason and Wendell crashed the party carrying antidiscriminatory placards.

And how is Susan handling motherhood? Like a duck to water. My sometimes crazy-making friend is besotted with her boy. She actually told me that maybe God in His wisdom chose to give her a boy because she probably would have transferred too much of her own stuff onto a girl. She has also appointed—not asked, appointed—both Edward and Wendell as godfathers. And she's done something else that put my own heart at peace. She has returned to the loving relationship she had with her mom and dad.

"I buried them, Quilla," she told me when I complimented her on her decision to make peace with her folks. "That day at our crazy mock funeral, I buried the ghosts of my birth parents. I can't begin to describe how frightening and liberating that was to do, but it's the best thing I could have done for me, Mom, Dad, and my baby."

Susan's story of liberation is not the only one. As I said before, 14 women showed up at my house for the "post funeral party." Have you ever been through a really awful day or experience, something so heavy you're totally dragged down with the weight of it, then someone invites you to a dinner, a funny movie, or just a get-together with friends, and you find yourself enjoying the respite from sorrow? You laugh harder, you sing more heartily, and you feel as though it's just a great day to be alive? That's what happened at our party.

Maybe the exuberance came from burdens laid down at our burial ceremony, but all those who came were ready to experience joy. And we did. Laughing, sharing jokes, and acting out. Natasha gave us a wonderful rendition of some kind of Polish jig—a cappella, during which she dragged the conservative Martha to her feet and danced her around the room to our claps and foot stomping.

Following Natasha's encore performance Clare rushed outside and came back with a guitar, on which she played beautiful pieces reminiscent of Chet Atkins and Liona Boyd. No one wanted the day to end, but by 8:00 the realities of the approaching workday forced us to begin looking ahead. Clare raised her hand to get our attention, and when that didn't work, she put her schoolmarm's skills into action. Everyone snapped to attention in under 10 seconds. Then standing her guitar beside her long legs, she told us how much the day meant to her.

"Sometimes you don't realize you need someone to share your load. Circumstances in my life forced me to rely mostly on myself. For years I didn't need anyone to hold my hand—until I did. I was never going to share with another the deep pain or the dark times in my life—until I did. Never would I be caught dead in a room with a bunch of women talking about their emotional stuff—until I did. And had someone told me that I would one day participate in a pretend funeral where I would bury the ugliness I've had to live with, I'd tell them they were crazy—until I did. I cannot begin to thank Quilla for not walking out on me during our interview. You've been the catalyst to my liberation.

"I don't know what the future holds for any of us, but I have begun to trust God with my future," Clare continued. "So before I cry in public, which would be another first, let me quickly wrap this up by saying thanks to all of you for being brave warriors in coming to terms with the cards life has dealt you. I am honored to be in your presence."

Mara, who was standing beside Clare, leaned in and whispered something in her ear. Clare nodded and picked up her guitar. As she strummed the first few chords, I knew I could not have picked a more fitting ending to our day.

Led out by Mara, who fed us the words, we held on to each other's hands and sang with great feeling that special song "Lean on Me." Even after all the others had left, I found myself humming the tune in the shower.

That night, in my private time with God, I thanked Him for giving me the courage to bury my low self-esteem as well as my nine-year-difference hang-up. He did for me, then, the one thing I could not resist. He welcomed me again to the heart of God.

When I called Edward later that night, the first thing I told him was how much I loved him. I told him all that he had come to mean to me and how precious he makes me feel. I promised him to do my very best to ensure he felt just as treasured by me in the days and years to come.

His silence on the line told me that I'd shut him up and that he was communing with God until he got his control back.

I was right. Moments later when he'd found his words, he said, "Woman of my heart, thank you, thank you, thank you."

Not bad for an outspoken guy, eh!

I have two more things to mention, and then I'm going back to the arms of my gently snoring husband.

About the project, just in case you're interested, I distributed copies of my report to all the women who participated—even the two married ones. At the back of the report I left space for each woman to write the things they had buried, similar to the format of those old-fashioned Bibles that people used to chronicle a family's genealogy of births, deaths, and marriages.

Why did I do that, you ask? Because sometimes when we give something up, or in our case do the burn and bury thing, we want to go pick it back up, especially when the new thing we are trying to replace it with is challenging us beyond our comfort zone. Recording our stuff under the burial section provides another way to imprint on the brain that we need to move on.

Finally, I had wrestled long and hard about how to break the news to the rest of the women that I was engaged. I was concerned, especially, about Clare and Lynn, as they were close to my age and I rub shoulders with them more frequently. And their pain is fresh and raw. I talked to Gloria about it, and she told me not to worry, she'd take care of it. And she did. I don't know what she told them or how she did it, but Clare, Lynn, as well as Mara, Danesha, Mia—all the ones from church—were there to support me and share my wedding day with me. And of course, Stelle and the new duo of mischief—Natasha and Martha.

And by the way, Mara and G. David are getting married this coming June! I can't wait.

God is good, and I am so very grateful. I pray that God will do for you what He has done for me—which is to secure me in the bosom of His love.

Till next time . . .

Quilla! (Almost tranquil)

PS: Just thought I'd let you know that Edward is not light-complexioned at all. He's quite dark. And during our whole courtship the fact never entered my mind. So much for it being an *important* criterion! The joke's on me, and I'm laughing. Hee! Hee!

---

* See Ps. 46:10.

Discussion Questions:

Quilla and her friends have raised some tough questions in this book. I encourage you to continue the discussion within your own community of friends.

- = *What issues not addressed in the book are just begging for some airtime?*
- = *What aspects of the story resonated with you?*

As usual I welcome your feedback and comments. It helps me keep the writing I do real. You can email your comments to rodneybooks@rogers.com. Now, here are a few questions to get your discussion group started . . .

Finding the Man

- = Would you consider marriage to a younger man? If so, what would be your age cutoff point?

- = What is it about marriage to a younger man that causes women to balk at the prospect?

- = When it comes to men, are women too picky?

- = What advice would you give to women such as Martha, who live in rural areas where there are few-to-zero men in the church from whom to select life partners?

- = Some women tell me they would never use a dating service. When asked why, they indicate that they are not that desperate, or that the men found on such sites are either predators or losers. What's your opinion of dating services? If you've used one, what's been your experience?

Getting to Know the Man

- = At what point in a dating relationship should the subject of marriage come up? Who do you think should initiate the discussion?

= Quilla discovered that many of the assumptions she had about her "dream guy" were unexamined. What qualities do you want in a husband? Which of the qualities are "must have" and which are the ones you could live without?

Sexual Feelings

= I've heard many Christian singles say that once you are in a committed relationship there is nothing wrong with having sex—especially if you are planning to get married. What are your thoughts on the subject? Should women hold out on sex to get the guy to the altar? Is it true that once a man has sex with a woman he has less desire to marry her?

= Is the biblical injunction to abstain from sex prior to marriage still relevant for our generation? If yes, how can singles avoid sexually compromising situations?

= A topic often associated with the sexuality question, but not addressed in this book, is that of masturbation. Some would argue that this is a way to appease sexual desire when it is overwhelming, and a better option than having unmarried sex. What are your thoughts on the subject? Is this an option for the Christian? Why or why not?

Marriage and Babies

= Is marriage for everyone?

= Would you marry someone outside your religious denomination if you shared most of the same fundamental beliefs?

= What are your thoughts about Susan's choice to have a baby through the sperm bank process? Both Quilla and Gloria raised

270 The Waiting Heart

some tough questions on this subject. Which side of the argument would you lean toward?

= If a marriage partner never materializes, and you long to have a child of your own, what options are open to you?

Men and Church

= Do you believe that there is something inherent in the religious experience that attracts women more so than men? If so, what is it?

= What could churches be doing to address the attrition problem with respect to men?

Learning to Forgive

a Story of Forgiveness

let it go

yvonne rodney

It was a terrible secret. A secret she'd kept for a long time.

Until the day she couldn't hold on to it any longer . . .

Let it Go: A Story of Forgiveness
Yvonne Rodney

This is a story of women overwhelmed with inconsolable grief and soul-consuming guilt—and their journey to redemption and healing. There's only one way, you know. Only one. 978-0-8127-0494-5